Maple 9
Introductory
Programming Guide

M. B. Monagan   K. O. Geddes   K. M. Heal
G. Labahn   S. M. Vorkoetter   J. McCarron
P. DeMarco

This document was produced using a special version of Maple that reads and updates LATEX files.

Printed in Canada

ISBN 1-894511-43-3

Contents

Preface

This manual introduces the basic Maple™ programming concepts, such as expressions, data structures, looping and decision mechanisms, procedures, input and output, debugging, and `Maplets`.

Audience

As a Maple user, you may have only used Maple interactively, written Maple programs, or programmed in another computer language.

You should be familiar with the following:

- Maple online help introduction

- Example worksheets

- How to use Maple interactively

- The *Maple Learning Guide*

Worksheet Graphical Interface

You can access the power of the Maple computation engine through a variety of user interfaces: the standard worksheet, the command-line[1] version, the classic worksheet (not available on Macintosh®), and custom-built Maplet™ applications. The full Maple system is available through all of these interfaces. In this manual, any references to the graphical Maple

---

[1] The command-line version provides optimum performance. However, the worksheet interface is easier to use and renders typeset, editable math output and higher quality plots.

interface refer to the standard worksheet interface. For more information on the various interface options, refer to the ?versions help page.

Manual Set

There are three other manuals available for Maple users, the *Maple Getting Started Guide*, the *Maple Learning Guide*, and the *Maple Advanced Programming Guide*.[2]

- The *Maple Getting Started Guide* contains an introduction to the graphical user interface and a tutorial that outlines using Maple to solve mathematical problems and create technical documents. It also includes information for new users about the online help system, New User's Tour, example worksheets, and the Maplesoft Web site.

- The *Maple Learning Guide* explains how Maple and the Maple language work. It describes the most important commands and uses them to solve technical problems. User hints for Maplet applications are also described in this guide.

- The *Maple Advanced Programming Guide* extends the basic Maple programming concepts to more advanced topics, such as modules, input and output, numerical programming, graphics programming, and compiled code.

In addition to the manuals, Maple has an online help system featuring examples that you can copy, paste, and execute immediately.

Conventions

This manual uses the following typographical conventions.

- courier font - Maple command, package name, and option name

- **bold roman** font - dialog, menu, and text field

---

[2]The Student Edition does not include the *Maple Introductory Programming Guide* and the *Maple Advanced Programming Guide*. These programming guides can be purchased from school and specialty bookstores or directly from Waterloo Maple Inc.

- *italics* - new or important concept, option name in a list, and manual titles

- **Note** - additional information relevant to the section

- **Important** - information that must be read and followed

The Maple Programming Language

Writing a Maple program can be very simple. It can be as straightforward as placing `proc()` and `end proc` around a group of Maple commands. However, using the Maple programming language, you can write Maple procedures that perform complex operations.

Writing code in Maple does *not* require expert programming skills. Because Maple has a large library of routines, writing useful programs from these powerful building blocks is easy. Unlike traditional programming languages, with the Maple programming language you can perform complicated tasks by using a single Maple library routine. In addition, you can use the Maple programming language to automate long or repetitive sets of instructions.

Ninety percent of the thousands of routines in the Maple language are Maple programs. You can examine these Maple programs and modify them to suit your needs, or extend them so that Maple can solve new types of problems. You can learn the fundamentals of the Maple programming language and write useful Maple programs in a few hours, rather than the days or weeks that it often takes to learn other languages. This efficiency is partly a result of the fact that Maple is interactive. This interaction makes it easier to test and correct programs.

Using This Book

Examples   Perform the examples shown in the manual as you read. To strengthen your knowledge, try variations or refer to the related online help page(s).

Troubleshooting   At the end of most chapters, there is a Troubleshooting section that lists common errors encountered while performing the examples in the chapter. See this section if you receive an error that you do not understand.

Exercises   Develop solutions to the problems posed in the Exercises at the end of each chapter. This consolidates and extends your learning.

Customer Feedback

Maplesoft welcomes your feedback. For suggestions and comments related to this and other manuals, email doc@maplesoft.com.

1 Introduction to Programming in Maple

Maple provides an interactive problem-solving environment, complete with procedures for performing symbolic, numeric, and graphical computations. At the core of the Maple computer algebra system is a powerful programming language, upon which the Maple libraries of mathematical routines are built.

In This Chapter

- Components of the Maple software

- Maple statements

- Procedures and other essential elements of the Maple language

- Contrasting the Maple language with traditional programming languages, which cannot perform symbolic calculations

1.1 The Maple Software

The Maple software consists of three distinct parts.

- User Interface

- Kernel

- Library

The *user interface* handles the input of mathematical expressions and commands, the display of output, and the control of the Maple *worksheet* environment options.[1]

The basic Maple system, the *kernel*, is a relatively small collection of compiled C code. When a Maple session is started, the entire kernel is loaded. It contains the essential facilities required to run Maple and perform basic mathematical operations. The components include the Maple programming language interpreter, arithmetic and simplification routines, print routines, memory management facilities, and a collection of fundamental functions. Its small size ensures that the Maple system is compact, portable, and efficient. In this guide, the kernel routines are referred to as *built-in* routines.

The *library* contains the majority of the Maple routines. It includes functionality related to calculus, linear algebra, statistics, graphics, and many other topics. The Maple library consists of individual routines and packages of routines. These routines are accessed and interpreted by the Maple system as required. As a result of this modularity, the computer consumes resources proportional to *only* the facilities that are used, enhancing the efficiency of the system. All library routines, which are implemented in the high-level Maple programming language, can be viewed and modified by users. Therefore, it is useful to learn the Maple programming language so that you can modify existing Maple code to produce customized routines.[2]

1.2   Maple Statements

Getting Started

The Maple software runs on many different platforms. Depending on the platform, you use its specialized worksheet interface or command-line interface. In both cases, when a Maple session is started, the Maple prompt character (>) is displayed.

>

---

[1] For more information about the Maple user interface and worksheets, refer to the *Maple Getting Started Guide* or *Maple Learning Guide*.

[2] For more information on the use of routines in the Maple library for mathematical and graphical computations, refer to the *Maple Learning Guide*.

This prompt character indicates that Maple is waiting to receive input in the form of a Maple statement.[3]

Maple Statements

There are many types of valid statements. Examples include statements that request help on a particular topic, display a text string, perform an arithmetic operation, use a Maple library routine, or define a procedure.[4]

Most Maple statements must have a trailing semicolon (;) or colon (:). If you enter a statement with a trailing semicolon, for most statements, the result is displayed. However, if you enter a statement with a trailing colon, the result is computed but *not* displayed.

> 2 + 3;

$$5$$

> 2 + 3:

Getting Help

To view an online help page for a particular topic, enter a question mark (?) followed by the corresponding topic name. For example, `?procedure` displays a help page that describes how to write a Maple procedure.[5] This type of Maple statement does not have a trailing colon or semicolon.

Displaying a Text String

The following statement returns a *string*. The text that forms the string is enclosed in *double quotes*, and the result (the text string) is displayed because the statement has a trailing semicolon. In the second example, no result is displayed because the statement has a trailing colon.[6]

> "Hello World";

"Hello World"

---

[3]Throughout this book, the *Maple notation* (or one-dimensional) input format is used to enter Maple statements. For more information on starting a Maple session, toggling between Maple notation (the default on most platforms) and standard math notation, and managing your files, refer to the *Maple Getting Started Guide* and *Maple Learning Guide* or enter `?managing` at the Maple prompt.

[4]For more information about statements in Maple, see chapter 3.

[5]For more information about getting help in Maple, refer to `?help` and `?HelpGuide`.

[6]For more information about strings in Maple, see chapter 2 or refer to `?string`.

```
> "Hello World":
```

Performing an Arithmetic Operation

The arithmetic operators in Maple are + (addition), − (subtraction), ∗ (multiplication), / (division), and ^ (exponentiation). A statement can be an arithmetic operation that contains any combination of these operators. The standard rules of precedence apply.

```
> 103993/33102;
```

$$\frac{103993}{33102}$$

Maple displays the result—in this case an exact rational number—in the worksheet or on the terminal in use, displaying the result as closely to standard mathematical notation as possible.

You can enter statements on one line (as in the previous example) or several lines.[7] You can even put the terminating semicolon on a separate line. It is not processed until you complete the command with a semicolon or a colon.[8]

```
> 103993
> / 33102
> ;
```

$$\frac{103993}{33102}$$

Assigning to a Name

By naming a calculated result or complicated expression, you can reference it. To assign to a name, use the assignment operator, :=.[9]

```
> a := 103993/33102;
```

$$a := \frac{103993}{33102}$$

---

[7]To enter a statement on more than one line, hold the SHIFT key and press ENTER at the end of each line.

[8]For more information about commands that control printing, see **Printing Output to the Screen** on page 257. For information about arithmetic operators, see page 70.

[9]For more information about names and assignment, see chapter 2.

```
> 2 * a;
```

$$\frac{103993}{16551}$$

Using Maple Library Routines

Once a value is assigned to a name, for example, the value assigned previously to a, you can use the name as if it were the assigned object. For example, you can use the Maple library routine evalf to compute a floating-point (decimal) approximation to 103993/33102 divided by 2 by entering the following statement.

```
> evalf(a/2);
```

$$1.570796326$$

You can use the Maple library of routines, introduced on page 6, for many purposes. For example, you can find the derivative of an expression by using the diff command.[10]

```
> diff(x^2 + x + 1/x, x);
```

$$2\,x + 1 - \frac{1}{x^2}$$

1.3   Procedures

This section formally introduces the concept of procedures in Maple. For more information about procedures, see chapter 6.

Defining a Simple Procedure

A Maple procedure (a type of program) is a prearranged group of statements processed together. The easiest way to create a Maple procedure is to encapsulate a sequence of commands, which can be used to perform a computation interactively, between the proc(...) and end proc statements.

---

[10]For more information about the Maple library routines, refer to the *Maple Learning Guide* or the online help.

Entering a Procedure Definition   The following procedure generates the string *"Hello World"*. Enter this procedure in a Maple session by entering its definition on one line.

```
> hello := proc() "Hello World"; end proc;
```

$$hello := \mathbf{proc}()\text{ ``Hello World'' } \mathbf{end\ proc}$$

For improved readability, enter the procedure on **multiple lines**: hold SHIFT and press ENTER at the end of each line.[11] Indent lines in the procedure by using the spacebar. When you enter the last line, which contains **end proc**, press ENTER.

```
> hello := proc()
>           "Hello World";
> end proc;
```

$$hello := \mathbf{proc}()\text{ ``Hello World'' } \mathbf{end\ proc}$$

To run this procedure, enter its name followed by a set of parentheses and a semicolon. Enclose any input to the procedure—in this case none—between the parentheses and delimited (separated) by commas (,).

```
> hello();
```

$$\text{``Hello World''}$$

The next example is a procedure that uses the **evalf** command.

```
> half := proc(x)
>           evalf(x/2);
> end proc;
```

$$half := \mathbf{proc}(x)\text{ evalf}(1/2 * x) \mathbf{end\ proc}$$

This procedure requires one input, **x**. The procedure computes the approximation of the value of **x** divided by 2. A Maple procedure returns the result of the last executed statement. Since **evalf(x/2)** is the last calculation performed in the procedure **half** (in fact, it is the only calculation), the approximation of **x/2** is returned.

---

[11]For more information, see **Unexpected End of Statement** on page 17.

The procedure is named **half** by using the := notation in the same manner that you would assign any other object to a name. Once you have named a procedure, you can use it as a command in the current Maple session with the same syntax used to run a Maple library routine.

```
> half(2/3);
```

$$0.3333333333$$

```
> half(a);
```

$$0.5000000000\,a$$

```
> half(1) + half(2);
```

$$1.500000000$$

By enclosing the **evalf(x/2)** statement between **proc()** and **end proc**, you create a procedure. In the next example, a new procedure is created that corresponds to the following two statements.

```
> a := 103993/33102;
```

$$a := \frac{103993}{33102}$$

```
> evalf(a/2);
```

$$1.570796326$$

The procedure definition for these statements does not explicitly require input, but it does include a *local variable*. A local variable **a** in a procedure is different from the variable **a** outside the procedure (if one exists). Thus, you can use **a** as a variable name outside of the procedure **f** without conflict.[12]

```
> f := proc() local a;
>         a := 103993/33102;
>         evalf(a/2);
> end proc;
```

---

[12]For more information about local variables, see **Variables** on page 201.

$$f :=$$
$$\textbf{proc}()\,\textbf{local}\,a;\ a := 103993/33102\,;\ \text{evalf}(1/2 * a)\,\textbf{end proc}$$

The interpretation of this procedure definition appears immediately after the statements that define it. Examine it carefully and note the following characteristics.

- The *name* of this procedure (program) is **f**.

- The procedure definition starts with **proc()**. The empty parentheses indicate that this procedure does not require input.

- Semicolons or colons separate the individual commands of the procedure.

- The **local a;** statement declares **a** as a local variable. As described previously, a local variable has meaning only inside the procedure definition.[13]

- The **end proc** keywords and colon or semicolon mark the end of the procedure.

- As you enter the procedure, the commands of the procedure do not display output. The procedure definition is displayed as output only after you complete it with **end proc** and a semicolon or colon.

- The procedure definition that displays as the value of the name f is equivalent to, but not identical to, the procedure definition you enter. The commands of the procedure are simplified if possible.

The procedure definition syntax is very flexible. You can:

- Enter each statement on one or more lines

- Enter multiple statements on one line, provided they are separated by colons or semicolons

- Place extra semicolons between statements

- Omit the semicolon (or colon) from the statement preceding **end proc**

---

[13]For more information about local variables, see **Variables** on page 201.

   To suppress the display resulting from a complicated procedure definition, use a colon instead of a semicolon at the end of the definition.

```
> g := proc() local a;
>        a := 103993/33102;
>           evalf(a/2);
> end proc:
```

Calling a Procedure   The execution of a procedure is referred to as an
invocation or a *procedure call.* When you invoke a procedure, Maple executes the statements that form the procedure body one at a time. The
result of the last computed statement within the procedure is returned as
the value of the procedure call.

   For example, to execute procedure f—that is, to cause the statements
that form the procedure to execute in sequence—type its name followed
by parentheses and a semicolon. No input is required to run the procedure,
so nothing is entered between the parentheses.

```
> f();
```

$$1.570796326$$

   Only the result of the last calculation performed within procedure f is
returned—the result of `evalf(a/2)`. The assignment `a:=103993/33102`
is executed, but the statement result is not displayed.

Maple Library Routines, Built-In Routines, and User-Defined Procedures

Maple routines are implemented in one of two formats—those written in
the C programming language and those written in the Maple programming
language. You can easily include complicated tasks in your user-defined
procedures by using the existing Maple routines instead of writing new
untested code.

   The routines that are written in C are compiled and built into the
Maple kernel. These built-in routines are those that are generally used in
computations, and those that are fundamental to the implementation of
the other Maple routines. Since the kernel is compiled, it is usually faster
to perform computations by using these built-in routines.[14]

---

[14]For more information about built-in kernel routines, see page 207 or refer to
`?builtin`.

The routines in the Maple library are written in the Maple programming language. These routines exist as individual routines or as packages of routines. They are accessed and interpreted by the Maple system as required.

The code for the library routines and the definitions of user-defined procedures can be viewed and modified. However, before exploring that, it is important that you learn about evaluation rules so that you understand the code.

Full Evaluation and Last Name Evaluation   For most named objects in Maple, such as e defined with the following command, you can obtain its value by entering its name.

```
> e := 3;
```

$$e := 3$$

```
> e;
```

$$3$$

This is called *full evaluation*—each name in the expression is fully evaluated to the last assigned expression in any chain of assignments. The following statements further illustrate how full evaluation works.

```
> c := b;
```

$$c := b$$

```
> b := a;
```

$$b := a$$

```
> a := 1;
```

$$a := 1$$

```
> c;
```

$$1$$

This group of statements creates the chain of assignments $c \Rightarrow b \Rightarrow a \Rightarrow 1$, and c fully evaluates to 1.

If you try this approach with a procedure, Maple displays only the *name* of the procedure instead of its true value (the procedure definition). For example, in the previous section, g is defined as a procedure. If you try to view the body of procedure g by referring to it by name, the procedure definition is *not* displayed.

> g;

$$g$$

This model of evaluation is called *last name evaluation* and it hides the procedure details. The reason for this approach is that procedures potentially contain many subobjects. To obtain the value of the name g, use the `eval` command, which forces full evaluation.[15]

> eval(g);

proc() **local** a; $a := 103993/33102$; evalf$(1/2 * a)$ **end proc**

Viewing Procedure Definitions and Maple Library Code   You can learn about programming in Maple by studying the procedure definitions of Maple library routines. To *print* the body of Maple library routines, set the Maple `interface` variable `verboseproc` to 2, and then use the `print` command.

Example   Look at the procedure definition for the Maple *least common multiple* routine, `lcm`, enter the following statements.[16]

> interface(verboseproc = 2):
> print(lcm);

---

[15]Last name evaluation applies to procedures, tables, and modules in Maple. For more information, refer to ?last_name_eval.

[16]For more information about `interface` variables, see page 258 or refer to ?interface.

```
proc(a, b)
local q, t;
option remember, 'Copyright (c) 1990 by the Unive\
rsity of Waterloo. All rights reserved.';
    if nargs = 0 then 1
    elif nargs = 1 then t := expand(a) ; sign(t) * t
    elif 2 < nargs then  lcm(a, lcm(op(2..nargs, [args])))
    elif type(a, integer) and type(b, integer) then ilcm(a, b)
    else gcd(a, b, q) ; q * b
    end if
end proc
```

Because the built-in kernel routines are written in the C programming language and compiled, you cannot view their definitions. If you print the definition of a built-in procedure, the procedure body is comprised of the option builtin statement and a positive integer that identifies the procedure.

```
> print(add);
```

$$\text{proc() option } builtin; \text{ 90 end proc}$$

1.4   Interrupting Computations and Clearing the Internal Memory

This section introduces two important concepts: interrupting a computation and clearing the internal memory.

Interrupting a Maple Computation

To stop a computation, for example, a lengthy calculation or infinite loop, use one of the following three methods.[17]

- Click the STOP icon[18] on the toolbar (in worksheet versions).

---

[17] Maple does not always respond immediately to an interrupt request if it is performing a complex computation. You may need to wait a few seconds before the computation is halted.

[18] For more information on toolbar icons, refer to ?worksheet,reference,toolbar.

- Hold the CTRL key and press the C key (in UNIX and Windows command-line versions).

- Hold the COMMAND key and press the period key (.) (in Macintosh command-line and worksheet versions).

To perform a *hard* interrupt, which stops the computation and exits the Maple session, in Windows command-line Maple, hold the CTRL key and press the BREAK key.

Clearing the Maple Internal Memory

Clear the internal memory during a Maple session by entering the `restart` command or clicking the restart icon[19] on the toolbar of the worksheet (in GUI versions). When you enter this command, the Maple session returns to its startup state; all identifiers (including variables and procedures) are reset to their initial values.[20]

```
> restart:
```

A Maple function that can be used to free space without resetting your session is the garbage collection facility `gc`. For information on `gc`, see page 335.

1.5   Troubleshooting

This section provides you with a list of common mistakes, examples, and hints that will help you understand and avoid common errors. Use this section to study the errors that you may encounter when entering the examples from this chapter in a Maple session.[21]

Unexpected End of Statement

Most valid statements in Maple must end in either a colon or a semi-colon. An error is returned if you press ENTER on an input region that is incomplete.

---

[19]For more information on toolbar icons, refer to `?worksheet,reference,toolbar`.

[20]For more information about clearing the Maple internal memory and the `restart` command, refer to `?restart`.

[21]You can use the `parse` routine for finding errors in statements, and the Maple debugger for finding errors in programs. For more information, see chapter 8, or refer to `?parse` and `?debugger`.

If you press ENTER to enter a procedure definition on multiple lines, the following error displays.

```
> p := proc()
```

Error, unexpected end of statement

To prevent this error message from displaying *as you enter* a procedure definition, hold the SHIFT key and press the ENTER key at the end of each line, instead of pressing only the ENTER key.

```
> p := proc()
>          "Hello World";
> end proc;
```

If you neglect to enter a trailing semicolon or colon, Maple inserts a semicolon and displays the following warning message.

```
> 1 + 2
```

Warning, inserted missing semicolon at end of statement,
1 + 2;

$$3$$

Maple also inserts a semicolon after **end proc** in procedure definition.

```
> p := proc()
>          "Hello World";
> end proc
```

Warning, inserted missing semicolon at end of statement,
...ld"; end proc;

```
                 p := proc() "Hello World" end proc;
```

Missing Operator

The most common error of this type is omitting the multiplication operator.

```
> 2 a + b;
```

Error, missing operator or ';'

You can avoid this error by using * to indicate multiplication.

> 2*a + b;

$$2\,a + b$$

Invalid, Wrong Number or Type of Arguments

An error is returned if the argument(s) to a Maple library command are incorrect or missing.

> evalf();

Error, wrong number (or type) of parameters in function evalf

> solve(y=3*x+4, 5);

Error, (in solve) a constant is invalid as a variable, 5

> cos(x, y);

Error, (in cos) expecting 1 argument, got 2

If such an error occurs, check the appropriate online help page for the correct syntax. Enter ?topic_name at the Maple prompt.

Unbalanced Parentheses

In complicated expressions or nested commands, it is easy to omit a closing parenthesis.

> [(1,0), (0,1];

Error, ']' unexpected

In a valid statement, each (, {, and [requires a matching), }, and], respectively.

> [(1,0), (0,1)];

$$[1, 0, 0, 1]$$

Assignment Versus Equality

When you enter statements in a Maple session, it is important that you understand the difference between equality (using =) and assignment (using :=).

The equal sign = creates an *equation*. An equation is commonly used to test whether two expressions (the left-hand side and the right-hand side) are equal. The test is usually performed by using the Maple `evalb` command.[22]

```
> x = 2;
```

$$x = 2$$

```
> x;
```

$$x$$

```
> evalb(x=2);
```

$$false$$

```
> x + 5;
```

$$x + 5$$

The assignment operator := assigns to the left-hand side the value of right-hand side. Once an assignment is made, the left-hand side can be used in place of the value of the right-hand side. The left-hand side must evaluate to a *name* (for example, the left-hand side *cannot* be a number).[23]

```
> x := 2;
```

---

[22] For more information about equations and Boolean testing, see page 84 or refer to `?evalb`.

[23] For more information about names and assignment, see pages 26 and 110, respectively.

$$x := 2$$

```
> x;
```

$$2$$

```
> evalb(x=2);
```

$$true$$

```
> x + 5;
```

$$7$$

1.6   Exercises

1. Assign the integers 12321, 23432, and 34543 to the names a, b, and c. Use these names to find the sum and difference of each pair of numbers.

2. Write two procedures. The first requires two inputs and finds their sum. The second requires two inputs and finds their product. Use these procedures to add and multiply pairs of numbers. How could you use these procedures to add and multiply three numbers?

3. Display your procedure definitions. Are they identical to the code you entered to write them? [24]

1.7   Conclusion

This chapter presented a basic overview of the Maple system and the Maple programming language. The Maple system consists of three main components: the kernel, which contains compiled built-in commands; the

---

[24] For more information about procedure definitions, see chapter 6.

library which contains routines written in the Maple programming language; and, the interface, which handles the input and output of mathematical expressions and functions. You were introduced to the essential elements of writing and executing Maple procedures, along with common syntax errors related to writing procedures.

To learn more about the Maple programming language, read the remaining chapters in this guide and, when you encounter other example programs, try to write variations. Study the details, exceptions, and options in these chapters, as the need arises. References to related topics in other chapters, manuals, and online help pages that provide additional information are included where relevant.

2   Maple Language Elements

Before programming in Maple, it is important to learn the properties and roles of the basic elements of the Maple language.

In This Chapter

- Basic elements of the Maple language: the character set and tokens

- Maple tokens: reserved words, operators, names, strings, and natural numbers; including the types of each and related functions

- Using special characters

- Maple data types related to the tokens

2.1   Character Set

The Maple character set consists of letters, digits, and special characters. The letters are the 26 lower case letters

```
a b c d e f g h i j k l m n o p q r s t u v w x y z
```

and the 26 upper case letters.

```
A B C D E F G H I J K L M N O P Q R S T U V W X Y Z
```

The 10 decimal digits are:

Table 2.1 Special Characters

	blank				(	left parenthesis
;	semicolon				)	right parenthesis
:	colon				[	left bracket
+	plus				]	right bracket
−	minus				{	left brace
*	asterisk				}	right brace
/	slash				`	left single quote (back quote)
ˆ	caret				'	right single quote (apostrophe)
!	exclamation				"	double quote
=	equal				|	vertical bar
<	less than				&	ampersand
>	greater than				_	underscore
@	at sign				%	percent
$	dollar				\	backslash
.	period				#	pound sign (sharp)
,	comma				?	question mark

```
0, 1, 2, 3, 4, 5, 6, 7, 8, 9
```

There are also 32 special characters, which are listed in Table 2.1. The use of special characters is discussed in **2.3 Using Special Characters**.

2.2   Tokens

The Maple language combines characters into tokens. The set of tokens consists of reserved words (also called *keywords*), programming-language operators, names, strings, and natural integers.

Reserved Words

The Maple *keywords* are reserved words that have special meanings. Thus, you cannot change them or use them as variables in procedures. The keywords are listed in Table 2.2. You can find information about a specific keyword in the subsequent chapters of this guide or in the online help pages.[1]

---

[1] For general information about reserved words in Maple, refer to ?keywords.

Table 2.2 Reserved Words

Keywords	Purpose
break, next	loop control
if, then, elif, else	if statement
for, from, in, by, to, while, do	for and while loops
proc, local, global, option, error, return options, description	procedures
export, module, use	modules
end	ends structures
assuming	assume facility
try, catch, finally	exception handling
read, save	read and save statements
quit, done, stop	ending Maple
union, minus, intersect, subset	set operators
and, or, not, xor	Boolean operators
implies	implication operator
mod	modulus operator

Programming-Language Operators

There are three types of Maple language operators: *nullary*, *unary*, and *binary*.[2]

In Maple, there are three nullary operators (operators that take no arguments and return values from the environment of the Maple session). They are constructed from the Maple *ditto* operator. The percent sign % is the ditto operator. It is a special Maple name used to refer to previously computed non-NULL expressions. Specifically, the following nullary operators are defined as:

```
%      last expression
%%     second-last expression
%%%    third-last expression
```

The % operator *re-evaluates* the last expression computed, the %% operator *re-evaluates* the second-last expression computed, and the %%% operator *re-evaluates* the third-last expression computed.

---

[2]For more information about the order of precedence of programming-language operators, see Table 3.4 on page 89 or refer to ?precedence.

Table 2.3 Programming Binary Operators

Operator	Meaning	Operator	Meaning
+	addition	<	less than
−	subtraction	<=	less or equal
*	multiplication	>	greater than
/	division	>=	greater or equal
ˆ	exponentiation	<>	not equal
$	sequence operator	->	arrow operator
@	composition	union	set union
@@	repeated composition	minus	set difference
&*string*	neutral operator	intersect	set intersection
,	expression separator	::	type declaration,
||	concatenation		pattern binding
.	non-commutative	and	logical and
	multiplication	or	logical or
..	ellipsis	xor	exclusive or
mod	modulo	implies	implication
:=	assignment	subset	subset

Note: The nullary operators do *not* reference the results of the lines located above the execution groups in which they are used. They reference the results of the *most recently performed* computations in the Maple session, regardless of the execution group or worksheet that contains them. Also, since the ditto operators do not recall the results of past computations, but *re-evaluate* the results of these computations, the use of local variables to save and recall computed expressions is preferred in procedures. For more information about local variables, see **Variables** on page 201.[3]

The Maple binary and unary operators, and their meanings, are listed in Table 2.3 and Table 2.4, respectively. For additional information about these operators, see page 70.

Names

A *name* in Maple is a sequence of one or more characters that uniquely identifies a command, file, variable, or other entity. There are two distinct types of names: *indexed names* and *symbols*, which are non-indexed

---

[3]For more information about the ditto operators, refer to `?ditto`.

Table 2.4 Programming Unary Operators

Operator	Meaning
+	unary plus (prefix)
−	unary minus (prefix)
!	factorial (postfix)
$	sequence operator (prefix)
not	logical not (prefix)
&*string*	neutral operator (prefix)
.	decimal point (prefix or postfix)
%*integer*	label (prefix)

names. For more information about indexed names, see page 34.

The simplest instance of a name consists of a sequence of letters, digits, and underscores. If you require a name that includes blank spaces, use left single quotes (for more information, see page 28).

```
> My_Name_1;
```

$$My\_Name\_1$$

You can confirm that the previous statement is a valid name (and symbol) by using the **whattype** command.

```
> whattype(%);
```

$$symbol$$

A name cannot begin with a number, and the maximum length of a name is system dependent.

```
> 1myname;

on line 258, syntax error, missing operator or ';':
1myname;
          ^
```

Maple is case-sensitive, so, for example, the name **Apple** is different from the name **apple**.

Other Maple names include:

- mathematical functions such as **sin** and **cos**

- Maple commands such as expand or simplify

- type names such as integer or list

- variables that represent values, for example, x and y in the expression x+y

- programming variables (A name becomes a programming variable only after Maple assigns it a value. Otherwise, the name remains an unknown.)

For example, in the first statement below, y is a name that does not have a value. In the second statement, the variable x has the value 3.

```
> 2*y - 1;
```

$$2y - 1$$

```
> x := 3; x^2 + 1;
```

$$x := 3$$

$$10$$

Names that *begin* with an underscore are reserved by Maple for internal use only, and names of the form ñame are permitted for spreadsheet references (refer to *cell references* in ?spreadsheet,references).

In general, names can also be formed by using left single quotes or concatenation. Other categories of names in Maple include indexed names, initially-known names, environment variables, constants, and protected names. These are discussed in the following sections.

Forming a Name By Using Left Single Quotes   You can form a name in Maple by enclosing any sequence of characters in left single quotes (also called back quotes). To form a name that includes blank spaces, use left single quotes.

```
> 'This is a name!';
```

$$This\ is\ a\ name!$$

```
> whattype(%);
```

symbol

Because the name is not indexed, it is of type symbol.

With the exception of keywords and names that contain blank spaces, any valid Maple name formed without using left single quotes is the same as the name formed by surrounding the name with left single quotes. For example, x and `x` refer to the same name x.

Name Concatenation   Names can be formed through concatenation by using the cat command or the superseded concatenation operator, ||.[4]

The cat Command   You can construct a name (or string) by using the cat command

```
cat( sequence )
```

where **sequence** contains any number of expressions, separated by commas.

The cat command is commonly used to concatenate names and strings, and the result returned has the type (name or string) of the first argument to cat. (In the following examples, any argument that is enclosed by double quotes is a string.)

```
> cat(a, b);
```

$$ab$$

```
> cat(a, "b");
```

$$ab$$

```
> cat("a", b);
```

"ab"

```
> cat(a, 2);
```

$$a2$$

---

[4]You can also use the cat command to form strings. For more information, see page 41 or refer to ?cat.

```
> cat("a", 2);
```

$$\text{``a2''}$$

If the result from the cat command evaluates to a name, then it is a *global* name—a name that can be recognized anywhere in the Maple session. To illustrate, consider the following procedures.[5]

```
> globalassign := proc()
>       local a;
>       a := 5;
>       assign( cat('a'), 2 );
> end proc:

> a;
```

$$a$$

```
> globalassign();
> a;
```

$$2$$

In procedure globalassign, the assignment statement[6] assigns 2 to the global name a. If the statement assign(cat('a'), 2) were assign('a', 2), the local variable a would be assigned 2, but the global variable a would be unchanged.[7]

The Concatenation Operator || You can also concatenate names by using the concatenation operator || in one of the following formats.

```
name || name
name || naturalInteger
name || string
name || ( expression )
```

---

[5]For more information about procedure syntax, see chapter 6.
[6]For more information about the assignment statement, see page 110.
[7]For more information about local and global variables, see **Variables** on page 201.

The concatenation operator is a binary operator that requires a name (or a string) as its left operand. Since a name can appear on the left-hand side of any concatenation operator, you can perform a succession of concatenations.

```
> i := 5;
```

$$i := 5$$

```
> i || 7;
```

$$i7$$

```
> p || "in";
```

$$pin$$

```
> a || (2*i);
```

$$a10$$

```
> a || i || b;
```

$$a5b$$

Maple *never* fully evaluates the left-most object, but evaluates it to a name. For example, study the result of i||7 and a||i||b in the previous examples. The i is evaluated to 5 only if it is *not* the left-most object in the concatenation.

In general, Maple evaluates expressions from left to right. However, Maple evaluates concatenations from *right to left*. Maple evaluates the right-most operand, then concatenates to the left operand.

Example 1 If the right operand evaluates to an integer, string, or name, then the result of the concatenation is a string or name (depending on the type of the left -most operand).

```
> n := 4: p || (2*n+1);
```

$$p9$$

Example 2 If the right operand evaluates to another type of object, for example, a general expression, the result of the operation is an *unevaluated* concatenated object.

> p || (2*m+1);

$$p||(2\,m+1)$$

Example 3 If the right-hand expression is a sequence or a range and the operands of the range are integers or character strings, then Maple returns a sequence of names.

> x || (a, b, 4, 67);

$$xa,\ xb,\ x4,\ x67$$

Example 4 If more than one range appears, the extended sequence of names is constructed.

> x || (1..2) || (1..3);

$$x11,\ x12,\ x13,\ x21,\ x22,\ x23$$

The use of the concatenation operator to form sequences has been superseded by the seq function. For more information, see page 183 or refer to ?seq.

Differences Between cat and || Although you can use both cat and || to concatenate, there are subtle differences in the way each performs. The concatenation operator does *not* evaluate its first argument, whereas cat does.[8]

> a := 2;

$$a := 2$$

> a || 4;

$$a4$$

---

[8]In this example, the result from cat(a,4) is the *name* 24 not the integer 24.

```
> cat(a, 4);
```

$$24$$

Also, the result of the statement that uses the concatenation operator is evaluated; this is *not* the case for the `cat` command.

```
> a4 := 5;
```

$$a4 := 5$$

```
> a || 4;
```

$$5$$

```
> cat(a, 4);
```

$$a4$$

Note: In general, it is recommended that you use `cat`.

Special Characters in Names To make the left single quote character appear in a name, enter a backslash character (\) followed by a left single quote (‘) where you want the left single quote character to appear. The backslash is the escape character in Maple. For more information, see **Escape Characters** on page 51 or refer to `?backslash`.

```
> 'a\'b';
```

$$a'b$$

Similarly, to cause a backslash to appear as one of the characters in a name, enter two consecutive backslashes, \. You must escape the backslash because the backslash also acts as a line continuation character. For more information, see page 47.

```
> 'a\\b';
```

$$a\backslash b$$

The special backslash character is only one character, as is demonstrated by using the `length` command.

```
> length(%);
```

$$3$$

Indexed Names Another form of a name in Maple is the *indexed* name (or subscripted name), which has the following syntax.

```
name [ sequence ]
```

Since an indexed name is itself a valid name, you can add a succession of subscripts.

```
> A[1,2];
```

$$A_{1,2}$$

```
> A[i,3*j-1];
```

$$A_{i,3j-1}$$

```
> b[1][1], data[Cu,gold][1];
```

$$b_{11}, \; data_{Cu,\,gold_1}$$

You can assign a value to an indexed name.

```
> f[Cu] := 1.512;
```

$$f_{Cu} := 1.512$$

```
> a[1]^2; a[1] := 3; a[1]^2;
```

$$a_1{}^2$$

$$a_1 := 3$$

$$9$$

Table 2.5 Initially Known Names

Name	Meaning	Name	Meaning
Catalan	Catalan's constant	lasterror	stores most recent error
constants	initially-known symbolic constants	libname	pathname of Maple library(ies)
Digits	number of digits in floating-point computations	NULL	empty expression sequence
FAIL	cannot determine value	Order	truncation order for series
false	Boolean evaluation	Pi	mathematical constant
gamma	Euler's constant	printlevel	control display of information
I	complex number	true	Boolean evaluation
infinity	mathematical infinity	undefined	undefined

Note: The use of an indexed name such as A[1,2] does not automatically imply that A is an array, as in some languages. The statement

> a := A[1,2] + A[2,1] - A[1,1]*A[2,2];

$$a := A_{1,2} + A_{2,1} - A_{1,1} A_{2,2}$$

forms a formula in four indexed names. However, if A does evaluate to an array, Array, or table, A[1,2] refers to element (1,2) of the array or table.[9]

Initially Known Names Maple ships with a collection of names that are initially known to the Maple system. These are names of global or environment variables and names of constants related to functions. Table 2.5 lists some of the initially known Maple names.[10]

Environment Variables Enviroment variables influence the execution of operations in a software program. You can display a sequence of all active environment variables by entering the following command.[11]

---

[9] For more information about arrays, Arrays, and tables, see chapter 4 or refer to ?array, Array, and ?table.

[10] For general information about initially known names, refer to ?ininames.

[11] For more information about assigned names, see pages 110–114 or refer to ?anames.

```
> anames('environment');
```

Testzero, UseHardwareFloats, Rounding, %, %%%, Digits,
index/newtable, mod, %%, Order, printlevel, Normalizer,
NumericEventHandlers

You can use environment variables in assignment statements. However, if an environment variable is assigned a value in a procedure body, its pre-procedure value is restored upon exit from the procedure. Also, the value of the environment variable is available to all subprocedures called from that procedure, unless locally superseded.[12,13,14]

```
> Digits;
```

$$10$$

```
> evalf(2/13);
```

$$0.1538461538$$

```
> envtest := proc()
>              Digits := 3;
>              evalf(2/13);
> end proc:
```

```
> envtest();
```

$$0.154$$

```
> Digits;
```

$$10$$

```
> evalf(2/13);
```

---

[12]For more information about environment variables, refer to **?envvar**. For more information about procedures, see chapter 6 or refer to **?procedures**.

[13]The **evalf** command is used to evaluate its argument to a floating-point (decimal) number. For more information, refer to **?evalf**.

[14]For more information on variable scoping, see **Variables** on page 201 or refer to chapter 1 of the *Maple Advanced Programming Guide*.

$$0.1538461538$$

Constants   You can display a sequence of all the currently active *symbolic* constants in Maple by using the global variable `constants`.

> `constants;`

$$false, \; \gamma, \; \infty, \; true, \; Catalan, \; FAIL, \; \pi$$

Maple also has *numeric* constants: integers, fractions, floating-point numbers, and complex numbers. For more information, see pages 63–68.[15]

Protected Names   A protected name has a predefined meaning. You cannot *directly* assign a value to it. For example, the names of built-in functions such as `sin` (the sine function), utility operations such as `degree` (computes the degree of a polynomial), commands such as `diff` (differentiation), and type names such as `integer` and `list`, are protected names. If you attempt to assign to any of these names, an error is returned.

> `list := [1,2];`

`Error, attempting to assign to 'list' which is protected`

The Maple system protects these names from re-assignment. However, even though it is *not* recommended, it is possible to make assignments to these names by first unprotecting them as illustrated by the following statements.[16]

> `unprotect(sin);`
> `sin := "a sin indeed";`

$$sin := \text{``a sin indeed''}$$

As a result, components of Maple that rely on the sine function do not work properly.

---

[15] For general information about constants in Maple, refer to `?constants`.

[16] You can usually undo assignments made to Maple system names by entering a `restart` command, or by ending the session. However, in general, it is dangerous to reassign Maple system names; using the `unprotect` command to modify Maple system names is *not* recommended.

```
> plot( 1, 0..2*Pi, coords=polar );
```

```
Plotting error, empty plot
```

To check whether a name is protected, use the **type** command.[17]

```
> type(diff, protected);
```

$$true$$

To display all the protected names, use the following command.[18]

```
select( type, unames(),anames(anything), protected);
```

To prevent a user from assigning a value to a name, use the **protect** command when writing programs.

```
> mysqr := x -> x^2;
```

$$mysqr := x \to x^2$$

```
> type(mysqr, protected);
```

$$false$$

```
> protect( mysqr );
> mysqr := 9;
```

```
Error, attempting to assign to 'mysqr' which is
protected
```

Strings

A *string* is a sequence of characters that evaluates to itself. To create a string, enclose any sequence of characters in double quotes.

```
> "This is a string";
```

$$\text{``This is a string''}$$

---

[17]You can perform type checking for many types of objects in Maple. For more information, see **2.4 Types and Operands** or refer to **?type**.

[18]For more information on the **select** function, see page 156.

You *cannot* assign to a string.

```
> "hello" := 5;
```

Error, invalid left hand side of assignment

Do not confuse the double quote character, which delimits a string, with the left single quote character (`), which forms a *name* (symbol), or right single quote ('), which *delays evaluation*. For more information on left and right single quotes, see pages 28 and 100, respectively.

In the following sections, strings and string operations are described. For information on the StringTools package, refer to ?StringTools.

Length of a String There is no practical limit on the length of a Maple string (the maximum string length is system dependent). On most Maple implementations, this means that a string can contain more than half a million characters.

Use the length command to determine the length of a string.

```
> length("What is the length of this string?");
```

$$34$$

All characters between, but excluding, the double quotes are counted. Each blank space is counted as one character.

The Empty String The empty string (or null string) is represented by two double quotation marks with no enclosed characters (not even a blank space).

```
> "";
```

""

```
> length(%);
```

$$0$$

```
> whattype(%%);
```

string

The null string is *not* the same as the global variable NULL, which is an empty expression sequence.[19] The output for the null string consists of zero printed characters.

Substrings   You can extract a substring of a string by using the substring command, or by using subscripts.

The substring command returns the string consisting of the characters specified by range.

```
substring( exprString, range );
```

If range is a nonzero integer m, then the mth character of exprString is returned as a one-character string. If range is specified as m..n, where m and n are nonzero integers, then the substring starting from the mth character and ending with the nth character of exprString is returned. Negative values in range indicate character positions counted from the right end of the string.

```
> S := "abcdef";
```

$$S := \text{``abcdef''}$$

```
> substring(S, 5);
```

$$\text{``e''}$$

```
> substring(S, 3..7);
```

$$\text{``cdef''}$$

```
> substring(S, -3..-1);
```

$$\text{``def''}$$

Alternatively, you can access a substring by using a string with a subscripted integer range (also called a *selection operation*).[20]

---

[19] For more information about expression sequences, refer to chapter 2 of the *Maple Learning Guide*.

[20] It is more efficient to use the selection operation than the substring command to access a substring of a string. Therefore, whenever possible, use a selection operation instead of the substring command for accessing substrings from procedures. For more information about selection, see page 114.

```
> S := "This is a string";
```

$$S := \text{``This is a string''}$$

```
> S[6];
```

$$\text{``i''}$$

```
> S[6..9];
```

$$\text{``is a''}$$

```
> S[-6..-1];
```

$$\text{``string''}$$

String Concatenation Like names, strings can also be formed through concatenation by using the **cat** command or the superseded concatenation operator, ||.[21]

The cat Command You can construct a string by using the **cat** command, where **sequence** contains any number of expressions, separated by commas.

```
cat( sequence )
```

The **cat** command is commonly used to concatenate strings with names and integers, and the result returned has the type (name or string) of the first argument to **cat**.

```
> cat("a", b);
```

$$\text{``ab''}$$

```
> cat("a", 2);
```

$$\text{``a2''}$$

---

[21] For more information on the differences between **cat** and ||, see pages 29–32 or refer to ?**cat**.

```
> i := 5;
```

$$i := 5$$

```
> cat( "The value of i is ", i, "." );
```

"The value of i is 5."

The Concatenation Operator || You can also concatenate strings by using the concatenation operator || in one of the following formats.

```
string || name
string || naturalInteger
string || string
string || ( expression )
```

The concatenation operator is a binary operator that requires a string (or a name) as its left operand. Since a string can appear on the left-hand side of any concatenation operator, Maple accepts a succession of concatenations.

```
> "The "|| "value of i is " || i;
```

"The value of i is 5"

In general, Maple evaluates expressions from left to right. However, Maple evaluates concatenations from *right to left*. Maple evaluates the right-most operand, then concatenates to the left operand. If the right operand evaluates to an integer, string, or name, the result of the concatenation is a string (or name, depending on the type of the left-most operand). If the right operand is evaluated to another type of object, for example, a general expression, the result of the operation is an *unevaluated* concatenated object.

```
> n := 4: "p" || (2*n+1);
```

"p9"

```
> "p" || (2*m+1);
```

$$\text{"p"} || (2m + 1)$$

If the right-hand expression is a sequence or a range, and the operands of the range are integers or character strings, Maple returns a sequence of strings.

```
> "var" || (a, b, 4, 67);
```

$$\text{"vara", "varb", "var4", "var67"}$$

If more than one range appears, an extended sequence of strings is constructed.

```
> "x" || (1..2) || (1..3);
```

$$\text{"x11", "x12", "x13", "x21", "x22", "x23"}$$

The use of the concatenation operator to form sequences has been superseded by the **seq** function. For more information, see page 183 or refer to **?seq**.

For examples that illustrate the differences between **cat** and **||**, see page 32.

Special Characters in Strings   To make the double quote character appear in a string, enter a backslash character (\) followed by a double quote (") where you want the double quote character to appear. You must do this since Maple does not know which double quote ends the string, and the backslash acts as the escape character in Maple. For more information, see page 51 or refer to **?backslash**.

```
> "a\"b";
```

$$\text{"a"b"}$$

Similarly, to cause a backslash to appear as one of the characters in a string, enter two consecutive backslashes, \. You must escape the backslash in this manner since the backslash also acts as a line continuation character in Maple. For more information, see page 47.

```
> "a\\b";
```

$$\text{"a\b"}$$

The special backslash character mentioned above counts as only one character, as is demonstrated by using the **length** command.

> length(%);

$$3$$

A reserved word enclosed in double quotes is a valid Maple string, distinct from its usage as a token.

> "while";

$$\text{``while''}$$

Parsing Strings The **parse** command accepts any Maple string and parses the string as if it had been entered or read from a file.

```
parse( exprString, option );
```

The string must consist of exactly *one* Maple expression. The expression is parsed, and returned unevaluated.

> parse("a+b");

$$a + b$$

> parse("a+b;");

$$a + b$$

If the string is syntactically incorrect, the **parse** command returns an error of the form "incorrect syntax in parse: ... (number)". The number indicates the offset in characters, counted from the beginning of the string, at which the syntax error was detected.

> parse("a++b");

Error, incorrect syntax in parse: '+' unexpected (4)

Partial statements or expressions cannot be parsed. Multiple statements or expressions cannot be parsed, unless they comprise one larger statement (such as a loop, or a procedure definition).

If the option `statement` is specified, the string must consist of exactly one Maple statement. In this case, the statement is parsed and evaluated, and then the result is returned.[22]

```
> parse("sin(Pi)");
```

$$\sin(\pi)$$

```
> parse("sin(Pi)", statement);
```

$$0$$

Searching a String   To perform case-sensitive and case-insensitive string searching, use the `SearchText` and `searchtext` commands, respectively.

```
SearchText( pattern, exprString, range );
searchtext( pattern, exprString, range );
```

The `SearchText` command searches for exact matches of `pattern` in `exprString`. The `searchtext` command performs the same search, but it is case-insensitive. If `pattern` is found, Maple returns an integer indicating the position of the first character in `pattern` in `exprString`. If the pattern is not found in `exprString`, 0 is returned.

```
> SearchText("my s", "This is my string.");
```

$$9$$

```
> searchtext("My S", "This is my string.");
```

$$9$$

The optional `range` restricts the search to the specified range. It is equivalent to performing a search on a substring, and it is useful when the pattern occurs more than once in the string.

```
> SearchText("is", "This is my string.", 4..-1);
```

$$3$$

---

[22]For more information about the `parse` command, see page 268 or refer to `?parse`.

Converting Expressions to Strings   To convert an expression to a string, use the `convert` command.[23]

```
> convert(a, string);
```

$$\text{``a''}$$

```
> convert(a+b-c*d/e, string);
```

$$\text{``a+b-c*d/e''}$$

Natural Integers

A *natural integer* is a sequence of one or more decimal digits.[24]

```
> 00003141592653589793238462643;
```

$$3141592653589793238462643$$

2.3   Using Special Characters

Token Separators

You can separate tokens by using white space characters or punctuation marks. The separator indicates the end of one token and the beginning of the next.

Blank Spaces, New Lines, Comments, and Continuation

The *white space characters* are space, tab, return, and line-feed. This guide uses the terminology *new line* to refer to a return or line-feed since the Maple system does not distinguish between these characters. The terminology *blank* refers to a space or tab.

The white space characters separate tokens, but are *not* themselves tokens. White space characters cannot normally occur *within* a token.

```
> a: = b;
```

---

[23] Maple has the facility to convert a variety of objects. For more information about expressions, see **3.2 Expressions** and **3.3 Using Expressions**. For more information about conversions in Maple, refer to `?convert`.

[24] For more information about integers in Maple, see page 62 or refer to `?integer`.

```
on line 26, syntax error, '=' unexpected:
a: = b;
  ^
```

However, you can use white space characters *between* tokens.

```
> a * x + x*y;
```

$$a\,x + x\,y$$

The only situation in which white space is part of a token is in a name or string formed by enclosing a sequence of characters in left single quotes or double quotes, respectively. For more information, see pages 28 and 38.

Except in a string, all characters that follow a pound sign "#" on a line are part of a *comment.*[25]

```
> a := 1 + x + x^2;   #This is a comment
```

$$a := 1 + x + x^2$$

Since white space and new line characters are functionally identical, you can continue *statements* from line to line, as described in chapter 1.

```
> a:= 1 + x +

> x^2;
```

$$a := 1 + x + x^2$$

To continue *numbers* and *strings* over multiple lines, use the backslash (\) as a line continuation character. The behavior of line continuation is as follows.

If the special character backslash \ immediately precedes a new line character, the Maple parser ignores both the backslash and the new line. If a backslash occurs in the middle of a line, Maple usually ignores it. [26]

---

[25] For information about comments in Maple procedures, see **6.5 Documenting Your Procedures**.

[26] For more information about the backslash and exceptions to this rule, refer to `?backslash`.

Table 2.6 Maple Punctuation Marks

;	semicolon	(	left parenthesis
:	colon	)	right parenthesis
'	left single quote	[	left bracket
'	right single quote	]	right bracket
|	vertical bar	{	left brace
<	left angle bracket	}	right brace
>	right angle bracket	,	comma

You can use this rule to break up a long sequence of digits into groups of smaller sequences, to enhance readability.

```
> "The input should be either a list of \

> variables or a set of variables";
```

"The input should be either a list of variables or a se \
t of variables"

```
>   G:= 0.57721566490153286060\

> 6512090082402\43104215933593992;
```

$$G := 0.57721566490153286060651209008240 2431\backslash$$
$$04215933593992$$

Punctuation Marks

The punctuation marks that act as token separators are listed in Table 2.6.

; and : Use the semicolon and the colon to separate statements. The distinction between these marks is that, during an interactive session, a colon prevents the result of the statement from printing.

```
> f:=x->x^2;
```

$$f := x \rightarrow x^2$$

```
> p:=plot(f(x), x=0..10):
```

'' Enclosing an expression, or part of an expression, in a right single quotes (also called *apostrophes*) delays evaluation of the expression (subexpression) by one level. For more information, see page 100.

```
> ''sin''(Pi);
```

$$\text{'sin'}(\pi)$$

```
> %;
```

$$\sin(\pi)$$

```
> %;
```

$$0$$

'' To form names, enclose an expression in left single quotes.

```
> limit(f(x), x=0, 'right');
```

$$0$$

() The left and right parentheses group terms in an expression and group parameters in a function call.

```
> (a+b)*c; cos(Pi);
```

$$(a+b)\,c$$

$$-1$$

```
> proc( x, y, z )
>    x+y+z;
> end proc:
```

[] Use the left and right square brackets to form indexed (subscripted) names and to select components from aggregate objects such as arrays, tables, and lists. For more information on data structures, see chapter 4.

```
> a[1]; L:=[2,3,5,7]; L[3];
```

$$a_1$$

$$L := [2,\ 3,\ 5,\ 7]$$

$$5$$

[] and {} Use the left and right square brackets to form lists, and the left and right braces to form sets. For more information on sets and lists, see chapter 4.

```
> L:=[2,3,5,2]; S:={2,3,5,2};
```

$$L := [2,\ 3,\ 5,\ 2]$$

$$S := \{2,\ 3,\ 5\}$$

<> and | The left and right angle brackets in conjunction with the vertical bar are used to construct Matrices and Vectors. For more information, refer to ?Matrix and ?MVshortcut.

```
> <<1,2,3> | <4,5,6>>;
```

$$\begin{bmatrix} 1 & 4 \\ 2 & 5 \\ 3 & 6 \end{bmatrix}$$

, Use the comma to form a sequence, and to separate the arguments of a function call or the elements of a list or set.

```
> sin(Pi), 0, limit(cos(xi)/xi, xi=infinity);
```

$$0,\ 0,\ 0$$

Escape Characters

An *escape character* indicates that the following character must be handled in a special manner. The escape characters in Maple are ?, !, #, and \.

? The question mark character, if it appears as the first nonblank character on a line, invokes the Maple help facility. The words following ? on the same line determine the arguments to the help procedure. Use either "," or "/" to separate the words in the argument. For more information, refer to **?help**.

! The exclamation mark character, if it appears as the first nonblank character on a line, passes the remainder of the line as a command to the host operating system. This facility is not available on all platforms. For more information, refer to **?system** and **?escape**.

The pound sign character indicates that the characters that follow it on the line are a comment. For more information, see **6.5 Documenting Your Procedures** or refer to **?comment**.

\ The backslash character is used for continuation of lines and grouping characters in a token. For more information, see page 47 or refer to **?backslash**.

2.4   Types and Operands

In most programming languages, data is divided into different classes of information—called *data types*. Types are important in Maple since they are used to decide whether an expression is a valid input in procedure calls and Maple commands. By definition, a *type* in Maple is any expression that is recognized by the **type** command. The **type** command has the following syntax.

```
type( expression, typeName );
```

If **expression** is of type **typeName**, the **type** command returns **true**. Otherwise, **false** is returned.

To determine the operands and the number of operands in an expression, use the **op** and **nops** commands, respectively. These commands have the following basic syntax.

Table 2.7 Integer Subtypes

Subtype	Meaning
negint	negative integer
posint	positive integer
nonnegint	non-negative integer
nonposint	non-positive integer
even	even integer
odd	odd integer

```
op( i, expression );
nops( expression );
```

If the optional first argument i to the op command is a positive integer, the ith operand of expression is returned.

The following sections introduce some elementary data types, for example, integers, strings, and names, but the Maple software contains many others.[27]

Integers

The type of an integer is integer. The type command also understands the subtypes of integers listed in Table 2.7.

An integer has only one operand, itself.

```
> x := 23;
```

$$x := 23$$

```
> type(x, prime);
```

$$true$$

```
> op(x);
```

$$23$$

```
> op(0, x);
```

[27]For more information about data types and operands in Maple, see chapter 3 or refer to ?type and ?op.

Integer

Strings

The type of a string is **string**. A string also has only one operand, itself.

```
> s := "Is this a string?";
```

$$s := \text{``Is this a string?''}$$

```
> type(s, string);
```

$$true$$

```
> nops(s);
```

$$1$$

```
> op(s);
```

$$\text{``Is this a string?''}$$

Names

The type of a name is **name**. However, the **type** command also understands the type names **symbol** and **indexed**. The type **name** is defined as **symbol** or **indexed**.

```
> x := 'my name';
```

$$x := my\ name$$

```
> type(x, name);
```

$$true$$

```
> type(x, symbol);
```

$$true$$

The type of an indexed name is **indexed**. The zeroth operand of an indexed name is the base name. The remaining operands are the indices (subscripts).

```
> x := A[1][2,3];
```

$$x := A_{12,3}$$

```
> type(x, name);
```

$$true$$

```
> type(x, indexed);
```

$$true$$

```
> nops(x);
```

$$2$$

```
> op(x);
```

$$2, 3$$

```
> op(0,x);
```

$$A_1$$

```
> y:=%;
```

$$y := A_1$$

```
> type(y, indexed);
```

$$true$$

```
> nops(y), op(0,y), op(y);
```

$$1, A, 1$$

Concatenations

The type of an *unevaluated* concatenation is "||". This type has two operands, the left-hand side expression and the right-hand side expression.

```
> c := p || (2*m + 1);
```

$$c := p||(2\,m+1)$$

```
> type(c, '||');
```

$$true$$

```
> op(0, c);
```

$$||$$

```
> nops(c);
```

$$2$$

```
> op(c);
```

$$p, 2\,m+1$$

2.5   Troubleshooting

This section provides you with a list of common mistakes, examples, and hints that will help you understand and avoid common errors. Use this section to study the errors that you may encounter when entering the examples from this chapter in a Maple session.

Attempting to Assign to a Protected Name

An error occurs if you attempt to assign a value to a protected name.[28]

```
> int := 10;

Error, attempting to assign to 'int' which is protected
```

---

[28]For more information about protected names, see page 37 or refer to ?protect.

Invalid Left-Hand Assignment

An error occurs if you attempt to assign a value to a string.[29]

```
> "my string" := 10;

Error, invalid left hand side of assignment
```

Use only valid names on the left-hand side of an assignment statement.

Incorrect Syntax in Parse

The `parse` command accepts a string as its argument. An error message is returned if the string is syntactically incorrect.[30]

```
> parse("a^2--b");

Error, incorrect syntax in parse: '-' unexpected (6)
```

The error message indicates the character number (counted from the left double quote) where error was detected. In this case, the 6th character (the second minus sign) caused the error.

White Space Characters within a Token

An error message is normally returned if a white space character occurs in a token.

```
> evalb(2 < = 3);

on line 71, syntax error, '=' unexpected:
evalb(2 < = 3);
         ^
```

The binary operator `<=` is a token in Maple. Therefore, it cannot contain a space.

```
> evalb(2 <= 3);
```

$$true$$

---

[29] For more information about strings, see page 38 or refer to `?string`.
[30] For more information about parsing, see page 44 or refer to `?parse`.

Incorrect Use of Double and Single Quotes

In Maple, double quotes form a string, left single quotes form a name, and right single quotes delay evaluation of an expression. Confusing a string with a name, or a name with delayed evaluation causes errors. Study the following examples to see the different uses of these quotes.[31]

To form a string, enclose the expression in double quotes.

```
> "2 + 3";
```

$$"2 + 3"$$

```
> whattype(%);
```

$$string$$

To form a name, enclose the expression in left single quotes.

```
> '2 + 3';
```

$$2 + 3$$

```
> whattype(%);
```

$$symbol$$

To delay the evaluation of an expression, enclose it in right single quotes. To evaluate the expression, omit these quotes.

```
> x := 2: y := 3: f := 'x + y';
```

$$f := x + y$$

```
> f := x + y;
```

$$f := 5$$

---

[31] For more information about using quotes, see **Punctuation Marks** on page 48 or refer to ?quotes.

2.6   Exercises

1. Using the %, %%, and %%% operators, find the:

   a) Sum of 5434 and 6342.

   b) Product of 92 and 310.

   c) Quotient of the result from a) divided by the result from b).

   d) Quotient of the result from b) divided by the result from a).

2. Estimate π to 10,000 digits.

3. Concatenate the three strings "int", "(x^2,", and "x)". Parse the resulting string. Evaluate the parsed string.

4. The Fibonacci numbers are a sequence of numbers. The first two numbers in the sequence are zero (0) and one (1). For n greater than two, the nth number in the sequence is the sum of the two preceding numbers. Assign values to indexed names representing the first, second, and general Fibonacci numbers.

5. Determine a random integer between 40 and 100 using the command rand(40..100). Concatenate this number with the string, "The student's grade is ". Extract the student's grade from the resulting string.

6. Assign the expressions x^2 and x*x to the names a and b. Find the three operands of a and b. Compare the results with those returned by using the dismantle function, that is, dismantle(a) and dismantle(b). The dismantle function displays the internal data structure used.

2.7   Conclusion

This chapter introduced the Maple language elements. In particular, tokens are the smallest meaningful elements in Maple. Tokens are used to form Maple expressions and statements. The next chapter shows how to use the information presented in this chapter to build expressions, and discusses how to form Maple statements.

3 Maple Expressions and Statements

You construct Maple statements, most importantly expressions, from tokens, which were discussed in chapter 2.

In This Chapter

- Syntax and semantics of the Maple language

- Expressions, the most important type of statement, including the use of expressions and the action of commands on expressions

- Other important types of statements

3.1 Syntax and Semantics

Syntax and semantics define a language. Syntax, or grammar, refers to the rules that are used to combine basic elements into statements. Semantics refers to the extra information or meaning that syntax cannot capture; it determines the actions Maple performs when you enter a command.

Syntax
Syntax defines valid forms of input, for example, expressions, statements, and procedures. It dictates, for example:

- Whether parentheses are required in the expression x^(y^z)

- How to enter a string that is longer than one line

- How to enter the floating-point number 2.3×10^{-3}

If the input is not syntactically correct, a syntax error is reported. Consider the following examples.

Adjacent minus signs are not valid.

```
> --1

on line 29, syntax error, '-' unexpected:
--1
 ^
```

You can enter floating-point numbers using many formats.

```
> 2.3e-3, 2.3E-03, +0.0023;
```

$$0.0023, 0.0023, 0.0023$$

However, you must place at least one digit between the decimal point and the exponent suffix.

```
> 2.e-3;

on line 42, syntax error, missing operator or ';':
2.e-3;
  ^
```

A correct way to enter this expression is `2.0e-3`.

Semantics

The semantics of a language specifies how expressions, statements, and programs execute—that is, the actions Maple performs with them. It controls:

- Whether `x/2*z` or `x/2/z` is equal to `x/(2*z)` or `(x/2)*z`

- The behavior when $\sin(x)/x$ is computed with `x=0`

- The return of 1, instead of an error, for $\sin(0)/\sin(0)$

- The value of `i` after executing the following loop

```
> for i from 1 to 5 do print(i^2) end do;
```

These are important concepts to understand before writing Maple programs.

A common mistake is to think that x/2*z is equal to x/(2*z). Following the operator precedence rules (see Table 3.4 on page 89), this is not true.

```
> x/2*z, x/(2*z);
```

$$\frac{1}{2}\,x\,z,\ \frac{1}{2}\frac{x}{z}$$

The remainder of this chapter focuses on the Maple programming language syntax.

3.2   Expressions

Expressions are the fundamental entities in the Maple language and the most important type of Maple statement. The types of expressions are the following:

- constants

- operator-based expressions

- data structures

- function calls

Procedures and modules[1] are also valid expressions because you can use them wherever an expression is accepted. This is an important feature of the Maple language. Procedures are described separately in chapter 6.

Expressions are now presented in detail, beginning with the numeric constants. The presentation shows how to input the expression, gives examples of how and where to use the expression, and illustrates the action of the type, nops, op, and subsop commands on the expression.

Constants

The Maple language contains both symbolic and numeric constants.

---

[1]For information on modules, refer to chapter 2 of the *Maple Advanced Programming Guide* or ?module.

Maple has a general concept of *symbolic* constants. The global variable constants is assigned the expression sequence containing the names of the initially known constants. For more information, see page 35.

Maple also has *numeric* constants. The numeric constants in Maple are integers, rational numbers (fractions), floating-point numbers (decimals), and the special values, infinity and undefined. The complex numeric constants are the complex integers (Gaussian integers), complex rationals, and complex floating-point numbers. The full set of real and complex numeric constants is exactly what is recognized by type(...,
complex(extended_numeric)).

Generally, a Maple expression is of type constant if it is:

- Of type complex(extended_numeric)

- One of the initially known constants

- An unevaluated function with all arguments of type constant

- A sum, product, or power with all operands of type constant.

For example, the following expressions are of type constant: 2, sin(1), f(2,3), exp(gamma), 4+Pi, 3+I, 2*gamma/Pi^(1/2).

```
> type(2, constant);
```

$$true$$

```
> type(sin(1), constant);
```

$$true$$

```
> type(2*gamma/Pi^(1/2), constant);
```

$$true$$

Integers In Maple, an *integer* is an optionally signed, arbitrary-length sequence of one or more decimal digits. However, the integer 0 (zero) does not have a sign.[2,3]

---

[2]The integer zero (0) does not have a sign. However, the floating-point zeros, +0.0 and -0.0, are signed. For more information, see page 65.

[3]The evalb command evaluates a Boolean expression. For more information, see page 86 or refer to ?evalb.

```
> evalb(0 = +0); evalb(0 = -0); evalb( +0 = -0);
```

$$true$$

$$true$$

$$true$$

In Maple, the maximum length of an integer is system dependent and can be obtained by entering `kernelopts(maxdigits)`. The number of digits is approximately:

```
> kernelopts(maxdigits);
```

$$268435448$$

A *natural integer* is any sequence of one or more decimal digits.

A *signed integer* is indicated by either +natural or −natural, where natural is any natural integer.

Hence, an *integer* is either a natural integer or a signed integer.

The type of an integer is `integer`.

```
> type(-36, integer);
```

$$true$$

To form arithmetic expressions involving integers in Maple, use the Maple arithmetic operators (see page 70 or refer to `?arithop`). In contrast with pocket calculators, when arithmetic expressions containing only integer operands are entered, Maple performs exact arithmetic—the integers are not converted to decimal numbers.[4]

Rational Numbers (Fractions)   A rational number (fraction) is the quotient of two integers, where the denominator is always nonzero.

```
integer/natural
```

As with integers, Maple does exact arithmetic with fractions. Maple simplifies fractions so that the denominator is positive, and reduces the fraction to lowest terms by dividing the greatest common divisor from the numerator and denominator.

---

[4]For more information about integers in Maple, refer to `?integer`.

```
> -30/12;
```

$$\frac{-5}{2}$$

If the denominator is 1 after simplifying the fraction, Maple converts the fraction to an integer.

```
> 25/5;
```

$$5$$

```
> whattype(%);
```

$$integer$$

The type of a fraction is `fraction`. The `type` command also accepts the composite type name `rational`, which is the union of `integer` and `fraction`–that is, rational numbers.

```
> x := 4/6;
```

$$x := \frac{2}{3}$$

```
> type(x, fraction);
```

$$true$$

```
> type(x, rational);
```

$$true$$

A fraction has two operands, the numerator and denominator. It is recommended that you use the `numer` and `denom` commands to extract the numerator and denominator of a fraction.

```
> op(1,x), op(2,x);
```

$$2, 3$$

```
> numer(x), denom(x);
```

2, 3

Floating-point Numbers (Decimals) An *unsigned float* has one of the
following six forms:

```
natural.natural
natural.
.natural
natural exponent
natural.natural exponent
.natural exponent
```

where `natural` is a natural integer, and `exponent` is the suffix containing the letter "e" or "E" followed by a signed integer with no spaces
between.

A *floating-point number* is an unsigned float or a signed float (`+unsigned`
`float` or `-unsigned float` indicates a signed float).

> 1.2, -2., +.2;

$$1.2, -2., 0.2$$

> 2e2, 1.2E+2, -.2e-2;

$$200., 120., -0.002$$

Note that

> 1.e2;

on line 229, syntax error, missing operator or ';':
1.e2;
  ^

is not valid, and that spaces are significant.

> .2e -1 <> .2e-1;

$$-0.8 \neq 0.02$$

The type of a floating-point number is `float`. The `type` command
also accepts the composite types `numeric` (which is the union of `integer`,

fraction, and float–that is, the real numbers), and extended_numeric (which is the union of integer, fraction, float, infinity, and undefined).[5]

A floating-point number has two parts, the *mantissa* (or *significand*) m and the *exponent* e, which represent the number $m \times 10^e$. The decimal point is placed after the right-most digit of m. To access the parts of a floating-point number, use the SFloatMantissa and SFloatExponent commmands.

```
> x := 231.3;
```

$$x := 231.3$$

```
> SFloatMantissa(x);
```

$$2313$$

```
> SFloatExponent(x);
```

$$-1$$

You can also use the Float command to construct floating-point numbers.

```
Float( m, e );
```

This constructs the floating-point number $m \times 10^e$. Again, m is the mantissa, e is the exponent, and the decimal point is located to the right of m.

```
> Float( 1.2, -3 );
```

$$0.0012$$

The mantissa m is a Maple integer. Hence, it is subject to the same restrictions in terms of number of digits as any Maple integer. Since Maple integers are machine dependent, the maximum number of digits in any integer, and therefore in m, is always at least $268, 435, 448$.[6]

---

[5]For information about the full suite of numeric types and subtypes, refer to ?numeric_type.

[6]For more information, see page 62 or refer to ?maxdigits.

The exponent **e** is subject to a smaller restriction, which is again machine dependent, but is always at least $2,147,483,646$. You can obtain the exact values of these limits by using the `Maple_floats` command. For more information, refer to `?Maple_floats`.

You can also enter a floating-point number $m \times 10^e$ by simply forming the expression `m * 10^e`.

```
> 1.2 * 10^(-3);
```

$$0.001200000000$$

Arithmetic with Floating-point Numbers For arithmetic operations and the standard mathematical functions, if one of the operands (or arguments) is a floating-point number or evaluates to a floating-point number, then floating-point arithmetic is used automatically. The global name `Digits`, which has the value 10 as its default, determines the number of digits (in the mantissa) that Maple uses for floating-point calculations.[7]

```
> x := 2.3: y := 3.7:
> 1 - x/y;
```

$$0.3783783784$$

In general, you can use the **evalf** command to force the evaluation of a non-floating-point expression to a floating-point expression, where possible.

```
> x := ln(2);
```

$$x := \ln(2)$$

```
> evalf(x);
```

$$0.6931471806$$

An optional index to the **evalf** command specifies the precision of the evaluation.[8]

---

[7]For more information, refer to `?Digits`.

[8]For more information about evaluation using floating-point arithmetic, refer to `?evalf`.

```
> evalf[15](x);
```

$$0.693147180559945$$

Complex Numerical Constants By default, I denotes the complex unit $\sqrt{-1}$ in Maple. Therefore, the following are equivalent.

```
> sqrt(-1), I, (-1)^(1/2);
```

$$I, I, I$$

You can enter a complex number a + bi as the sum a + b*I or by using the Complex command as Complex(a, b).

```
> 2 + 3*I;
```

$$2 + 3I$$

```
> Complex(2, 3);
```

$$2 + 3I$$

Maple uses a special representation for complex numeric constants, such as 1.3 + 4.2*I. To select the real and imaginary parts, use the Re and Im commands.[9]

```
> z := 2+3*I;
```

$$z := 2 + 3I$$

```
> Re(z), Im(z);
```

$$2, 3$$

The type of a complex number is complex(numeric). This means that the real and imaginary parts are of type numeric—that is, integers, fractions, or floating-point numbers. Other possible type names are listed in Table 3.1.

---

[9] In an expression such as x + y*I, where x and y are symbols, Maple does not assume that x is the real part and y is the imaginary part.

Table 3.1 Types of Complex Numbers

Complex Type Name	Meaning
complex(integer)	both a and b are integers, possibly 0
complex(rational)	both a and b are rationals
complex(float)	both a and b are floating-point constants
complex(numeric)	any of the above

Arithmetic with complex numbers is done automatically.

```
> x := (1 + I); y := 2.0 - I;
```

$$x := 1 + I$$

$$y := 2.0 - 1.I$$

```
> x + y;
```

$$3.0 + 0.I$$

Maple can evaluate elementary functions and many special functions over the complex numbers. Maple evaluates the result automatically if **a** and **b** are numeric constants and one of **a** or **b** is a decimal number.

```
> exp(2+3*I), exp(2+3.0*I);
```

$$e^{(2+3I)}, \; -7.315110095 + 1.042743656\,I$$

If the arguments are not complex floating-point constants, you can expand the expression in some cases into the form **a+bi**, where **a** and **b** are real, by using the **evalc** command.

For example, the result of the following statement is not in the form **a+bi** because **a** is not of type **numeric**.

```
> 1/(a - I);
```

$$\frac{1}{a - I}$$

```
> evalc(%);
```

Table 3.2 The Arithmetic Operators

Operator	Meaning
+	addition
−	subtraction
*	multiplication
.	non-commutative multiplication
/	division
^	exponentiation

$$\frac{a}{a^2 + 1} + \frac{I}{a^2 + 1}$$

Note: The `evalc` command assumes that the symbol a is *real*.

To use another letter, say j, to represent the imaginary unit, use the `interface` command as follows.

```
> interface(imaginaryunit = j);
> solve( {z^2 = -1}, {z} );
```

$$\{z = j\}, \{z = -j\}$$

The following command reinstates I as the imaginary unit.

```
> interface(imaginaryunit = I);
> solve( {z^2 = -1}, {z} );
```

$$\{z = I\}, \{z = -I\}$$

Operators

A Maple operator is a symbol indicating that a mathematical operation is to be performed. This section discusses the Maple operators, and how to create expressions involving them.

The Arithmetic Operators The six Maple arithmetic operators are listed in Table 3.2. They can all be used as binary operators. However, you can also use the operators + and − as prefix operators representing unary plus and unary minus, respectively.

The types and operands of the arithmetic operations follow.

- The type of a sum or difference is '+'.

- The type of a product or quotient is '*'.

- The type of a power is '^'.

- The operands of the sum $x - y$ are the terms x and $-y$.

- The operands of the product xy^2/z are the factors x, y^2, and z^{-1}.

- The operands of the power x^a are the base x and the exponent a.

> whattype(x-y);

$$+$$

> whattype(x^y);

$$\hat{} \;$$

Arithmetic   Maple always computes the result to the five arithmetic operations $x + y$, $-y$, $x \times y$, x/y, and x^n, *if* n is an integer, and x and y are numbers. For example, you cannot prevent Maple from simplifying 2 + 3 to 5 in output.[10] If the operands are floating-point numbers, Maple performs the arithmetic computation in the floating-point environment.

> 2 + 3, 6/4, 1.2/7, (2 + I)/(2 - 2*I);

$$5, \; \frac{3}{2}, \; 0.1714285714, \; \frac{1}{4} + \frac{3}{4}I$$

> 3^(1.2), I^(1.0 - I);

$$3.737192819, \; 0. + 4.810477381\,I$$

For numerical constants, Maple reduces fractional powers of integers and fractions as follows.

- For integers n, m and fraction b,

$$(n/m)^b \to (n^b)/(m^b).$$

---

[10]For information on displaying output that appears unsimplified, refer to the examples in section 1.3 of the *Maple Advanced Programming Guide*.

- For integers n, q, r, d and fraction $b = q + r/d$ with $0 < r < d$,

$$n^b = n^{q+r/d} \rightarrow n^q \times n^{r/d}.$$

For example,

```
> 2^(3/2), (-2)^(7/3);
```

$$2\sqrt{2},\ 4\,(-2)^{(1/3)}$$

Automatic Simplifications   Maple automatically performs the following simplifications for any symbol x or arbitrary expression.

```
> x - x, x + x, x + 0, x*x, x/x, x*1, x^0, x^1;
```

$$0,\ 2\,x,\ x,\ x^2,\ 1,\ x,\ 1,\ x$$

Note the following exceptions.

```
> infinity - infinity;
```

$$undefined$$

```
> infinity/infinity;
```

$$undefined$$

```
> 0/0;
```

```
Error, numeric exception: division by zero
```

To perform additional simplifications, use the `simplify` command.[11]
In Maple, addition and multiplication are associative and commutative. Therefore, the following simplifications are performed where a, b, and c denote numerical constants, and x, y, and z denote general symbolic expressions.

$$ax + bx \rightarrow (a + b)x$$

$$x^a \times x^b \rightarrow x^{a+b}$$

---

[11] For more information, refer to `?simplify`.

$$a(x + y) \rightarrow ax + ay$$

The first two simplifications mean that Maple adds like terms in polynomials automatically. The third simplification means that Maple distributes numerical constants (integers, fractions, and floating-point numbers) over sums, but does not do the same for non-numerical constants.

```
> 2*x + 3*x, x*y*x^2, 2*(x + y), z*(x + y);
```

$$5\,x,\ x^3\,y,\ 2\,x + 2\,y,\ z\,(x + y)$$

To force Maple to display an expression in expanded form, use the `expand` command.[12]

The simplifications that are most confusing to Maple users relate to simplifying powers x^y for non-integer exponents y.

Simplification of Repeated Exponentiation In general, Maple does not perform the simplification $(x^y)^z \rightarrow x^{(yz)}$ automatically because it does not always provide an accurate answer. For example, letting $y = 2$ and $z = 1/2$, the simplification would imply that $\sqrt{x^2} = x$, which is not necessarily true. Maple performs the transformation only if it is provably correct for all complex x with the possible exception of a finite number of values, such as 0 and ∞. Maple simplifies $(x^a)^b \rightarrow x^{ab}$ if b is an integer, $-1 < a \leq 1$, or x is a positive real constant.

```
> (x^(3/5))^(1/2), (x^(5/3))^(1/2);
```

$$x^{(3/10)},\ \sqrt{x^{(5/3)}}$$

```
> (2^(5/3))^(1/2), (x^(-1))^(1/2);
```

$$2^{(5/6)},\ \sqrt{\frac{1}{x}}$$

Similarly, Maple does not simplify $a^b c^b \rightarrow (ac)^b$ automatically. This simplification may introduce more unique roots.

```
> 2^(1/2)+3^(1/2)+2^(1/2)*3^(1/2);
```

---

[12]For more information, refer to `?expand`.

$$\sqrt{2} + \sqrt{3} + \sqrt{2}\sqrt{3}$$

Simplifying $\sqrt{2}\sqrt{3}$ to $\sqrt{6}$ in the previous expression would create a third unique square root. Calculating with roots is, in general, difficult and expensive. Therefore, new roots are avoided.

Use the `combine` command to combine roots.[13]

The Non-commutative Multiplication Operator .   The . (dot) operator performs (non-commutative) multiplication on its arguments. It is left associative.

```
A . B;
```

If A and B are numbers (including complex and extended numerics such as `infinity` and `undefined`), then A . B = A*B. If one of A and B is a Matrix or a Vector, and the other is a Matrix, Vector, or constant, their product is computed by using the `LinearAlgebra[Multiply]` command. Arguments that are not of type Matrix, Vector, or constant are ignored, and A . B remains unevaluated. There is also a dot product operator in the `VectorCalculus` package.[14]

> 7 . 6;

$$42$$

> M:=<<1,0,2>|<0,1,2>|<0,0,2>>;

$$M := \begin{bmatrix} 1 & 0 & 0 \\ 0 & 1 & 0 \\ 2 & 2 & 2 \end{bmatrix}$$

> V:=<10,0,0>;

$$V := \begin{bmatrix} 10 \\ 0 \\ 0 \end{bmatrix}$$

---

[13]For more information, refer to `?combine`.

[14]For more information about Matrix, Vector, and the `LinearAlgebra` package in Maple, refer to `?LAOverview`. For more information about the non-commutative multiplication operator, refer to `?dot`. For more information about the `VectorCalculus` dot product operator, refer to `?VectorCalculus[DotProduct]`.

```
> M . V;
```

$$\begin{bmatrix} 10 \\ 0 \\ 20 \end{bmatrix}$$

```
> lambda . M . V;
```

$$\lambda \cdot \begin{bmatrix} 10 \\ 0 \\ 20 \end{bmatrix}$$

In Maple, . (dot) can be interpreted as a decimal point (for example, 2.3), as part of a range operator (for example, x..y), or as the (non-commutative) multiplication operator. To distinguish between these three circumstances, Maple uses the following rule.

Any dot with spaces before and/or after it that is not part of a number is interpreted as the non-commutative multiplication operator.

For example, 2.3 is a number, 2 . 3 and 2 .3 return 6, and 2. 3 returns an error.[15]

```
> 2.3, 2 . 3, 2 .3;
```

$$2.3, 6, 6$$

```
> 2. 3;

on line 739, syntax error, unexpected number:
2. 3;
   ^
```

The Composition Operators @ and @@   The composition operators are @ and @@.

The @ operator represents function composition. For example, f@g denotes $f \circ g$.

```
> (f@g)(x);
```

---

[15] For more information about floating-point numbers, see page 65 or refer to **?Float**. For more information about the range operator, see page 77 or refer to **?range**.

$$f(g(x))$$

```
> (sin@cos)(Pi/2);
```

$$0$$

The @@ operator represents repeated functional composition. For example, f@@n denotes $f^{(n)}$.

```
> (f@@2)(x);
```

$$(f^{(2)})(x)$$

```
> expand(%);
```

$$f(f(x))$$

```
> (D@@n)(f);
```

$$(D^{(n)})(f)$$

There is no single notational rule used by mathematicians. Usually $f^n(x)$ denotes composition. For example, D^n denotes the differential operator composed n times. Also, $\sin^{-1}(x)$ denotes the inverse of the sin function, that is, composition to the power -1. However, some mathematicians use $f^n(x)$ to denote ordinary powering, for example, $\sin^2(x)$ is the square of the sine of x. In Maple $f^n(x)$ always denotes repeated composition and $f(x)^n$ always denotes powering.

```
> sin(x)^2, (sin@@2)(x), sin(x)^(-1), (sin@@(-1))(x);
```

$$\sin(x)^2,\ (\sin^{(2)})(x),\ \frac{1}{\sin(x)},\ \arcsin(x)$$

```
> sin(Pi)^2, (sin@@2)(Pi);
```

$$0, 0$$

The Ditto Operators %, %%, and %%% The sequence of expressions assigned to the three *ditto* nullary operators is the last three non-NULL results generated in the Maple session independent of where they are located in the session.[16,17]

The Range Operator .. A range expression is represented by using the binary operator .. (two consecutive periods) between two expressions.

expression1 .. *expression2*

It is important to note that this only *represents* a range, that is, it is a notational tool. For example, the range 1..3 is *not* equivalent to the expression sequence 1, 2, 3. However, the seq command can be used to yield the expression sequence.[18]

> 1..3;

$$1..3$$

> seq(i, i = 1..3);

$$1, 2, 3$$

A range has type '..' or **range**.

> r:=3..7;

$$r := 3..7$$

> type(r, '..');

true

A range has two operands, the left-hand limit and the right-hand limit. You can access these limits by using the **op** command or the **lhs** and **rhs** commands.

---

[16]For more information about the ditto operator and nullary operators, see page 25 or refer to ?ditto.

[17]The ditto operators are technically *not* operators.

[18]For more information about the seq command, see page 183 or refer to ?seq.

```
> op(1,r), op(2,r);
```

$$3, 7$$

```
> lhs(r), rhs(r);
```

$$3, 7$$

You can also use the **range** construct in conjunction with the **op** command to extract a sequence of operands from an expression.

```
> a := [ u, v, w, x, y, z ];
```

$$a := [u, v, w, x, y, z]$$

```
> op(2..5,a);
```

$$v, w, x, y$$

The Factorial Operator ! Maple uses the unary operator ! as a postfix operator that denotes the factorial function of its operand **n**.

```
n!
```

The expression **n!** is shorthand for the command **factorial(n)**.

```
> 0!, 5!;
```

$$1, 120$$

For floating-point n, generalized factorial function values **n!** are calculated by using **GAMMA(n+1)**.

```
> 2.5!;
```

$$3.323350970$$

```
> (-2)!;
```

```
Error, numeric exception: division by zero
```

The type of an unevaluated factorial is !. Note that in Maple, n!! does *not* denote the double factorial function.[19] It denotes *repeated* factorial, n!! = (n!)!.

> 3!!;

$$720$$

The mod Operator The mod operator evaluates an expression modulo m, for a nonzero integer m.

```
e mod m;
```

The operator syntax e mod m is equivalent to the 'mod'(e,m) command.[20]

> 5 mod 2;

$$1$$

Maple has two representations for an *integer modulo m*: modp and mods. You can assign the environment variable 'mod' to either modp or mods.

modp In the *positive representation,* e mod m is an integer between 0 and $m - 1$, inclusive. The following assignment explicitly selects the positive representation.

> 'mod' := modp;

$$mod := modp$$

> 9 mod 5;

$$4$$

This is the default representation.

---

[19] For information on the Maple doublefactorial command, refer to ?doublefactorial.

[20] Use left single quotes around mod when it is not used as an operator because it is a reserved word. For more information about reserved words, see page 24 or refer to ?keyword.

mods In the *symmetric representation*, e mod m is an integer between
-floor((abs(m)-1)/2) and floor(abs(m)/2). The following assignment selects the symmetric representation.[21]

> 'mod' := mods;

$$mod := mods$$

> 9 mod 5;

$$-1$$

Alternatively, you can invoke the modp and mods commands directly.

> modp(9,5), mods(9,5);

$$4, -1$$

The mod operator accepts the inert operator &^ for powering. That is, i&^j mod m calculates i^j mod m. Instead of separately computing the integer i^j , which may be too large to compute, and then reducing modulo m, Maple computes the power by using binary powering with remainders.

> 2^(2^100) mod 5;

Error, numeric exception: overflow

> 2 &^ (2^100) mod 5;

$$1$$

The first operand of the mod operator can be a general expression. Maple evaluates the expression over the ring of integers modulo m. For polynomials, it reduces rational coefficients modulo m. The mod operator accepts many functions for polynomial and matrix arithmetic over finite rings and fields, for example, Factor for polynomial factorization and Nullspace for matrix null spaces.[22]

---

[21] For more information on the floor function, refer to ?floor.

[22] Do not confuse the commands factor and Factor or int and Int. The former evaluate immediately; the latter are *inert* commands which Maple does not evaluate until you make the call to mod. For more information on inert functions, refer to ?inert.

```
> 1/2 mod 5;
```

$$3$$

```
> 9*x^2 + x/2 + 13 mod 5;
```

$$4\,x^2 + 3\,x + 3$$

```
> Factor(4*x^2 + 3*x + 3) mod 5;
```

$$4\,(x+3)\,(x+4)$$

The mod command can also compute over a Galois field $GF(p^k)$, that is, the finite field with p^k elements.[23]

The Neutral Operators &name   Maple has a neutral operator (or user-defined) facility. You can form a neutral operator symbol by using the ampersand character "&" followed by one or more characters. There are two varieties of &-names: alphanumeric and non-alphanumeric.

alphanumeric The & character followed by any Maple name not requiring left single quotes, for example, &wedge.

non-alphanumeric The & character followed by one or more non-alphanumeric characters, for example, &+ or &++.

The following characters *cannot* appear in an &-name

& | ( ) [ ] { } ; : ’ ‘ # \ %

plus the new line and blank characters.

You can use neutral operators as unary prefix operators, binary infix operators, or function calls. In any of these cases, they generate function calls with the name of the function being that of the neutral operator. (In the standard pretty-printing (output format) mode, these function calls are printed in binary operator format when exactly two operands exist, and in unary operator format when exactly one operand exists. However, the internal representation is an unevaluated function.) Consider the following example.

---

[23]For more information and a list of commands that mod accepts, refer to ?mod.

```
> a &~ b &~ c;
```

$$(a \,\&^{\sim} b) \,\&^{\sim} c$$

```
> op(%);
```

$$a \,\&^{\sim} b, \, c$$

```
> op(0,%%);
```

$$\&^{\sim}$$

Maple imposes no semantics on the neutral operators. The user can define the operator to have a meaning by assigning the name to a Maple procedure. You can define manipulations on expressions containing such operators by using the interface to user-defined procedures for standard library commands, including `simplify`, `diff`, `combine`, `series`, `evalf`, and many others. For more information on neutral operators, refer to **Neutral Operators** in section 1.5 of the *Maple Advanced Programming Guide*.

The Relational Operators <, >, <=, >=, and <> You can form new types of expressions from ordinary algebraic expressions by using the relational operators <, >, <=, >=, and <>. The semantics of these operators depend on whether they occur in an algebraic context or in a Boolean context.

In an *algebraic* context, the relational operators are simply placeholders for forming equations or inequalities. Maple fully supports addition of equations or inequalities, and multiplication of an equation or inequality by an algebraic expression. To add or subtract two equations, for example, Maple applies the addition or subtraction to each side of the equations, yielding a new equation. In the case of multiplying an equation by an expression, Maple distributes the multiplication to each side of the equation. You can perform similar operations with inequalities.

```
> e := x + 3*y = z;
```

$$e := x + 3y = z$$

```
> 2*e;
```

$$2\,x + 6\,y = 2\,z$$

The type of an equation is = or `equation`. Use the `op(0,...)` or `whattype` command to return the principal type.

```
> op(0,e);
```

$$=$$

```
> whattype(e);
```

$$=$$

An equation has two operands, the left-hand side and the right-hand side. In addition to using the `op` command to select the operands of an equation, you can use the `lhs` and `rhs` commands.

```
> lhs(e);
```

$$x + 3\,y$$

The `type` command also accepts the types `<>`, `<`, and `<=`. Maple automatically converts inequalities involving `>` or `>=` to `<` and `<=`, respectively. All the relational types have two operands.

```
> e := a > b;
```

$$e := b < a$$

```
> op(e);
```

$$b,\, a$$

In a *Boolean* context, Maple evaluates expressions to the value **true** or the value **false**. A Boolean context includes the condition in an **if** statement and the condition in the **while** clause of a loop.[24]

---

[24]For more information about **if** statements and **while** clauses, see chapter 5, or refer to ?if and ?while.

In the case of the operators <, <=, >, and >=, the difference of the operands, in general, evaluates to a numeric constant that Maple compares with zero.

```
> if 2<3 then "less" else "not less" end if;
```

$$\text{``less''}$$

You can also use the relational operators to compare strings.

```
> if "f" <= "m" then "first half" else "second half" end if;
```

$$\text{``first half''}$$

In the case of the relations = and <>, the operands can be arbitrary expressions (algebraic or non-algebraic). This equality test for expressions tests object equality of the Maple representations of the expressions, which is *not* the same as mathematical equivalence.

To evaluate a relation in a Boolean context, use the **evalb** command.

```
> evalb( x + y = y + x );
```

$$true$$

```
> evalb( x^2 - y^2 = (x - y)*(x + y) );
```

$$false$$

For the latter example, apply the **expand** command to show that the equation is **true**.

```
> evalb( x^2 - y^2 = expand( (x - y)*(x + y) ) );
```

$$true$$

You can also use the **is** command, instead of **evalb**, to evaluate relations in a Boolean context.

```
> is( x^2 - y^2 = (x - y)*(x + y) );
```

$$true$$

```
> is( 3<Pi );
```

$$true$$

The Logical Operators and, or, xor, implies, **and** not   Generally, you can form an expression by using the logical operators and, or, xor, implies, and not. The first four are binary operators and the last is a unary (prefix) operator. An expression containing one or more logical operators is automatically evaluated in a Boolean context.

```
> 2>3 or not 5>1;
```

$$false$$

```
> 3 < evalf(Pi) xor evalf(exp(1)) < evalf(Pi);
```

$$false$$

The precedence of the logical operators and, or, and not is analogous to that of multiplication, addition, and exponentiation, respectively. Here no parentheses are necessary.[25]

```
> (a and b) or ((not c) and d);
```

$$a \text{ and } b \text{ or } \text{ not } c \text{ and } d$$

The xor operator is of lower precedence than or. The implies operator has the lowest precedence of the logical operators.

The type names for the logical operators and, or, xor, implies, and not are and, or, xor, implies, and not, respectively. The first four have two operands, the last has one operand.

```
> b := x and y or z;
```

$$b := x \text{ and } y \text{ or } z$$

```
> whattype(b);
```

---

[25] For more information about precedence of Maple operators, see Table 3.4 on page 89 or refer to ?precedence.

or

```
> op(b);
```

$$x \text{ and } y, z$$

In expressions with operators of the same precedence, the evaluation of Boolean expressions that involve the logical operators **and** and **or** proceeds from left to right, and terminates once Maple can determine the truth of the whole expression. Consider the evaluation of the following.

```
a and b and c
```

If the result of evaluating a is `false`, the result of the entire Boolean expression is `false`, regardless of the value of b and c. Therefore, Maple stops evaluating the expression. These evaluation rules are commonly known as *McCarthy* evaluation rules and they are quite crucial for programming. Consider the following statement.

```
if x <> 0 and f(x)/x > 1 then ... end if;
```

If Maple always evaluated both operands of the **and** clause, when x is 0, evaluation would result in a *division by zero* error. The advantage of the above code is that Maple attempts to check the second condition only when $x \neq 0$.

Boolean Expressions In general, a Boolean context requires a Boolean expression. Therefore, you must use the Boolean constants `true`, `false`, and `FAIL`, the relational operators, and the logical operators to form Boolean expressions. The **type** command accepts all these for the name `boolean`.

The evaluation of Boolean expressions in Maple uses *three-valued logic*. In addition to the special names `true` and `false`, Maple also understands the special name `FAIL`. Maple sometimes uses the value `FAIL` when it is unable to completely solve a problem. You can interpret it as the value "*unknown.*"

```
> is(sin(1),positive);
```

true

Table 3.3 Truth Tables

and	false	true	FAIL
false	false	false	false
true	false	true	FAIL
FAIL	false	FAIL	FAIL

or	false	true	FAIL
false	false	true	FAIL
true	true	true	true
FAIL	FAIL	true	FAIL

not	false	true	FAIL
	true	false	FAIL

```
> is(a1,positive);
```

false

In the context of the Boolean clause in an **if** statement or a **while** statement, Maple determines the branching of the program by treating the value **FAIL** as if it were the value **false**. With three-valued logic, you do not need to test for **FAIL** separately when using the **is** command. Otherwise, you would need to write

```
if is( a - 1, positive) = true then ...
```

The three-valued logic allows you to write

```
if is( a - 1, positive) then ...
```

The evaluation of a Boolean expression yields **true**, **false**, or **FAIL** according to Table 3.3.

It is important to note that three-valued logic leads to asymmetry in the use of **if** statements and **while** statements. For example, the following two statements are not equivalent.

```
if condition then statseq1 else statseq2 end if;
if not condition then statseq2 else statseq1 end if;
```

If **condition** has the value **FAIL**, **statseq2** is executed in the first structure and **statseq1** is executed in the second structure.

The Set Operators union, minus, intersect, **and** subset The **union**, **intersect**, **minus**, and **subset** commands are used for the set union, intersection, difference, and subset operations. The **union** and **intersect**

commands are infix n-ary operators. The **minus** and **subset** commands are binary infix operators.

```
> A:={1,2,3}; B:={2,3,4};
```

$$A := \{1, 2, 3\}$$

$$B := \{2, 3, 4\}$$

```
> A union B;
```

$$\{1, 2, 3, 4\}$$

```
> A intersect B;
```

$$\{2, 3\}$$

```
> A minus B;
```

$$\{1\}$$

```
> A subset B;
```

false

Associated with each set operator, there is a type of the same name. For more information, refer to **?type**.

The assuming **Operator**   The **assuming** operator performs a single computation under assumptions on the name(s) in the expression. For more information about the **assuming** command, refer to chapter 6 of the *Maple Learning Guide* or **?assuming**.

Precedence Rules   The order of precedence of all the operators in this section is shown in Table 3.4, from highest to lowest binding strengths.[26]

---

[26] For more information about precedence in Maple, refer to **?precedence**.

Table 3.4 Operator Precedence Order

Operator	Associativity
%	non-associative
&-operators	left associative
!	left associative
^, @@	non-associative
., *, /, @, intersect	left associative
+, -, union	left associative
mod	non-associative
subset	non-associative
..	non-associative
<, <=, >, >=, =, <>, in	non-associative
$	non-associative
not	right associative
and	left associative
or	left associative
xor	left associative
implies	non-associative
assuming	non-associative

Data Structures

The Maple system includes many data structures. The more common ones are mentioned here in the context of expressions. For a thorough discussion on sequences, sets, lists, tables, arrays, Arrays, and others, see chapter 4.

Sequences, Sets, and Lists   A *sequence* is a group of expressions separated by commas.

```
expression1, expression2, expression3
```

Example   The parameter s forms the sequence containing the expressions 5, 6, and 7.

> s := 5, 6, 7;

$$s := 5, 6, 7$$

> whattype(%);

exprseq

You can also use the **seq** operator to form sequences.

```
> seq( i, i=5..7 );
```

$$5, 6, 7$$

Sequences occur in many Maple expressions. In particular, a sequence is the basic element for forming sets, lists, and function calls. For more information on sequences, refer to chapter 2 of the *Maple Learning Guide*.

A *set* is an unordered sequence of unique expressions. A set is formed by enclosing a sequence in braces (**{}**).

```
> myset := {s};
```

$$myset := \{5, 6, 7\}$$

```
> whattype(%);
```

$$set$$

A *list* is an ordered sequence of expressions. The expressions in the list need not be unique. A list is formed by enclosing a sequence in square brackets (**[]**).

```
> mylist := [s];
```

$$mylist := [5, 6, 7]$$

```
> whattype(%);
```

$$list$$

Tables, arrays, and Arrays The table data structure in Maple is a special object for representing data in tables. You can create a table either explicitly by using the **table** command or implicitly by assignment to an indexed name. The following statements are equivalent.

```
> T := table([(Na,11) = 23]);
```

$$T := \text{table}([(Na, 11) = 23])$$

> T[Na,11] := 23;

$$T_{Na, 11} := 23$$

They both create a table object with one component. The purpose of a table is to allow fast access to data.

> T[Na,11];

$$23$$

The array data structure in Maple is a specialization of the table data structure. An array is a table with specified dimensions, where each dimension is an integer range. To create an array, use the **array** command.

> a := array(1..2,1..2);

$$a := \text{array}(1..2, \ 1..2, \ [])$$

An Array is a table-like data structure with fixed dimensions and integer indices.[27] To create an Array, use the **Array** command.

> A := Array([[1,2],[3,4]]);

$$A := \begin{bmatrix} 1 & 2 \\ 3 & 4 \end{bmatrix}$$

For more information about tables, arrays, and Arrays, see chapter 4.

Functions

A *function* expression represents a function call, or in other words, an application of a function or procedure to arguments. Such an expression is said to be of type **function**. A typical example of an expression of type **function** is the expression **f(x)**, which represents the application of the expression **f** to the argument sequence **x**. The *entire* expression **f(x)** is of type **function** (that is, a *function call* or *function application*), while

---

[27] For information on the differences between arrays and Arrays, see **4.4 arrays and Arrays**.

the expression f is typically *not* itself of type `function` (but it is often of type `procedure`).

A function call in Maple takes the following form.

---

f(*sequence*)

Often f is a procedure, or a name that evaluates to a procedure.

```
> sin(x);
```

$$\sin(x)$$

```
> min(2,3,1);
```

$$1$$

```
> g();
```

$$g()$$

```
> a[1](x);
```

$$a_1(x)$$

Maple executes a function call as follows. First, f is evaluated (typically yielding a procedure). Next, Maple evaluates the operands of `sequence` (the arguments) in an unspecified order. If any of the arguments evaluates to a sequence, Maple flattens the sequence of evaluated arguments into one sequence. If f evaluates to a procedure, Maple invokes this procedure on the argument sequence.[28]

```
> x := 1:
> f(x);
```

$$f(1)$$

```
> s := 2,3;
```

---

[28] In the example below, the arrow (->) notation is used. For more information about creating procedures using the arrow notation, see page 207.

$$s := 2, 3$$

```
> f(s,x);
```

$$f(2, 3, 1)$$

```
> f := g;
```

$$f := g$$

```
> f(s,x);
```

$$g(2, 3, 1)$$

```
> g := (a,b,c) -> a+b+c;
```

$$g := (a, b, c) \rightarrow a + b + c$$

```
> f(s,x);
```

$$6$$

As mentioned previously, a function object's type is **function**. The operands are the arguments. The zeroth operand is the name of the function.

```
> m := min(x,y,x,z);
```

$$m := \min(1, y, z)$$

```
> op(0,m);
```

$$min$$

```
> op(m);
```

$$1, y, z$$

```
> type(m,function);
```

$$true$$

```
> f := n!;
```

$$f := n!$$

```
> type(f, function);
```

$$true$$

```
> op(0, f);
```

$$factorial$$

```
> op(f);
```

$$n$$

In general, the function name **f** can be one of the following.

- name

- procedure definition

- integer

- float

- parenthesized algebraic expression

- function

- module selection, for example, `module_name:-f(sequence)`

If **f** is a procedure definition, you can write, for example,

```
> proc(t) t*(1-t) end proc (t^2);
```

$$t^2 \left(1 - t^2\right)$$

instead of the following two statements.

```
> h := proc(t) t*(t-1) end proc;
```

$$h := \mathbf{proc}(t)\, t * (t - 1) \,\mathbf{end\ proc}$$

```
> h(t^2);
```

$$t^2 \left(t^2 - 1 \right)$$

If `f` is an integer or a float, Maple treats `f` as a constant operator. That is, `f(x)` returns `f`.

```
> 2(x);
```

$$2$$

The following rules define the meaning of a parenthesized algebraic expression.

```
> (f + g)(x), (f - g)(x), (-f)(x), (f@g)(x);
```

$$f(x) + g(x),\ f(x) - g(x),\ -f(x),\ f(g(x))$$

Recall that the `@` sign denotes functional composition, that is, `f@g` denotes $f \circ g$. These rules together with the previous rule mean the following.

```
> (f@g + f^2*g +1)(x);
```

$$f(g(x)) + f(x)^2\, g(x) + 1$$

Recall that `@@` denotes functional exponentiation, that is, `f@@n` denotes $f^{(n)}$ which means `f` composed with itself `n` times.

```
> (f@@3)(x);
```

$$\left(f^{(3)} \right)(x)$$

```
> expand(%);
```

$$f(f(f(x)))$$

Finally, f can be a function, as in the following statements.[29]

```
> cos(0);
```

$$1$$

```
> f(g)(0);
```

$$f(g)(0)$$

```
> D(cos)(0);
```

$$0$$

3.3   Using Expressions

Investigating the Parts of an Expression

When programming with expressions, it is important to be able to:

- Determine whether an expression has a given type[30]

- Determine the number of operands in an expression

- Select operands from an expression

- Replace operands in an expression

The commands have been introduced previously, but they are now formally presented in Table 3.5.

Consider the following formula.

```
> f := sin(x) + 2*cos(x)^2*sin(x) + 3;
```

$$f := \sin(x) + 2\cos(x)^2 \sin(x) + 3$$

```
> type(f, '+');
```

---

[29] For more information about how to define a function by using functional operators, see page 231 or refer to ?unapply.

[30] An expression can have multiple types.

Table 3.5 Type and Operand Commands

Command	Description
type(f, t)	tests if f is of type t
nops(f)	returns the number of operands of f
op(i, f)	selects the ith operand of f
subsop(i=g, f)	replaces the ith operand of f with g

$$true$$

```
> type(f, '*');
```

$$false$$

```
> nops(f);
```

$$3$$

```
> op(1, f);
```

$$\sin(x)$$

```
> subsop(2=0, f);
```

$$\sin(x) + 3$$

The op command has several other useful forms.
The command

```
op(i..j, f)
```

returns the sequence

```
op(i, f), op(i+1, f), ..., op(j-1, f), op(j, f)
```

of operands of f between i and j inclusive.
The command

```
op([i, j, k], f)
```

is an abbreviation of

```
op(k, op(j, op(i, f)))
```

The last object in the list can also be a range.
The command

```
op([i1, ..., iN, j..k], f)
```

is an abbreviation of

```
op(j..k, op(iN, ..., op(i1, f)...))
```

To see the whole sequence of operands of an expression, use

```
op(f)
```

which is equivalent to `op(1..nops(f),f)`.

The special operand `op(0,f)` generally returns the primary **type** of an expression.[31] However, if `f` is a function, it returns the name of the function.

```
> op(0, f);
```

$$+$$

```
> op(1..3, f);
```

$$\sin(x),\ 2\cos(x)^2\sin(x),\ 3$$

```
> op(0, op(1,f));
```

$$\sin$$

```
> op(0, op(2,f));
```

$$*$$

---

[31] For a complete description of `op(0,f)`, refer to ?op.

Using the results of these commands, you can start to develop an *expression tree* of *nodes*, *branches*, and *leaves* for f.

$$\sin(x) + 2\cos(x)^2 \sin(x) + 3$$

The complete tree is:

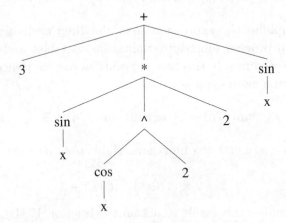

The first "node" of the expression tree labeled "+" is a sum. This indicates the expression's type (from op(f, 0)).

This expression has three branches corresponding to the three terms in the sum (from op(1..3, f))—that is, $\sin(x)$, $2\cos(x)^2\sin(x)$, and 3.

The nodes of each branch indicate the type of each term in the sum. The leaves of the tree are the names and integers in this example.[32,33]

Evaluating and Simplifying Expressions
Example 1   To understand how Maple evaluates and simplifies expressions, consider the following example.

```
> x := Pi/6:
> sin(x) + 2*cos(x)^2*sin(x) + 3;
```

---

[32] The idea of an expression tree *closely* models how Maple interprets expressions. More precisely, Maple uses DAGs (directed acyclic graphs) to represent arbitrary expressions. While similar to this idea of an expression tree, they have the additional property that all common subexpressions are identified by Maple *only once*. As a result, since all like subexpressions are shared, expressions are nonmutable, and changing an expression involves a copy operation. For more information about DAGs, refer to chapter 6 of the *Maple Advanced Programming Guide*.

[33] For more information about the display of Maple data structures, refer to ?dismantle.

$$\frac{17}{4}$$

Maple first reads and parses the input. As the input is parsed, Maple builds an expression tree to represent the value

$$\sin(x) + 2\cos(x)^2\sin(x) + 3.$$

Maple simplifies the expression tree, and then evaluates the result. The evaluation process substitutes values for variables and invokes any functions or procedures. In this case, x evaluates to $\pi/6$. Hence, with these substitutions, the expression is:

$$\sin(\pi/6) + 2\cos(\pi/6)^2\sin(\pi/6) + 3$$

Invoking the **sin** and **cos** functions, Maple obtains a new "expression tree",

$$1/2 + 2 \times (1/2\sqrt{3})^2 \times 1/2 + 3.$$

Maple simplifies this result to obtain the fraction 17/4.

Example 2   Alternatively, consider the next example: evaluation occurs, but no simplification is possible.

```
> x := 1;
```

$$x := 1$$

```
> sin(x) + 2*cos(x)^2*sin(x) + 3;
```

$$\sin(1) + 2\cos(1)^2\sin(1) + 3$$

Unevaluated Expressions

In general, Maple evaluates all expressions immediately. In some situations, it is necessary to delay evaluation. An expression enclosed in right single quotes is called an *unevaluated* expression.

```
'expression'
```

For example, the statements

```
> a := 1; x := a + b;
```

$$a := 1$$

$$x := 1 + b$$

assign the value 1 + b to the name x, while the statements

```
> a := 1; x := 'a' + b;
```

$$a := 1$$

$$x := a + b$$

assign the value a + b to the name x if b has no value.

Evaluating an expression enclosed in right single quotes removes one level of quotes, so in some cases nested quotes are useful.

Note: There is a distinction between evaluation and simplification of statements.

Example Consider the following

```
> x := '2 + 3';
```

$$x := 5$$

which assigns the value 5 to the name x though the expression is enclosed in right single quotes. First '2+3' simplifies to '5'. The evaluator removes the quotes, returning 5.

The result of evaluating an expression with two levels of quotes is an expression of type uneval. This expression has only one operand, namely the expression inside the outermost pair of quotes.

```
> op(''x - 2'');
```

$$x - 2$$

```
> whattype(''x - 2'');
```

$$uneval$$

To reset the value of a name, assign the unevaluated name (its initial value) to the name.[34]

```
> x := 'x';
```

$$x := x$$

Now the value of x is reset to x.

Another special case of unevaluation arises in the function call

```
'f'(sequence)
```

Suppose the arguments evaluate to the sequence a. Since the result of evaluating 'f' is not a procedure, Maple returns the unevaluated function call f(a).

```
> ''sin''(Pi);
```

$$\text{'sin'}(\pi)$$

```
> %;
```

$$\sin(\pi)$$

```
> %;
```

$$0$$

You will find this facility useful when writing procedures that implement simplification rules—refer to the section 1.4 of the *Maple Advanced Programming Guide*.[35]

Substituting Subexpressions

To combine the acts of substitution and evaluation, use the two-parameter version of the eval command.

The eval command has the following syntax, where s is an equation, list, or set of equations.

---

[34] For more information about unassigning names, see page 110.

[35] For more information and examples regarding unevaluated expressions in Maple, refer to ?uneval.

```
eval( expr, s );
```

```
> expr := x^3 + 3*x + 1;
```

$$expr := x^3 + 3\,x + 1$$

```
> eval( expr, x=y );
```

$$y^3 + 3\,y + 1$$

```
> eval( expr, x=2 );
```

$$15$$

```
> eval( sin(x) + x^2, x=0 );
```

$$0$$

The **subs** command performs *syntactic* substitution. It replaces subexpressions in an expression with a new value; the subexpressions must be operands in the sense of the **op** command.

The **subs** command has the following syntax where **s** is an equation, list, or set of equations.

```
subs( s, expr );
```

The **subs** command traverses the expression **expr** and compares each operand in **expr** with the left-hand side(s) of the equation(s) **s**. If an operand is equal to a left-hand side of an equation in **s**, **subs** replaces the operand with the right-hand side of the equation. If **s** is a list or set of equations, Maple makes the substitutions indicated by the equations simultaneously.

```
> f := x*y^2;
```

$$f := x\,y^2$$

```
> subs( {y=z, x=y, z=w}, f );
```

$$y\,z^2$$

The general syntax of the subs command is

```
subs( s1, s2, ..., sn, expr );
```

where s1, s2, . . . , sn are equations, or sets or lists of equations, $n > 0$, and expr is an expression. This is equivalent to the following sequence of substitutions.

```
subs( sn, ..., subs( s2, subs( s1, expr ) ) ) ;
```

Thus, subs substitutes according to the given equations from left to right. Notice the difference between the previous example and the following one.

```
> subs( y=z, x=y, z=w, f );
```

$$y\, w^2$$

The difference between the eval and subs commands is demonstrated in the following example.

```
> subs( x=0, cos(x) + x^2 );
```

$$\cos(0)$$

```
> eval( cos(x) + x^2, x=0 );
```

$$1$$

In the preceding subs command, Maple substitutes 0 (zero) for x and simplifies the result. Maple simplifies cos(0) + 0^2 to cos(0). By using the eval command, Maple evaluates cos(0) to 1 (one).

Substitution compares only operands in the expression tree of expr with the left-hand side of an equation.

```
> eval( a*b*c, a*b=d );
```

$$a\, b\, c$$

The substitution does not result in d*c because the operands of the product a*b*c are a, b, c. That is, the products a*b, b*c, and a*c do not appear explicitly as operands in the expression a*b*c. The easiest way to make such substitutions is to solve the equation for one unknown and substitute for that unknown.

```
> eval( a*b*c, a=d/b );
```

$$d c$$

You cannot always do this, and you may find that it does not always produce the results you expect. The **algsubs** routine provides a more powerful substitution facility.

```
> algsubs( a*b=d, a*b*c );
```

$$d c$$

Displaying Large Expressions: Labels

A label in Maple has the following form.

```
%natural
```

That is, it consists of the unary operator % followed by a natural integer.[36]

A label is only valid after Maple introduces it. The purpose of labels is to name (label) common subexpressions to decrease the size of the printed output, increasing comprehensibility. After the **prettyprinter** displays it, you can use a label like an assigned name.

```
> solve( {x^3 - y^3 = 2, x^2 + y^2 = 1}, {x, y});
```

$$\{y = \%1, \ x = -\frac{1}{3} \%1 \left(-4 \%1^3 - 3 - \%1^2 + 6 \%1 + 2 \%1^4\right)\}$$

$$\%1 := \text{RootOf}(3 \_Z^2 + 3 - 3 \_Z^4 + 2 \_Z^6 + 4 \_Z^3)$$

After Maple executes this statement, the label %1 is an assigned name with a value of the preceding RootOf expression.

---

[36]The percent sign performs two roles in the Maple program: a label indicator and the ditto operator, which represents the result of the last, second last, and third last result. For more information on the ditto operator, see page 25.

```
> %1;
```

$$\text{RootOf}(3\,\_Z^2 + 3 - 3\,\_Z^4 + 2\,\_Z^6 + 4\,\_Z^3)$$

Two facilities are available for use with labels. The command

```
interface( labelwidth=n );
```

specifies that Maple should not display expressions less than (approximately) n characters wide as labels. The default value is 20 characters. The command

```
interface( labeling=truefalse );
```

enables the use of %1, %2, ... labels for output subexpressions. You can turn off this facility by using the following command.

```
> interface(labeling=false);
```

Structured Types

A simple type check may not provide sufficient information. For example, the command

```
> type( x^2, '^' );
```

$$\textit{true}$$

verifies that x^2 is an exponentiation, but it does not indicate whether the exponent is, say, an integer. To do so, you must use *structured* types. Consider the following example.

```
> type( x^2, name^integer );
```

$$\textit{true}$$

Because x is a name and 2 is an integer, the command returns true.
To learn more about structured types, study the following examples. The square root of x does not have the structured type name^integer.

```
> type( x^(1/2), name^integer );
```

false

The expression (x+1)^2 does not have type name^integer, because x+1 is not a name.

> type((x+1)^2, name^integer);

false

The type **anything** matches any expression.

> type((x+1)^2, anything^integer);

true

An expression matches a *set* of types if the expression matches one of the types in the set.

> type(1, {integer, name});

true

> type(x, {integer, name});

true

The type set(type) matches a *set* of elements of type **type**.

> type({1,2,3,4}, set(integer));

true

> type({x,2,3,y}, set({integer, name}));

true

Similarly, the type list(type) matches a *list* of elements of type **type**.

> type([2..3, 5..7], list(range));

true

Note that e^2 is not of type `anything^2`.

```
> exp(2);
```

$$e^2$$

```
> type( %, anything^2 );
```

false

Because e^2 is the pretty-printed (output formatted) version of `exp(2)`, it does not match the type `anything^2`.

```
> type( exp(2), 'exp'(integer) );
```

true

The next example illustrates the need to use right single quotes (') to delay evaluation when including Maple commands in `type` expressions.[37]

```
> type( int(f(x), x), int(anything, anything) );
Error, testing against an invalid type
```

An error is returned because Maple evaluates `int(anything, anything)`.

```
> int(anything, anything);
```

$$\frac{1}{2}\ anything^2$$

This is not a valid type. If you enclose the `int` command in right single quotes, the type checking works as intended.

```
> type( int(f(x), x), 'int'(anything, anything) );
```

true

The type `specfunc(type, f)` matches the function `f` with zero or more arguments of type `type`.

---

[37]For more information on delayed evaluation, see page 100.

```
> type( exp(x), specfunc(name, exp) );
```

$$true$$

```
> type( f(), specfunc(name, f) );
```

$$true$$

The type function(type) matches any function with zero or more arguments of type type.

```
> type( f(1,2,3), function(integer) );
```

$$true$$

```
> type( f(1,x,Pi), function( {integer, name} ) );
```

$$true$$

In addition to testing the type of arguments, you can test the number of arguments. The type anyfunc(t1, ..., tn) matches any function with n arguments of the listed types in the correct order.

```
> type( f(1,x), anyfunc(integer, name) );
```

$$true$$

```
> type( f(x,1), anyfunc(integer, name) );
```

$$false$$

```
> type( f(x), anyfunc(integer, name) );
```

$$false$$

Another useful variation is to use the And, Or, and Not type constructors to create Boolean combinations of types. Note that these are different from the logical operators and, or, and not discussed on page 85.[38]

---

[38] For more information on structured types, refer to ?type,structured. For more information on how to define your own types, refer to ?type,definition.

```
> type(Pi, 'And( constant, numeric)');
```

$$false$$

Pi is of type symbol, not of type numeric.

```
> type(Pi, 'And( constant, Not(numeric))');
```

$$true$$

3.4   Statements

The statement is an important component in the Maple language. There are many types of statements in Maple.

- assignment statement

- selection statements

- repetition statements

- read and save statements

- break and next statements

- error and return statements

- use statement

- quit statement

- expressions

Expressions have been discussed at length earlier in this chapter. The remainder of this chapter discusses the assignment statement in detail, and introduces the other statements listed previously.

The Assignment Statement

An assignment statement can take one of the following forms, where expr is any expression.

```
name := expr;
(name1, ..., namen) := (expr1, ..., exprn);
```

Once an assignment statement is entered, the left-hand side of the assignment operator is evaluated to a name. Then, the right-hand side is evaluated to an expression. Finally, the assignment is performed.[39]

> a := 0;

$$a := 0$$

You can perform multiple assignments in one statement. If the left-hand side is a sequence of names enclosed in parentheses, the right-hand side must evaluate to a sequence of expressions (with the same number of components) enclosed in parentheses. The assignments are then performed, matching each name with the corresponding expression.

> (a, b) := (1,2);

$$a, b := 1, 2$$

> a; b;

$$1$$

$$2$$

A common error is to confuse an assignment statement with an equation. An assignment statement uses the assignment operator (:=) to assign an evaluated expression to a name. An equation uses an equal sign (=) to represent the equality of two operands, the right-hand side and the left-hand side.

Consider the following examples. You can use equations as arguments to the solve command. The first statement assigns the equation on the right-hand side of the assignment statement to the name eq1. The second statement solves the equation.

> eq1 := y = 3*x - 4;

---

[39]You can also use the assign command to make an assignment. For more information, refer to ?assign.

$$eq1 := y = 3\,x - 4$$

```
> solve(eq1, x);
```

$$\frac{1}{3}\,y + \frac{4}{3}$$

Testing for Assignment   You can test whether a name has an assigned value by using the `assigned` command.

```
assigned( name );
```

The `assigned` command returns `true` if `name` has a value different from its name. Otherwise, `false` is returned.

```
> assigned(a);
```

false

To return an expression sequence of names that are currently assigned values different from their names, use the `anames` command. It has the following syntax.

```
anames();
```

```
> a := 0:   b:=1:
> anames();
```

a, b

You can also use `anames` to return an expression sequence of names assigned values of certain types, or the current environment variables in the session. For more information, refer to `?anames`.

Unassigning a Name   There are many ways to unassign a name (reset its value to its name).

If a name is unassigned, it acts as an *unknown*. After a name is assigned a value, it acts as a *variable*. However, it is often desirable to unassign an assigned name, so that you can use the name as an unknown again.

One method of unassigning a name is to assign the unevaluated name (its initial value) to the name. To do this, enclose the name in right single quotes to delay evaluation.

```
> a := 4;
```

$$a := 4$$

```
> a;
```

$$4$$

```
> a := 'a';
```

$$a := a$$

```
> a;
```

$$a$$

You can also unassign names by using the **unassign** command.

```
unassign( name1, name2, ... );
```

The arguments to **unassign** must be *unevaluated* names.

```
> i := 1;
```

$$i := 1$$

```
> unassign(i);
```

```
Error, (in unassign) cannot unassign '1' (argument must
be assignable)
```

```
> unassign('i');
```

The value returned by **unassign** is NULL.

Another way you can unassign a name is by using the **evaln** command.

```
evaln( name );
```

The **evaln** command evaluates **name** to a *name* (as opposed to evaluating **name** to its *value* as in other calls). Therefore, you can unassign a name by using **evaln** in the following manner.

```
> a := 4;
```

$$a := 4$$

```
> a := evaln(a);
```

$$a := a$$

```
> a;
```

$$a$$

Selection Statements

Selection is an important operation in programming. To perform selection, use the *conditional* or **if** statement. It has the following syntax.

```
if Boolean expression then
   statement sequence
elif Boolean expression then
   statement sequence
else
   statement sequence
end if
```

The construct **elif conditional expression then statement sequence** can be repeated any number of times.

```
> a := sin(1.8): b := ln(1.8):
> if a > b then
>    print( "a is larger" );
> else
>    print( "a is not larger" );
> end if;
```

$$\text{"a is larger"}$$

For more information about selection and the `if` statement, see **5.1 Selection and Conditional Execution**.

Repetition Statements

Looping constructs, such as the `for` loop and the `while` loop, are used to repeat similar actions a number of times.

Example 1   Without using looping constructs, the following statements are necessary to calculate the sum of the first four natural numbers.

```
> total := 0;
```

$$total := 0$$

```
> total := total + 1;
```

$$total := 1$$

```
> total := total + 2;
```

$$total := 3$$

```
> total := total + 3;
```

$$total := 6$$

```
> total := total + 4;
```

$$total := 10$$

Example 2   The same calculation is simpler if you use the `for` loop.

```
> total := 0;
```

$$total := 0$$

```
> for i from 1 to 4 do
>     total := total + i;
> end do;
```

$$total := 1$$

$$total := 3$$

$$total := 6$$

$$total := 10$$

The initial value of i is 1. After each execution of the assignment statement (the body of the loop), the value of i is increased by 1. The value of i is compared to 4 before the body is re-executed. If i is less than or equal to 4, Maple executes the body of the loop again. After the execution of the loop finishes, the value of **total** is 10 and the value of i is 5.

```
> total;
```

$$10$$

Example 3 Alternatively, you can calculate the sum of the first four natural numbers by using the **while** loop.

```
> total := 0; i := 0;
```

$$total := 0$$

$$i := 0$$

```
> while i <= 4 do
>     total := total + i;
>     i := i + 1;
> end do;
```

$$total := 0$$

$$i := 1$$

$$total := 1$$

$$i := 2$$

$$total := 3$$

$$i := 3$$

$$total := 6$$

$$i := 4$$

$$total := 10$$

$$i := 5$$

Before each cycle through the while loop, Maple checks whether i is greater than 4. If it is not, then Maple executes the body of the loop. When the execution of the loop finishes, the value of total is 10 and the value of i is 5.

Note: In the for loop, i is incremented in the for i from 1 to 4 do part of the statement. In the while loop, i is incremented by the i := i+1 statement in the loop body.

The while and the for loop are both special cases of a more general repetition statement. It has the following syntax.

```
for name from expr by expr to expr while expr do
    statement sequence
end do;
```

For more information about repetition using loops, see **5.2 Repetition**.

The read and save Statements
You can interact with Maple either directly by entering a command using the keyboard, or indirectly by accessing information from a file. The read and save statements read and save Maple data and procedures to and from files. For more information about these statements, see chapter 7.

The break and next Statements

The **break** and **next** statements are used for controlling how a repetition statement is executed.

The **break** statement causes Maple to exit from the repetition statement. Execution then proceeds with the first statement *that follows* the repetition statement.

```
> L := [9,8,7,6]:
```

```
> for i in L do
>     if i=8 then
>         break
>     end if;
>     print(i);
> end do;
```

$$9$$

The **next** statement causes Maple to immediately proceed to the *next iteration* in the repetition statement.

```
> for i in L do
>     if i=8 then
>         next
>     end if;
>     print(i);
> end do;
```

$$9$$

$$7$$

$$6$$

An error occurs if Maple evaluates **break** or **next** in a context outside a repetition statement. For more information about the **break** or **next** statement, see page 179.

The error and return Statements

The **error** and **return** statements control flow in procedures. The **error** statement raises an exception and interrupts the execution of the current statement in a procedure. For more information about the **error** statement, see page 219. The **return** statement causes an immediate return to the point where the current procedure was invoked. For more information about the **return** statement, see page 217.

The use Statement

The use statement specifies local bindings of names, module exports, and operator overloading. It has the following syntax:

```
use exprseq in stateseq end use;
```

where stateseq is a sequence of statements and exprseq is a sequence of expressions. The expressions can be any of the following.

- equation of the form name = expression

- module member selection m:-e, which is equivalent to the equation e=m:-e

- module expression m, which is equivalent to the equations e=m:-e for all exports e of m.

```
> use StringTools in
>    a:=Random(10);
>    Encode(a, 'encoding' = 'base64');
> end use;
```

$$a := \text{``d8p!¡v''}$$

$$\text{``/9BkOHAhPHaEzw==''}$$

The quit Statement

The quit statement terminates the current Maple session. It has the following syntax.

```
quit;
```

The keywords done and stop are equivalent to quit.

You can also use quit as a procedure to return a specific integer value to the operating system

```
> 'quit'(0);
```

3.5   Troubleshooting

This section provides you with a list of common mistakes, examples, and hints that will help you understand and avoid common errors. Use this section to study the errors that you may encounter when entering the examples from this chapter in a Maple session.

Syntax Errors

If input is not syntactically correct, Maple reports a syntax error.

```
> 2+-3;

on line 22, syntax error, '-' unexpected:
2+-3;
 ^
```

If the error occurs in a Maple expression and you cannot determine the cause, use the **parse** command to indicate the location of the error. For more information, see page 44 or refer to **?parse**.

```
> parse("2+-3");

Error, incorrect syntax in parse: '-' unexpected (4)
```

If Maple returns an error after you enter a Maple command, refer to the corresponding online help page, by using **?topic**, to determine the correct calling sequence.

```
> plot(x^2);

Plotting error, empty plot
> ?plot
```

Reserved Word Unexpected

An error occurs in Maple if you try to improperly use a reserved word.[40]

```
> mod(4, 2);

on line 61, syntax error, reserved word 'mod'
unexpected:
mod(4, 2);
 ^
```

---

[40]For more information about reserved words, see page 24 or refer to **?keyword**.

To avoid this error, use left single quotes when you must use reserved words as a name, for example, in function calls.

```
> 'mod'(4,2);
```

$$0$$

Break or Next Not in Loop

An error occurs if Maple evaluates **break** or **next** in a context different from a repetition statement.[41]

```
> break;
```

```
Error, break or next not in loop
```

3.6   Exercises

1. Find the numerator and denominator of the irreducible form of 4057114691 divided by 4404825097799.

2. Construct floating-point numbers using the floating-point number constructor. Construct the number 917.3366 using a positive exponent, and then using a negative exponent. Construct a floating-point approximation of 1/3.

3. Without using the **Digits** environmental variable, find the difference between π estimated to 20 digits and 10 digits.

4. Calculate the negative complex root of -1369, and then sum 3 and the root. Find the inverse of this complex sum. Find the inverse of (a*b)/c+((a-d)/(b*e))*I) in standard form, where a, b, c, d, and e are real.

5. Using the **time** command, determine the time required to multiply two ten-by-ten matrices.

6. Compute 3^(3^98) modulo 7.

---

[41]For more information about **break** and **next**, see page 179.

7. Use Maple to verify de Morgan's laws.

8. Contrast the behavior of functions and expressions by performing the following commands.

   a) Define a function f equal to x^3. Define an expression g equal to x^3.

   b) Evaluate f and g at 2.

   c) Evaluate f and g at y.

   d) Assign the value 2 to x. Evaluate f and g.

9. Swap the values of two variables using one statement.

10. Sum the smallest 100 prime integers.

    Hint: Use the `ithprime` or `nextprime` function.

3.7   Conclusion

This chapter discussed the syntax and semantics of Maple expressions and statements. There are many expression types in Maple, and by using expression trees you can understand the types and the operands in an expression. Expressions are commonly used in Maple statements. Maple has many types of statements in its language, including assignments, conditional and looping statements, and statements to read from and save to files.

With the knowledge of how to form valid Maple statements, you can proceed to the next chapter which discusses Maple data structures.

4   Basic Data Structures

Maple supports a variety of data structures such as tables, arrays (a special case of tables), Arrays, stacks, and queues. Two basic data structures commonly used in Maple are sets and lists.

In This Chapter

- Defining and manipulating sets, lists, tables, arrays, and Arrays

- Selecting elements from basic data structures

- Converting between data structures

- Stacks and queues, two additional data structures that are implemented using tables

4.1   Sets

A *set* is an *unordered* sequence of *unique* expressions enclosed in braces ({}). Recall that a sequence is a group of expressions separated by commas. For more information about sequences, refer to chapter 2 of the *Maple Learning Guide*.

{ *sequence* }

Maple removes duplicate members and reorders them in a manner convenient for internal storage. The **sequence** can be empty, so {} represents an empty set.[1]

> {x, y, y};

---

[1]Compare the results of these examples to those in **4.2 Lists**.

$$\{x, y\}$$

```
> {a, 1, b, 2};
```

$$\{1, 2, b, a\}$$

```
> {y[1],x,x[1],y[1]};
```

$$\{x, y_1, x_1\}$$

Manipulating a Set

There are a variety of commands that perform operations on sets.

Set Arithmetic The most commonly used built-in set arithmetic operators are `union`, `minus`, and `intersect`. These operators perform set union, set difference, and set intersection, respectively.

```
> s := {x, y, z};
```

$$s := \{x, y, z\}$$

```
> t := {w, y, z};
```

$$t := \{y, z, w\}$$

```
> s union t;
```

$$\{x, y, z, w\}$$

```
> s minus t;
```

$$\{x\}$$

```
> s intersect t;
```

$$\{y, z\}$$

Testing Set Equality   You can force the evaluation of expressions that involve relational operators by using `evalb`. To perform equality testing with sets, use the `evalb` command in conjuction with the relational operator =.

> evalb(s = t);

false

Testing Set Membership   To test for set membership, use the `member` command or the `in` operator.

> member(x, s);

true

> evalb (x in s);

true

> member(w, s);

false

Applying a Function to the Members of a Set   To apply a function to the members of a set, use the `map` command. The simplest form of the `map` command syntax, where `f` is a function or procedure and `S` is a set, is:

```
map( f, S );
```

In this form, the `map` command replaces each member `Si` of `S` with `f(Si)`.

> map(f, {a,b,c});

$$\{f(a), f(b), f(c)\}$$

> S := {1,-2,3,-4};

$$S := \{-4, -2, 1, 3\}$$

```
> map(abs,S);
```

$$\{1, 2, 3, 4\}$$

```
> map(x->x^2, S);
```

$$\{1, 4, 9, 16\}$$

You can also apply a function to the members of a set by using the in command.

```
> for elem in S do
>    elem^3;
> end do;
```

$$-64$$

$$-8$$

$$1$$

$$27$$

4.2   Lists

A *list* is an *ordered* sequence of expressions enclosed in square brackets ([]).

[*sequence*]

The ordering of the list is the same as the **sequence** ordering (specified by the user). Also, unlike sets, duplicate entries are retained in the list. In the case where **sequence** is empty, [] represents an empty list.[2]

```
> [x, y, y];
```

$$[x, y, y]$$

---

[2] Compare the results of these examples to those in **4.1 Sets**.

```
> [a, 1, b, 2];
```

$$[a, 1, b, 2]$$

```
> [y[1],x,x[1],y[1]];
```

$$[y_1, x, x_1, y_1]$$

The elements of a list can be any expression, even other lists.

```
> L := [[1], [2, a], [X, Y, Z]];
```

$$L := [[1], [2, a], [X, Y, Z]]$$

Maple gives nested lists whose inner lists have the *same* number of elements a special name—`listlist`.[3]

```
> M := [[a,b], [1,2], [3, 4]];
```

$$M := [[a, b], [1, 2], [3, 4]]$$

```
> type(M, list);
```

$$true$$

```
> type(L, listlist);
```

$$false$$

```
> type(M, listlist);
```

$$true$$

The following command creates a list of sets.

```
> [seq( { seq( i^j, j=1..3) }, i=-2..2 ) ];
```

$$[\{-8, -2, 4\}, \{-1, 1\}, \{0\}, \{1\}, \{2, 4, 8\}]$$

---

[3]For more information about nested lists, refer to `?listlist`.

By changing the braces and brackets, you can create a set of lists, list of lists, or set of sets.

```
> {seq( [ seq( i^j, j=1..3) ], i=-2..2 ) };
```

$$\{[-2, 4, -8], [-1, 1, -1], [0, 0, 0], [1, 1, 1], [2, 4, 8]\}$$

Manipulating a List

There are a variety of commands that perform operations on lists.

Testing List Membership To test whether an element is in a list, use the member command.

```
> L := [1,2,3];
```

$$L := [1, 2, 3]$$

```
> member(2, L);
```

true

```
> member(5, L);
```

false

You can also determine the position of an element in a list. If member returns true and a third argument, for example 'p', is included in the calling sequence, the element's position in the list is assigned to p.

```
> member(2, L, 'p');
```

true

```
> p;
```

2

Concatenating Lists Use the op command to extract the expression sequence of elements from the individual lists. Concatenate two lists by creating a new list from the expression sequences.

```
> L1 := [a,b,c];
```

$$L1 := [a, b, c]$$

```
> L2 := [y,z];
```

$$L2 := [y, z]$$

```
> L3 := [op(L1), op(L2)];
```

$$L3 := [a, b, c, y, z]$$

You can also concatenate parts of lists with another list by using the op command to select particular elements from a list.[4]

```
> L4 := [op(2, L1), op(L2)];
```

$$L4 := [b, y, z]$$

Inserting Elements into a List   To prepend and append elements to a list, use the previous concatenation method.

```
> L1 := [grape];
```

$$L1 := [grape]$$

```
> [banana, op(L1)];   # prepend element
```

$$[banana, grape]$$

```
> [op(L1), orange];   # append element
```

$$[grape, orange]$$

You can also insert elements in a list by using the **nops** command.[5]

---

[4]For more information about selection using the op command, see page 155.

[5]The nops command determines the number of operands in an expression. For more information about nops, refer to ?nops.

```
> L1 := [banana, grape, orange, peach, pear, plum];
```

$$L1 := [banana, grape, orange, peach, pear, plum]$$

```
> [ op(1..2, L1), kiwi, op(3..nops(L1), L1) ];
```

$$[banana, grape, kiwi, orange, peach, pear, plum]$$

Replacing Elements in a List   To replace an element in a list, use a selection operation in an assignment statement.[6]

```
> L1 := [banana, grape, orange];
```

$$L1 := [banana, grape, orange]$$

```
> L1[2] := kiwi;
```

$$L1_2 := kiwi$$

```
> L1;
```

$$[banana, kiwi, orange]$$

To replace all occurrences of an expression in a list, use the `eval` command.

```
> L1 := [banana, grape, orange, grape];
```

$$L1 := [banana, grape, orange, grape]$$

```
> eval(L1, grape=kiwi);
```

$$[banana, kiwi, orange, kiwi]$$

---

[6]For more information about the selection operation, see page 152 or refer to `?selection`.

Table 4.1 Sorting Options

List Element Type	*F*	*Resulting sort Order*
numeric	<	ascending
numeric	>	descending
string or symbol	lexorder	lexiographic

Reversing the Order of Elements in a List   To reverse the order of the elements in a list, use a combination of the selection operation, and the seq and nops commands.[7]

```
> L1 := [banana, grape, orange];
```

$$L1 := [banana,\ grape,\ orange]$$

```
> [ seq( L1[-i], i=1..nops(L1) ) ];
```

$$[orange,\ grape,\ banana]$$

Sorting a List   To sort the elements in a list, use the **sort** command. It has the following syntax where L is a list and F is an optional parameter that specifies the sort order.

```
sort( L, F );
```

If F is not specified, the elements of the list L are sorted in *ascending* order. Otherwise, Table 4.1 displays the permissible values of F and the resulting sort order for lists containing elements of a particular type.[8]

```
> sort([z,e,b]);
```

$$[b,\ e,\ z]$$

```
> sort([2.5, 7/3, 10]);
```

---

[7]For more information on the **seq** command, see page 183 or refer to **?seq**.

[8]The algorithm that Maple uses for **sort** is a recursive implementation of merge sort with an early detection of sorted sequences. For more information about sorting lists, refer to **?sort**.

$$[\frac{7}{3}, 2.5, 10]$$

```
> sort([2.5, 7/3, 10], '>');
```

$$[10, 2.5, \frac{7}{3}]$$

Applying a Function to the Elements of a List Two commonly used commands that apply functions to the elements of a list are the map command and the zip command.

You can apply a function to the elements of a list by using the map command. The simplest map command syntax, where f is a function or procedure and L is a list, is:

```
map( f, L );
```

In this form, the map command replaces each element Li of L with f(Li).

```
> map(f, [a,b,c]);
```

$$[f(a), f(b), f(c)]$$

```
> L := [1, -2, 3, -4];
```

$$L := [1, -2, 3, -4]$$

```
> map(abs, L);
```

$$[1, 2, 3, 4]$$

```
> map(x->x^2, L);
```

$$[1, 4, 9, 16]$$

You can apply a binary (two parameter) function to the elements of *two lists* by using the zip command. It has the following syntax where f is any binary function, and L1 and L2 are lists. If the optional argument d is specified, it is used as the default value in f when L1 and L2 are not the same size.

```
zip( f, L1, L2, d );
```

If d is specified and L1 and L2 are the same size, d is ignored.

```
> zip((x,y)->x+y, [1,2,3], [4,5,6]);
```

$$[5, 7, 9]$$

```
> zip((x,y)->x+y, [1,2,3], [4,5], 10);
```

$$[5, 7, 13]$$

4.3   Tables

The `table` data structure in Maple is used for representing data in a *table*—an arrangement of rows and columns. To create a table explicitly, use the `table` command. The optional parameters F and L specify an indexing function, and a list or set that specifies the initial values of the table, respectively.

```
table( F, L);
```

If L is a *list of entries*[9], the indices are set to the natural integers 1, 2, ...[10]

```
> T := table([a, b, c]);
```

$$T := \text{table}([1 = a, 2 = b, 3 = c])$$

```
> T0 := table([cos, sin, tan]);
```

$$T0 := \text{table}([1 = \cos, 2 = \sin, 3 = \tan])$$

---

[9]The use of a *set* of initial values is ambiguous because there is no fixed ordering of set elements. Hence, the ordering of the entries in the result may not correspond to the ordering in which the entries are given.

[10]You can also create a table implicitly by using an indexed name. For more information, see page 135 or refer to `?table`.

If L is a *list of equations* or a *set of equations*, the left-hand side of each equation is the *table index* (key), and the right-hand side is the *table entry* (value). Unlike arrays and Arrays (see **4.4 arrays and Arrays** or refer to **?array** or **?Array**), in which indices must be integers, the indices of a table can be any value.

```
> T1 := table([0=alpha, 1=beta]);
```

$$T1 := \text{table}([0 = \alpha, \, 1 = \beta])$$

```
> T2 := table({y1=x, y3=x^2, y2=x^3});
```

$$T2 := \text{table}([y1 = x, \, y3 = x^2, \, y2 = x^3])$$

```
> T3 := table([(shirt, S) = 12, (shirt, M) = 8, (shirt, L) = 9]);
```

$$T3 := \text{table}([(shirt, \, S) = 12, \, (shirt, \, M) = 8, \, (shirt, \, L) = 9])$$

If L is not specified, an empty table is created.

```
> table();
```

$$\text{table}([])$$

The optional indexing function F can be a procedure or a name that describes the semantics of indexing in the table. If F is not specified, then ordinary indexing (integer) is assumed. The built-in indexing functions are: **symmetric**, **antisymmetric**, **sparse**, **diagonal**, and **identity**. For more information about indexing functions, refer to **?indexingfunctions**.

The purpose of a table is to enable fast access to data. To access the value of a table entry, enter the table name followed by a table key (in square brackets).[11]

```
> T0[3];
```

$$\tan$$

---

[11] For more information about table entry selection, see **4.5 Selecting Elements from a Data Structure** or refer to **?selection**.

```
> T3[shirt,M];
```

$$8$$

An Alternate Method for Generating a Table

A table can be created implicitly by making an assignment to an indexed name T, where T does not have a previous value.

```
T[ indexExpr ] = entryValue ;
```

In this format, T is the name of the table, indexExpr is the index of the entry, and entryValue is the actual value of the entry in the table.

For example, the following statements have the same effect.

```
> T4 := table([(Cu,1) = 64]);
```

$$T4 := \text{table}([(Cu,\, 1) = 64])$$

```
> T4[Cu,1] := 64;
```

$$T4_{Cu,\, 1} := 64$$

Both statements create a table object with one component.

Table Evaluation Rules

Tables have special evaluation rules. If the name T is assigned to a table, the result of evaluating T is the name T, not the value of T (contents of the table).[12]

```
> T5 := table([1,2,3,4]);
```

$$T5 := \text{table}([1 = 1,\, 2 = 2,\, 3 = 3,\, 4 = 4])$$

```
> T5;
```

$$T5$$

---

[12]In Maple, an expression is normally evaluated by using full recursive evaluation—that is, the result of the expression is the fully evaluated expression. For more information about evaluation rules, see page 14 or refer to ?last_name_eval.

To access the value of a table object, apply the `eval` command.

```
> eval(T5);
```

$$\text{table}([1 = 1, \, 2 = 2, \, 3 = 3, \, 4 = 4])$$

Manipulating a Table

There are a variety of commands that perform operations on tables.

Inserting Entries   To add new entries to a table, use subscript notation. Thus, `T := table([4])` is equivalent to `T[1] := 4` (implicit creation).

```
> mytable[1] := apple;
```

$$mytable_1 := apple$$

If there is no entry in the table at the specified key, a new entry is created.

```
> mytable[2] := banana;
```

$$mytable_2 := banana$$

```
> eval(mytable);
```

$$\text{table}([1 = apple, \, 2 = banana])$$

If there is already an entry value for the specified key, it is updated to the new value.

```
> mytable[2] := orange;
```

$$mytable_2 := orange$$

```
> eval(mytable);
```

$$\text{table}([1 = apple, \, 2 = orange])$$

Example To assign a value to a table key, use a procedure that accepts an indexed name. Consider the following procedure.

```
> keyvalues := proc(b)
>                    b^3
> end proc:
```

If the first parameter to procedure **keyvalues** is valid, the assignment is made.

```
> newtable := table():  #create an empty table
> newtable[1]:= keyvalues(2):  #assign the value 8 to newtable[1]
> eval(newtable);
```

$$\text{table}([1 = 8])$$

To automatically assign values to table keys, use a flow control statement.[13]

```
> newtable := table();
```

$$newtable := \text{table}([])$$

```
> for i to 5 do newtable[i]:= keyvalues(i) end do:
> eval(newtable);
```

$$\text{table}([1 = 1, 2 = 8, 3 = 27, 4 = 64, 5 = 125])$$

To determine whether a table component is assigned, use the **assigned** command.

```
> assigned(newtable[1]);
```

$$true$$

Removing Entries To remove an entry from a table, assign an unevaluated table entry to its name by using right single quotes on the right-hand side of an assignment statement, or use the **evaln** command. For example, `T[1] := 'T[1]'` removes the first entry from T. Alternatively, you can use `evaln(T[1])` or `unassign('T[1]')`.

---

[13]For more information about flow control statements, see **5.1 Selection and Conditional Execution**.

```
> T5[3] := 'T5[3]';
```

$$T5_3 := T5_3$$

```
> eval(T5);
```

$$\text{table}([1 = 1,\ 2 = 2,\ 4 = 4])$$

Displaying Table Indices To return the sequence of the table entries, use the `indices` command, where T is a table.[14]

```
indices(T);
```

```
> T := table([[shirt,S]=42,[shirt,M]=16,[shirt,L]=36]);
```

$$T := \text{table}([[shirt,\ S] = 42,\ [shirt,\ M] = 16,\ [shirt,\ L] = 36])$$

```
> indices(T);
```

$$[[shirt,\ S]],\ [[shirt,\ M]],\ [[shirt,\ L]]$$

Displaying Table Entries To return a sequence of the table values, use the `entries` command, where T is a table.[15]

```
entries(T);
```

```
> entries(T);
```

$$[42],\ [16],\ [36]$$

Alternatively, you can use the **op** command to return the operands of a table, for example, its entries and indexing function. (If no indexing function has been specified, NULL is returned.) Table 4.2 lists the operands

---

[14]The order of the keys in the returned sequence does not necessarily correspond to the order of the keys in the table because tables in Maple are implemented by using *hash tables*. However, there is a one-to-one correspondence between the order of the indices and the order of the entries.

[15]The order of the entries in the returned sequence does not necessarily correspond to the order of the entries in the table.

Table 4.2 Table Operands

Operand	*op Command*
table structure	op(T)
data type	op(0, eval(T))
indexing function	op(1, eval(T))
table entries	op(2, eval(T))

and corresponding op command that you can use to access them. In the op commands shown, T is the name of the table.[16]

The call op(T) returns the actual table structure.

```
> op(T4);
```

$$\text{table}([(Cu,\ 1) = 64])$$

The object assigned to T4 is a table.

```
> op(0,eval(T4));
```

$$table$$

The table T4 has no indexing function and the list of entries has only one key/value pair.

```
> op(1,eval(T4));
> op(2,eval(T4));
```

$$[(Cu,\ 1) = 64]$$

Copying a Table   If two names evaluate to the same table, an assignment to a component of *either* affects *both*.

```
> T6 := table([w, x, y, z]);
```

$$T6 := \text{table}([1 = w,\ 2 = x,\ 3 = y,\ 4 = z])$$

---

[16]Tables have special evaluation rules. To access the table object, you must apply the eval command. For more information, see page 135.

```
> b := T6:
> b[1] := 7;
```

$$b_1 := 7$$

```
> eval(T6);
```

$$table([1 = 7, 2 = x, 3 = y, 4 = z])$$

```
> eval(b);
```

$$table([1 = 7, 2 = x, 3 = y, 4 = z])$$

In this example, there is only *one* table. The name b points to the name T6 which points to the table structure.

To create a copy of a table that is independent of the original, use the copy command.

```
copy( T );
```

```
> c := copy(T6);
```

$$c := table([1 = 7, 2 = x, 3 = y, 4 = z])$$

```
> c[1] := 10:
> eval(T6);
```

$$table([1 = 7, 2 = x, 3 = y, 4 = z])$$

```
> eval(c);
```

$$table([1 = 10, 2 = x, 3 = y, 4 = z])$$

Applying a Function to the Entries of a Table   To apply a function to the entries of a table to create a new table, use the map command. The indices of the table remain the same.

In the following example, the first statement creates a table of polynomials, and the second statement creates a (new) table of their derivatives by using the map command.[17]

```
> T7 := table([x, x^2 + 2, x^3 - x + 1, 1/x^2]):
> map(diff, T7, x);
```

$$\text{table}([1 = 1,\ 2 = 2\,x,\ 3 = 3\,x^2 - 1,\ 4 = -\frac{2}{x^3}])$$

To modify the values in-place, that is, change the values in the original table, use the following method.

```
> for entry in op(2,eval(T6)) do
>    T6[lhs(entry)] := 2*rhs(entry)
> end do;
```

$$T6_1 := 14$$

$$T6_2 := 2\,x$$

$$T6_3 := 2\,y$$

$$T6_4 := 2\,z$$

```
> eval(T6);
```

$$\text{table}([1 = 14,\ 2 = 2\,x,\ 3 = 2\,y,\ 4 = 2\,z])$$

4.4   arrays and Arrays

In Maple, there are two kinds of *arrays*: *arrays* and *Arrays*.

An array is a specialization of the table data structure, with zero or more specified dimensions B, where each dimension is an integer range (index bound). As in the case of tables (see **4.3 Tables** or refer to ?table), F is the optional indexing function, and L is the initial list of values.

---

[17]For more information about the map command, refer to ?map.

```
array( F, B, L );
```

The number of ranges in B is called the *dimension* of the array. If no index bound is specified in B, it is deduced from the intitial list of values. The list of initial values L can be a:

- list of equations (similar to tables)

- list of values (one-dimensional)

- nested list of lists (row-by-row representation)

If L is the empty list, the array is zero-dimensional and the index bound is NULL (a sequence of zero integer ranges). If L is given as a list of n values, the array is one-dimensional and the index bound is the range 1..n. If L is a list of lists, the number of dimensions can be deduced from the level of nesting of the lists and each dimension is indexed from 1.

All parameters to the **array** command are optional and can appear in any order, but at least one bound or one list must appear. If the bounds are not specified, they are deduced from the list of initial values. If the bounds are specified without an initialization list, the array values are unassigned.

```
> a2 := array(1..3); #empty 1-d array
```

$$a2 := \text{array}(1..3, [])$$

```
> a3 := array(1..3, [a,b,c]); #1-d array
```

$$a3 := [a, b, c]$$

```
> a4 := array([a,b,c]); #1-d array
```

$$a4 := [a, b, c]$$

```
> a5 := array(1..3, 1..2); #empty 3 x 2 array
```

$$a5 := \text{array}(1..3, 1..2, [])$$

```
> a6 := array([[1,2,3],[4,5,6]]); #2-d array
```

$$a6 := \begin{bmatrix} 1 & 2 & 3 \\ 4 & 5 & 6 \end{bmatrix}$$

Similarly, an Array is a table-like structure with fixed dimensions and integer indices. The difference between arrays and Arrays is the underlying data structure. An array uses a hash table, while an Array uses a fixed size data block.

The **Array** command has the same form as **array**, but accepts more optional parameters. If the bounds are specified without an initialization list, all Array values are assigned 0 (zero). For more information, refer to **?Array**.

```
Array( F, B, L );
```

```
> A2 := Array(1..3); #empty 1-d Array
```

$$A2 := [0, 0, 0]$$

```
> A3 := Array(1..3, [a,b,c]); #1-d Array
```

$$A3 := [a, b, c]$$

```
> A4 := Array([a,b,c]); #1-d Array
```

$$A4 := [a, b, c]$$

```
> A5 := Array(1..3, 1..2); #empty 3 x 2 Array
```

$$A5 := \begin{bmatrix} 0 & 0 \\ 0 & 0 \\ 0 & 0 \end{bmatrix}$$

```
> A6 := Array([[1,2,3],[4,5,6]]); #2-d Array
```

$$A6 := \begin{bmatrix} 1 & 2 & 3 \\ 4 & 5 & 6 \end{bmatrix}$$

As in the creation of a table, the optional indexing function F can be a procedure or a name that describes the semantics of indexing in the array or Array. If F is not specified, ordinary indexing (integer) is implied. The built-in indexing functions are: `symmetric`, `antisymmetric`, `sparse`, `diagonal`, and `identity`.[18] For more information about indexing functions, refer to `?indexingfunctions`.

> a7 := array(symmetric, 1..2, 1..2, [(1,1) = 3]);

$$a7 := \begin{bmatrix} 3 & a7_{1,2} \\ a7_{1,2} & a7_{2,2} \end{bmatrix}$$

Evaluation Rules for arrays

There are special evaluation rules for arrays. If the name `a` has been assigned to an array, the result of evaluating `a` is the *name* `a`, not the *value* of `a` (contents of the array). As with a table, to access the value of the array object, apply the `eval` command.[19]

> a := array([1,2,3,4]);

$$a := [1, 2, 3, 4]$$

> a;

$$a$$

> eval(a);

$$[1, 2, 3, 4]$$

In contrast, it is *not* necessary to use `eval` for Arrays.

> A6;

$$\begin{bmatrix} 1 & 2 & 3 \\ 4 & 5 & 6 \end{bmatrix}$$

---

[18]There are additional built-in indexing function names for Arrays. For a complete list, refer to `?rtable_indexingfunctions`.

[19]For more information about evaluation rules, see page 14 or refer to `?last_name_eval`.

Manipulating arrays and Arrays

There are a variety of commands that perform operations on arrays and Arrays. You manipulate arrays and Arrays in a manner that is similar to that used for tables.

Inserting Entries To assign entries in arrays and Arrays, use subscript notation, that is, square brackets.

> a3[3] := d;

$$a3_3 := d$$

> eval(a3);

$$[a, b, d]$$

> A3[3] := d;

$$A3_3 := d$$

> A3;

$$[a, b, d]$$

> a7 := array(symmetric,1..2,1..2);

$$a7 := \text{array}(symmetric, 1..2, 1..2, [])$$

> a7[1,1] := 3;

$$a7_{1,1} := 3$$

> a7[1,2] := 4;

$$a7_{1,2} := 4$$

> eval(a7);

$$\begin{bmatrix} 3 & 4 \\ 4 & ?_{2,2} \end{bmatrix}$$

Removing Entries To remove entries from an array, assign an unevaluated array entry to its name by using right single quotes on the right-hand side of an assignment statement, or use the `evaln` command. For example, `a[1] := 'a[1]'` removes the first entry from `a`. Similarly, you can use `evaln(a[1])`.

```
> a3[3] := 'a3[3]';
```

$$a3_3 := a3_3$$

```
> eval(a3);
```

$$[a, b, ?_3]$$

Entries cannot be removed from Arrays. Unless you specify `storage=sparse` in its definition[20], each entry must have an assigned value.

Displaying array Indices To return a sequence of the indices to the array, use the `indices` command, where `a` is an array (*not* an Array).

```
indices( a );
```

The order of the indices in the returned sequence does not necessarily correspond to the order of the indices in the array.

```
> indices(a3);
```

$$[1], [2]$$

Displaying array Entries To return a sequence of the array entries, use the `entries` command, where `a` is an array (*not* an Array).

```
entries( a );
```

The order of the entries in the returned sequence does not necessarily correspond to the order of the entries in the array.

```
> entries(a3);
```

---

[20]For a list of Array storage formats, refer to `?Array`.

Table 4.3 array Operands

Operand	op Command
array structure	op(a)
data type	op(0, eval(a))
indexing function	op(1, eval(a))
array bounds	op(2, eval(a))
array entries	op(3, eval(a))

$[a]$, $[b]$

Alternatively, you can use the op command to return the operands of an array, that is, its entries, data type, indexing function, and bounds. (If no indexing function has been specified, nothing is returned.) Table 4.3 lists these operands and the corresponding op command that you can enter to access them. In the op commands, a is the name of the array.[21]

The object assigned to a7 is the actual array structure.

```
> op(a7);
```

$$\begin{bmatrix} 3 & 4 \\ 4 & ?_{2,2} \end{bmatrix}$$

The type of object assigned to a7 is an array.

```
> op(0,eval(a7));
```

array

As with tables, the first operand is the indexing function (if any).

```
> op(1,eval(a7));
```

symmetric

The second operand is the sequence of ranges that indicate the bounds.

---

[21]Recall that arrays (like tables) have special evaluation rules. To access the array object, apply the **eval** command.

Table 4.4 Array Operands

Operand	op Command
all operands	op(A)
data type	op(0, A)
indexing function	op(1, A)
Array bounds	op(2, A)
Array entries	op(3, A)
other operands	op(4, A)

```
> op(2,eval(a7));
```

$$1..2, \; 1..2$$

The third operand is a *list* of the entries in the array.

```
> op(3, eval(a7));
```

$$[(1, 1) = 3, \; (1, 2) = 4]$$

The example above displays only two entries in array **a7** because the values of the entries located at **(2, 1)** and **(2, 2)** are implicitly specified by the **symmetric** indexing function.

Similarly, you can use the **op** command to return the operands of an Array, that is, the data type, indexing function, bounds, entries, entry data type, storage type, and order. Table 4.4 lists the operands and the corresponding **op** commands.

```
> op(A6);
```

$$1..2, \; 1..3, \{(1, 3) = 3, \; (2, 1) = 4, \; (2, 2) = 5, \; (2, 3) = 6,$$
$$(1, 1) = 1, \; (1, 2) = 2\}, \; datatype = anything,$$
$$storage = rectangular, \; order = Fortran\_order$$

Copying arrays and Arrays If two names evaluate to the same array or Array, an assignment to a component of *either* affects *both*.

```
> a8 := array([w,x,y,z]);
```

$$a8 := [w, \; x, \; y, \; z]$$

```
> b := a8;
```

$$b := a8$$

```
> b[1] := 7;
```

$$b_1 := 7$$

```
> eval(a8);
```

$$[7,\ x,\ y,\ z]$$

```
> eval(b);
```

$$[7,\ x,\ y,\ z]$$

```
> A8 := Array([1,2,4,8]);
```

$$A8 := [1,\ 2,\ 4,\ 8]$$

```
> B := A8;
```

$$B := [1,\ 2,\ 4,\ 8]$$

```
> B[1] := 0;
```

$$B_1 := 0$$

```
> A8;
```

$$[0,\ 2,\ 4,\ 8]$$

```
> B;
```

$$[0,\ 2,\ 4,\ 8]$$

In the preceding examples, there is only one array (or Array). The name b (B) points to the name a8 (A8) that points to the array (or Array) structure.

To create a copy of an array that is independent of the original, use the copy command.

```
copy( a );
```

```
> c := copy(a8);
```

$$c := [7,\ x,\ y,\ z]$$

```
> c[1] := 10;
```

$$c_1 := 10$$

```
> eval(a8);
```

$$[7,\ x,\ y,\ z]$$

```
> eval(c);
```

$$[10,\ x,\ y,\ z]$$

To create a copy of an Array that is independent of the original, use the Array command.

```
> C := Array(A8);
```

$$C := [0,\ 2,\ 4,\ 8]$$

```
> C[1] := Pi;
```

$$C_1 := \pi$$

```
> A8;
```

$$[0,\ 2,\ 4,\ 8]$$

```
> C;
```

$$[\pi,\ 2,\ 4,\ 8]$$

Applying a Function to the Entries of an array or Array To apply a function to the *entries* of an array or Array to create a new array or Array, use the `map` command.

In the following example, the first statement creates an array of polynomials, and the second statement creates an array of the factored polynomials by using the `map` command.[22]

```
> a8 := array([2*x^4 - x^2, x^2 + 2*x, x^3 - x + 2*x]);
```

$$a8 := [2\,x^4 - x^2,\ x^2 + 2\,x,\ x^3 + x]$$

```
> map(factor, a8);
```

$$[x^2\,(2\,x^2 - 1),\ x\,(x + 2),\ x\,(x^2 + 1)]$$

The `Map` command in the `LinearAlgebra` package applies a function to the entries in an *Array*, returning a new Array.

```
> A8 := Array([x,23,y-2]);
```

$$A8 := [x,\ 23,\ y - 2]$$

```
> LinearAlgebra[Map](x->x*y,A8);
```

$$[x\,y,\ 23\,y,\ (y - 2)\,y]$$

To modify the values in-place, that is, change the values in the original array or Array, use the following method.[23]

```
> for entry in op(3,A8) do
>    A8[lhs(entry)] := rhs(entry) + 1
> end do;
```

$$A8_1 := x + 1$$

$$A8_2 := 24$$

$$A8_3 := y - 1$$

---

[22] For more information about the `map` command, refer to `?map`.
[23] This method (with `op(2,...)`) is used to modify tables in-place.

> A8;

$$[x + 1,\ 24,\ y - 1]$$

4.5 Selecting Elements from a Data Structure

Selecting elements from a data structure is most commonly achieved by performing a selection operation. However, there are a number of other methods by which you can choose an element.

The Selection Operation []

The selection operation, [], selects components from aggregate objects, for example, sequences, sets, lists, tables, arrays, and Arrays. The selection operation uses the following syntax, where **name** represents the object and **sequence** indicates the selected entry (or entries).[24]

```
name [ sequence ]
```

Sequences, Sets, and Lists If **name** evaluates to a sequence, set, or list, and **sequence** evaluates to an integer, a range, or NULL, Maple performs a selection operation.[25]

If **sequence** evaluates to an integer i, then Maple returns the ith operand of the set, list, or sequence. Negative integers cause elements to be counted from the end of the sequence, set, or list. For example, -1 indicates the last element.

```
> s := x,y,z:
> L := [s,s];
```

$$L := [x,\ y,\ z,\ x,\ y,\ z]$$

```
> S := {s,s};
```

$$S := \{x,\ y,\ z\}$$

---

[24]For more information about selecting elements, refer to **?selection**.

[25]Although you can use the selection operation to select elements of a set, the order of elements in a set is *session dependent*. Do not make any assumptions about this order.

```
> S[2];
```

$$y$$

```
> L[-4];
```

$$z$$

If **sequence** evaluates to a range, the lower bound must be less than or equal to one more than the upper bound. Specifically, `A[3..3]` selects a single element, `A[3..2]` produces an empty selection, and `A[3..1]` is not permitted.

```
> L[2..3];
```

$$[y, z]$$

```
> L[3..3];
```

$$[z]$$

```
> L[3..2];
```

$$[]$$

```
> L[3..1];
```

```
Error, invalid subscript selector
```

If **sequence** evaluates to **NULL**, Maple returns a sequence containing all operands of the aggregate object.

```
> S[];
```

$$x, y, z$$

Tables, arrays, and Arrays If name evaluates to a table, Maple returns the value in the table entry, if there is one. If there is not an entry with sequence as its key, the value returned is an indexed name. However, if sequence evaluates to a range, the selection remains unevaluated.

```
> T := table([(1,1)=Bob, (1,2)=Mary, (2,1)=Sally, (2,2)=Joe]);
```

$$T := \text{table}([(1,\ 1) = Bob,\ (1,\ 2) = Mary,\ (2,\ 1) = Sally,$$
$$(2,\ 2) = Joe$$
$$])$$

```
> T[2,2];
```

$$Joe$$

```
> T[3,1];
```

$$T_{3,1}$$

Because arrays are implemented as tables, the array behavior is the same.

```
> a := array([w,x,y,z]);
```

$$a := [w,\ x,\ y,\ z]$$

```
> a[3];
```

$$y$$

```
> a[1..3];
```

$$a_{1..3}$$

In this case, Arrays behave like lists. The range selection evaluates to a subArray.

```
> B := Array([[1,2,3],[4,5,6],[7,8,9]]);
```

$$B := \begin{bmatrix} 1 & 2 & 3 \\ 4 & 5 & 6 \\ 7 & 8 & 9 \end{bmatrix}$$

```
> B[1..2,1..2];
```

$$\begin{bmatrix} 1 & 2 \\ 4 & 5 \end{bmatrix}$$

The op Command

You can use the op command to extract operands from sets, lists, tables, and arrays.[26] To use op in this manner, use the following syntax, where i is an integer or integer range that represents the operand(s) to extract and e is the data structure.[27]

```
op( i, e );
```

Sets and Lists   Notice that if negative integers are used to indicate the operands in a set or list, the elements are counted from the end: using -1 indicates the last element, using -2 indicates the second last, and so on.

```
> S := {10,11,12,13};
```

$$S := \{10, 11, 12, 13\}$$

```
> op(1, S);
```

$$10$$

```
> op(2..3, S);
```

$$11, 12$$

---

[26]In general, the use of op to extract operands from a list or set is less efficient than using the selection operation because the *entire* list or set is evaluated. Therefore, if possible, use the selection operation.

[27]You cannot use the op command on a sequence because Maple interprets the elements of the sequence as individual arguments to op. Instead, you must access elements of a sequence by using the selection operation []. For more information on sequence selection, see page 152 or refer to ?sequence.

```
> L := [a,b,c,d,e];
```

$$L := [a,\ b,\ c,\ d,\ e]$$

```
> op(3..-1, L);
```

$$c,\ d,\ e$$

Tables, arrays, and Arrays Unlike sets, lists, and Arrays, tables and arrays have special evaluation rules. For more information on using op with tables, see **4.3 Tables**. For more information on using op with arrays and Arrays, see **4.4 arrays and Arrays**.

The select, remove, and selectremove Commands

You can also use the select, remove, and selectremove commands to select the elements of a *list* or *set* that satisfy a criterion.

The simplest forms are:

```
select( f, x )
remove( f, x )
selectremove( f, x )
```

where f is a Boolean-valued function and x is an expression which must be a sum, product, list, set, function, or indexed name.

The select command returns a new object of the same type as x that contains only the operands of x for which the Boolean-valued function f returns true.

```
>  X := [seq(i,i=1..10)];
```

$$X := [1,\ 2,\ 3,\ 4,\ 5,\ 6,\ 7,\ 8,\ 9,\ 10]$$

```
> select(isprime,X);
```

$$[2,\ 3,\ 5,\ 7]$$

The remove command is (almost) the complement of select. It returns a new object of the same type as x that contains only the operands of x for which the Boolean-valued function f returns false.

```
> remove(isprime,X);
```

$$[1, 4, 6, 8, 9, 10]$$

The `selectremove` function returns two new objects of the same type as x, the first containing the operands for which the Boolean-valued function f returns `true` and the second containing the operands for which f returns `false`. The result is computed more efficiently than using both `select` and `remove` because it evaluates f(xi) once for each operand.

```
> selectremove(isprime,X);
```

$$[2, 3, 5, 7], [1, 4, 6, 8, 9, 10]$$

Note: If f(xi) returns `FAIL`, none of `select`, `remove`, and `selectremove` returns an object containing xi.

The general forms of these commands are

```
select( f, x, y1, ..., yn )
remove( f, x, y1, ..., yn )
selectremove( f, x, y1, ..., yn )
```

where f is a function, x is a sum, product, list, set, function or indexed name, and y1, ..., yn are expressions. The expressions y1, ..., yn are passed to the function f. That is, for each operand of x, the Boolean evaluation f(xi, y1, ..., yn) is calculated.

```
> X := {2, sin(1), exp(2*x), x^(1/2)};
```

$$X := \{2, \sin(1), e^{(2\,x)}, \sqrt{x}\}$$

```
> select(type, X, 'function');
```

$$\{\sin(1), e^{(2\,x)}\}$$

```
> remove(type, X, 'constant');
```

$$\{e^{(2\,x)}, \sqrt{x}\}$$

```
> integers := [$10..15];
```

$$integers := [10, 11, 12, 13, 14, 15]$$

```
> select(isprime, integers);
```

$$[11, 13]$$

```
> remove(isprime, integers);
```

$$[10, 12, 14, 15]$$

```
> selectremove(isprime, integers);
```

$$[11, 13], [10, 12, 14, 15]$$

4.6   Converting Between Data Structures

You can convert the structure of the result by using a variety of methods. This is useful because some results are in the form of a data structure that is not accepted by other Maple commands.

Converting a Sequence to a Set or a List

Many Maple commands return results in the form of a sequence. To convert a sequence into a set or list, enclose the result in braces or square brackets, respectively.

For example, the solve command returns a sequence of values if it finds multiple solutions.

```
> s := solve(x^4 - 2*x^3 - x^2 + 4*x - 2, x);
```

$$s := 1, 1, \sqrt{2}, -\sqrt{2}$$

The result is a sequence of values, not an equation. Enclosing the solutions in square brackets creates a list.

```
> [s];
```

$$[1, 1, \sqrt{2}, -\sqrt{2}]$$

Alternatively, you can convert the result to a set by enclosing s in braces. Note that duplicate solutions do not appear in the set.

```
> {s};
```

$$\{1, \sqrt{2}, -\sqrt{2}\}$$

Converting Other Data Structures

In general, to convert the structure of one result to another, use the convert command.

Example Convert a table to a list.

```
> T := table([x, x^2, x^3, x^4]);
```

$$T := \text{table}([1 = x, 2 = x^2, 3 = x^3, 4 = x^4])$$

```
> convert(T, 'list');
```

$$[x, x^2, x^3, x^4]$$

For a complete list of conversions between data structures, refer to ?convert.

4.7   Other Maple Data Structures

In addition to the data structures already discussed in this chapter, Maple has a wide variety of other data structures. In particular, two data structures commonly used in programming are stacks and queues.

Stacks

A *stack* is a data structure in which the removal order of the elements is the reverse of the entry order. You can only insert (or *push*) and delete (or *pop*) elements from the *top* of the stack. This behavior is referred to as LIFO (last in, first out). Stacks are implemented as tables in Maple. They are created by using the `stack` commands.[28]

Begin by creating a new (empty) stack.

```
> s := stack[new]();
```

$$s := \text{table}([0 = 0])$$

Push the letters h, a, t onto the stack.

```
> stack[push](h, s);
```

$$h$$

```
> stack[push](a, s);
```

$$a$$

```
> stack[push](t, s);
```

$$t$$

Check the `depth`, the value of the `top` element, and the contents of the stack.

```
> stack[depth](s);
```

$$3$$

```
> stack[top](s);
```

$$t$$

```
> eval('s');
```

$$\text{table}([0 = 3, 1 = h, 2 = a, 3 = t])$$

---

[28]For more information about stacks in Maple, refer to ?stack.

Pop the letters off the stack. The original order of the letters is re-versed.[29]

```
> while not stack[empty](s) do stack[pop](s); end do;
```

$$t$$

$$a$$

$$h$$

Queues

A *queue* is a data structure in which the removal order of elements is the same as the entry order. This behavior is referred to as FIFO (first in, first out). Queues are implemented as tables in Maple and are created by using the queue commands.[30]

Create a new (empty) queue.

```
> q := queue[new]();
```

$$q := \text{table}([0 = 0])$$

Place the letters h, a, t in the queue.

```
> queue[enqueue](q, h);
```

$$h$$

```
> queue[enqueue](q, a);
```

$$a$$

```
> queue[enqueue](q, t);
```

$$t$$

Check the length, the value of the front element, and the contents of the queue.

---

[29] The order of this result is the reverse of that in the example in the following subsection **Queues**.

[30] For more information about queues in Maple, refer to ?queue.

```
> queue[length](q);
```

$$3$$

```
> queue[front](q);
```

$$h$$

```
> eval('q');
```

$$\text{table}([0 = 3,\ 1 = h,\ 2 = a,\ 3 = t])$$

Remove the letters from the queue. The original order of the letters is maintained.[31]

```
> while not queue[empty](q) do queue[dequeue](q); end do;
```

$$h$$

$$a$$

$$t$$

Other important data structures are the connected graph and adjacency matrix. For more information on these data structures, see **6.10 Using Data Structures to Solve Problems**.

There are many other data structures in Maple. For example, the `matrix`[32] and `vector`[33] constructors create special cases of arrays, and the `Matrix`[34] and `Vector`[35] constructors create special cases of Arrays.

4.8   Troubleshooting

This section provides you with a list of common mistakes, examples, and hints that will help you understand and avoid common errors. Use this

---

[31]The order of this result is the reverse of that in the example in the preceding subsection **Stacks**.

[32]For information on the `matrix` constructor, refer to `?matrix`.

[33]For information on the `vector` constructor, refer to `?vector`.

[34]For information on the `Matrix` constructor, refer to `?Matrix`.

[35]For information on the `Vector` constructor, refer to `?Vector`.

section to study the errors that you may encounter when entering the examples from this chapter in a Maple session.

Wrong Number of Parameters in Function

Maple generates an error if a sequence is used as a parameter to op or nops.[36]

```
> s := a, b, c;
```

$$s := a,\, b,\, c$$

```
> op(2, s);
```

```
Error, wrong number (or type) of parameters in function
op
```

To avoid this error, convert s to a list (by enclosing s in square brackets) in the call to op or nops.

```
> op(2, [s]);
```

$$b$$

Invalid Subscript Selector

Maple generates an error if, during a selection operation, an invalid range is specified. An invalid range occurs if the following rule is broken: *the lower bound must be less than or equal to one more than the upper bound.* In the case that the range is an integer in a selection operation from a list, you cannot access the zeroth operand because lists are indexed by natural integers 1, 2, ...[37]

```
> L := [a, b, c, d];
```

$$L := [a,\, b,\, c,\, d]$$

```
> L[3..1];
```

```
Error, invalid subscript selector
```

---

[36] For more information, refer to ?op.

[37] For more information about selection and ranges, refer to ?selection.

```
> L[0];
```

Error, invalid subscript selector

To avoid this error, use a range with a lower bound that is less than the upper bound.

```
> L[1..3];
```

$$[a, b, c]$$

Requires Range or Initialization List for Building arrays

Maple generates an error if no parameters are specified in a call to **array**.

```
> a := array();
```

Error, needs ranges or initialization list for building arrays

Unlike a table (for which an empty parameter list is permissible), in a call to **array** you must specify either the bound or an initialization list.

```
> a := array(1..3);
```

$$a := \mathrm{array}(1..3, [])$$

Error in array Bound or Array Index out of Range

Maple generates an error if you try to assign a value to an array or Array index that is outside the array bound.

```
> a := array(1..3);
```

$$a := \mathrm{array}(1..3, [])$$

```
> a[4] := p;
```

Error, 1st index, 4, larger than upper array bound 3

```
> A := Array(1..2);
```

$$A := [0, 0]$$

```
> A[4] := x^2;
```

```
Error, Array index out of range
```

To avoid this error, assign the entry to an index within the bound.

```
> a[3] := 100;
```

$$a_3 := 100$$

```
> eval(a);
```

$$[?_1, ?_2, 100]$$

```
> A[2] := x-y;
```

$$A_2 := x - y$$

```
> A;
```

$$[0, x - y]$$

4.9   Exercises

1. Define a set with elements that are the powers of 13 modulo 100 for exponents ranging from 1 to 1000. Is 5 a member of the set? Why is it beneficial to use a set instead of a list?

   Hint: You can determine the set by using one statement if you use the **seq** command.

2. Generate the sums of 4 and the first 100 multiples of 3. Determine the sums that are square-free composite numbers.

   Hint: The **numtheory** package has a function that you need to use.

3. Find floating-point approximations for the sum of the square root and cubic root of each of the first 15 powers of 2.

   Hint: Use `map`, `seq`, and `zip`.

4. Write a procedure that implements the sieve of Eratosthenes: Count the number of integers (less than or equal to a given integer) that are prime.

4.10 Conclusion

When you write a procedure, you generally have freedom to choose the data structure used for the data. The choice of data structure can have a great impact on the complexity and efficiency of the procedure. This chapter presented a variety of data structures that you can use to write procedures in Maple.

Procedures were introduced in chapter 1. Detailed information about procedures is provided in chapter 6.

The next chapter formally discusses the statements and other constructs that control the number of times and order in which operations are executed. These include the `for...while...do` looping construct, and the `if...then...else` selection statement.

5 Flow Control

In the Maple programming language, there are control structures that direct the flow of execution in a procedure. In particular, you can organize the Maple statements in a procedure by *sequence*, *selection*, or *repetition*. You have primarily used sequential flow in the preceding chapters. This chapter describes the Maple control structures for selection and repetition.[1]

In This Chapter

- Selection and conditional execution control structures, the `if` statement and the `'if'` operator

- Repetition control (looping) structures, the `for` and `while` statements

- Looping commands: `map`; `select`, `remove`, and `selectremove`; `zip`; `seq`, `add`, and `mul`; and `$`, `sum`, and `product`

5.1   Selection and Conditional Execution

A selection (or conditional execution) control structure selects one statement to execute from many listed. In Maple, to control the selection of a statement, use the `if` statement, or the `'if'` operator.

The `if` Statement
The most general form of the `if` statement has the following syntax.

---

[1]Procedure calls and exception handlers (`try...catch...finally` statements) are also forms of flow control in Maple. For more information about procedure calls, see chapter 6. For more information about handling exceptions, see chapter 8.

```
if conditional expression then
    statement sequence
elif conditional expression then
    statement sequence
else
    statement sequence
end if
```

The `elif conditional expression then` construct can appear zero, one, or many times. The `else` construct can be excluded.

This section describes various forms of this general `if` statement.

Simple Forms of the `if` Statement   The following is the syntax of two simpler forms of the general `if` statement.

```
if expr then
    statseq
end if
```

```
if expr then
    statseq1
else
    statseq2
end if
```

Maple executes these selection statements as follows.

1. The conditional expression (`expr`) in the `if` clause is evaluated. The conditional expression can be any Boolean expression, which evaluates to `true`, `false`, or `FAIL`, formed by using:

   • relational operators: <, <=, >, >=, =, and <>
   • logical operators: **and**, **or**, and **not**
   • logical names: **true**, **false**, and **FAIL**

   Otherwise, the `if` statement returns an error.

```
    > x := -2:
> if x then
>    0
> else
>    1
> end if;
```

```
Error, invalid boolean expression
```

2. If the result of the **if** clause is the Boolean value **true**, Maple executes the statement sequence in the **then** clause. If the result of the **if** clause is the Boolean value **false** or **FAIL**, Maple executes the statement sequence in the **else** clause (if there is one).[2]

```
> if x<0 then
>    0
> else
>    1
> end if;
```

$$0$$

You can omit the **else** clause if you do not want to specify an action if the condition is **false**.

```
> if x>0 then
>    x := x-1
> end if;
```

Nested Selection Statements A selection statement can be nested— that is, the statement sequence in the **then** clause or **else** clause can be any statement (or sequence of statements), including an **if** statement.

```
> if x>0 then
>    print("Positive")
> else
>    if x=0 then
>       print("Zero")
>    else
>       print("Negative")
>    end if
> end if;
```

"Negative"

The following example demonstrates the behavior of **if** statements in the case that the conditional expression evaluates to **FAIL**.

```
> r := FAIL:
```

---

[2]For more information about Boolean expressions in Maple, see page 86 or refer to **?boolean**.

```
> if r then
>    print(1)
> else
>    if not r then
>       print(0)
>    else
>       print(-1)
>    end if
> end if;
```

$$-1$$

General Forms of the if Statement   For more complicated scenarios, use one of the following two forms of the if statement.

```
if expr then
    statseq
elif expr then
    statseq
end if
```

```
if expr then
    statseq
elif expr then
    statseq
else
    statseq
end if
```

The elif expr then statseq construct can appear more than once.

The following example implements the mathematical sign function by using an elif clause.

```
> x := -2;
```

$$x := -2$$

```
> if x<0 then
>    -1
> elif x=0 then
>    0
> else
>    1
> end if;
```

$$-1$$

Maple does not have a formal *case* statement. However, you can use the **if** statement as a case statement with the optional **else** clause as the default case. For example, to write a program that accepts a parameter n with four possible values (0, 1, 2, and 3), use the following code.[3],[4]

```
> n := 5;
```

$$n := 5$$

```
> if n=0 then
>    0
> elif n=1 then
>    1/2
> elif n=2 then
>    sqrt(2)/2
> elif n=3 then
>    sqrt(3)/2
> else error "bad argument: \%1", n;
> end if;
```

```
Error, bad argument: 5
```

The 'if' Operator

The operator form `'if'` requires three arguments and it returns the evaluation of the second or third argument, depending on the truth value of the first.

```
'if'(conditional expr,true expr,false expr)
```

The first argument must evaluate to **true, false,** or **FAIL**. If the first argument evaluates to **true**, the second argument is evaluated and returned. If the first argument evaluates to **false** or **FAIL**, the third argument is evaluated and returned. When the operator form is used, the

---

[3]A *case* statement is one that directs a program to choose one action from a list of alternatives, depending on the value of a given variable. Case statements (or similar constructs) are common to most programming languages.

[4]For more information about the **error** statement, see page 219 or refer to ?error.

name of this function must be enclosed in right single quotes (') because if is a Maple reserved word.[5]

```
> b:=4;
```

$$b := 4$$

```
> 'if'(b>5, 10, 11);
```

$$11$$

This 'if' operator statement is equivalent to the following if statement.

```
> if b>5 then
>    10
> else
>    11
> end if;
```

$$11$$

5.2   Repetition

A loop structure (repetition statement) executes a section of code multiple times. Maple has two general forms of repetition statements that you can use to perform looping in procedures. They have the following syntax.

```
for name from expr by expr to expr while expr do
    statement sequence
end do
```

---

[5]For more information about reserved words in Maple, see page 24 or refer to ?reserved.

```
for name in expr while expr do
    statement sequence
end do
```

Many of the clauses in these general repetition statements are optional. As a result, you can extract two special cases of loop-control statements—the `for` and the `while` statements. These special cases provide the ability to execute a statement sequence repeatedly, either for a counted number of times (by using the `for` clause) or until a condition is satisfied (by using the `while` clause).[6]

The for Loop

The `for` loop is used to repeatedly execute a sequence of statements for a counted number of times. The `for` loop has two forms: the `for...from` loop and the `for...in` loop.

The for...from Loop   A typical `for...from` loop has the following syntax.

```
for name from expr by expr to expr
while expr do
    statseq
end do
```

The following clauses are optional.

- for name

- from expr

- by expr

- to expr

- while expr

You can also omit the sequence of statements `statseq`. Excluding the `for` clause, which must appear first, the clauses can appear in any order. If you omit a clause, it has the default value shown in Table 5.1.

A typical `for...from` loop is used to generate a sequence of results.

---

[6]You can replace many of the loops that use `for` or `while` statements with more efficient and concise special forms. For more information, see **5.3 Looping Commands**.

Table 5.1 for Clauses and Their Default Values

Clause	Default Value
for	*dummy_variable*
from	1
by	1
to	infinity
while	true

```
> for i from 2 to 5 do
>    i^2
> end do;
```

$$4$$

$$9$$

$$16$$

$$25$$

This sequence of results is generated as follows.

- Maple assigns i the value 2.

- Because 2 is less than 5, Maple executes the statement between the do and the end do.

- Then i is incremented by 1 to 3, and tested again.

- The loop executes until i is strictly larger than 5. In this case, the final value of i is 6.

```
> i;
```

$$6$$

You can also write the previous example by using the following statement.

```
> for i from 2 by 1 to 5
> while true do
>    i^2
> end do:
```

When the by clause is negative, the for loop counts down.

```
> for i from 5 to 2 by -1 do
>    i^2
> end do;
```

$$25$$

$$16$$

$$9$$

$$4$$

Example To find the first prime number greater than 10^7, you could write:

```
> for i from 10^7
> while not isprime(i) do
> end do;
```

After this statement is executed, i is the first prime larger than 10^7.

```
> i;
```

$$10000019$$

Notice that the body of the loop is empty. Maple permits the empty statement. Improve the program by considering only odd numbers.

```
> for i from 10^7+1 by 2
> while not isprime(i) do
> end do;
```

```
> i;
```

$$10000019$$

The following code demonstrates how to repeat an action n times, in this case, throwing a die five times.

```
> die := rand(1..6):
```

```
> to 5 do
>    die();
> end do;
```

$$4$$

$$3$$

$$4$$

$$6$$

$$5$$

If all of the clauses in the `for` statement are omitted, an infinite loop is produced.

```
do statseq end do
```

This has the same effect as the following code, but the `do` loop does not assign a value to a dummy variable each iteration.

```
for dummy_variable from 1 by 1 to infinity
while true do
    statseq
end do
```

Such a loop statement repeats indefinitely unless Maple encounters a `break` statement (see page 179), `return` statement (see page 219), `quit` statement (see page 119), or error.

The `for...in` Loop   The `for...in` loop has the following syntax.

```
for name in expr
while expr do
    statseq
end do
```

The loop index `name` is assigned the operands of the first `expr`. You can test the value of the index in the optional `while` clause, and, of course, the value of the index is available when you execute the `statseq`. If the object in `expr` contains at least one operand, then the value of the index variable `name` remains assigned at the end of the loop .

For example, given a list L of integers, to find the integers that are less than or equal to 7, use the following `for` loop.

```
> L := [7,2,5,8,7,9];
```

$$L := [7, 2, 5, 8, 7, 9]$$

```
> for i in L do
>   if i <= 7 then
>     print(i)
>   end if;
> end do;
```

$$7$$

$$2$$

$$5$$

$$7$$

This code cycles through the operands of object L, in this case, a list. The object can be, for example, a set, sum of terms, product of factors, or string of characters.

The while Loop

The `for` loop is used to repeatedly execute a sequence of statements until a condition is satisfied. The `while` loop is a `for` loop with all of its clauses omitted except the `while` clause.

```
while expr do
    statseq
end do
```

The expression `expr` is called the *while condition*. It must be a Boolean-valued expression. That is, it must evaluate to `true`, `false`, or `FAIL`.

```
> x := 256;
```

$$x := 256$$

```
> while x>1 do
>   x := x/4
> end do;
```

$$x := 64$$

$$x := 16$$

$$x := 4$$

$$x := 1$$

The `while` loop behaves as follows.

- Maple evaluates the *while condition*. An error occurs if the while condition does not evaluate to `true`, `false`, or `FAIL`.

- If the condition evaluates to `true`, Maple executes the body of the loop.

- The loop repeats until the while condition evaluates to `false` or `FAIL`.[7]

```
> x := 1/2:
```

```
> while x>1 do
>     x := x/2
> end do;
```

```
> x;
```

$$\frac{1}{2}$$

```
> while x do
>     x := x/2
> end do;
```

```
Error, invalid boolean expression
```

Control within Loops

Within the Maple language reside two additional loop control constructs: `break` and `next`.

---

[7]Maple evaluates the while condition before it executes the body of the loop.

The break Statement   When Maple executes a **break** statement, the result is to exit from the repetition statement in which it occurs. Execution then proceeds with the first statement following this repetition statement.[8]

```
> L := [2, 5, 7, 8, 9];
```

$$L := [2, 5, 7, 8, 9]$$

```
> for i in L do
>    print(i);
>    if i=7 then
>       break
>    end if;
> end do;
```

$$2$$

$$5$$

$$7$$

The next Statement   When Maple executes a **next** statement, it proceeds immediately to the next iteration. For example, to skip the elements in a list that are equal to 7, use the following **for** loop.

```
> L := [7,2,5,8,7,9];
```

$$L := [7, 2, 5, 8, 7, 9]$$

```
> for i in L do
>    if i=7 then
>       next
>    end if;
>    print(i);
> end do;
```

$$2$$

$$5$$

$$8$$

$$9$$

---

[8]For more information about the **break** statement, refer to **?break**.

An error occurs if Maple encounters the names **break** or **next** in a context different from a repetition statement.

```
> next;
```

Error, break or next not in loop

5.3   Looping Commands

The previous section described the **for** and **while** loops. Some processes that involve loops are used so often that Maple provides special-purpose commands for them. These commands help to make writing programs simpler and more efficient. You can group these eight loop−based Maple commands into three categories.[9]

1. map, select, remove, selectremove

2. zip

3. seq, add, mul

The map Command

The **map** command applies a function to every element of an aggregate object. The simplest form of the **map** command is

```
map( f, x )
```

where **f** is a function and **x** is an expression. The **map** command replaces each operand x_i of the expression x with $f(x_i)$.[10]

```
> map( f, [a,b,c] );
```

---

[9]When possible, use these Maple commands instead of a generic **for** or **while** loop since the code for these commands is built into the Maple kernel. Therefore, it is usually more efficient to perform computations by using them. However, there are circumstances in which it is not desirable to use these special looping commands. For more information, see page 185.

[10]The exceptions are for a table, array, Array, or rtable. Maple applies the function to the entries of the table, array, or Array not the operands or indices. For an rtable, the function is applied to each element of the rtable, and then returns a new rtable of the mapped result.

$$[f(a),\ f(b),\ f(c)]$$

Example Given a list of integers, you can create a list of their absolute values and of their squares by using the `map` command.

```
> L := [ -1, 2, -3, -4, 5 ];
```

$$L := [-1,\ 2,\ -3,\ -4,\ 5]$$

```
> q:=map(abs, L);
```

$$q := [1,\ 2,\ 3,\ 4,\ 5]$$

```
> map(x->x^2, L);
```

$$[1,\ 4,\ 9,\ 16,\ 25]$$

The general syntax of the `map` command is

```
map( f, x, y1, ..., yn )
```

where `f` is a function, `x` is any expression, and `y1`, ..., `yn` are expressions. The action of `map` is to replace each operand x_i of `x` by `f(xi, y1, ..., yn)`.

```
> map( f, [a,b,c], x, y );
```

$$[f(a,\ x,\ y),\ f(b,\ x,\ y),\ f(c,\ x,\ y)]$$

```
> map( (x,y) -> x^2+y, L, 1);
```

$$[2,\ 5,\ 10,\ 17,\ 26]$$

The `select`, `remove`, and `selectremove` **Commands**

The `select` command returns the operands for which the specified Boolean-valued function returns `true`. The `remove` command returns the operands for which the specified Boolean-valued function returns `false`. The `selectremove` command returns two objects: the operands for which the specified Boolean-valued function returns `true` and the operands for which the specified Boolean-valued function returns `false`. The `select`, `remove`, and `selectremove` commands have the same syntax as the `map` command.

```
> X := 2*x*y^2 - 3*y^4*z + 3*z*w + 2*y^3 - z^2*w*y;
```

$$X := 2\,x\,y^2 - 3\,y^4\,z + 3\,z\,w + 2\,y^3 - z^2\,w\,y$$

```
> select(has, X, z);
```

$$-3\,y^4\,z + 3\,z\,w - z^2\,w\,y$$

```
> remove( x -> degree(x)>3, X );
```

$$2\,x\,y^2 + 3\,z\,w + 2\,y^3$$

For more information about these commands, see page 156 or refer to `?select`.

The `zip` Command

The `zip` command merges two lists or vectors, and then applies a binary function. The `zip` command has two forms

```
zip(f, u, v)
zip(f, u, v, d)
```

where `f` is a binary function, `u` and `v` are both lists or vectors, and `d` is any value. The `zip` command takes each pair of operands u_i, v_i, and creates a new list or vector from `f(u_i, v_i)`.[11]

```
> zip( (x,y) -> x || y, [a,b,c,d,e,f], [1,2,3,4,5,6] );
```

$$[a1,\ b2,\ c3,\ d4,\ e5,\ f6]$$

If the lists or vectors are not the same length, the length of the result depends on whether you provide the argument `d`.

If you do not specify `d`, the length of the result is the same as the length of the smaller list or vector.

---

[11] There is a similar command for rtable-based Matrices and Vectors. For more information, refer to `?Zip`.

```
> zip( (x,y) -> x+y, [a,b,c,d,e,f], [1,2,3] );
```

$$[a+1,\, b+2,\, c+3]$$

If d is specified, the length of the result of the zip command is the same as the length of the longer list or vector. Maple replaces the missing value(s) with d.

```
> zip( (x,y) -> x+y, [a,b,c,d,e,f], [1,2,3], xi );
```

$$[a+1,\, b+2,\, c+3,\, d+\xi,\, e+\xi,\, f+\xi]$$

The seq, add, and mul Commands

The seq, add, and mul commands form sequences, sums, and products, respectively. They have the following syntax.

```
seq(f, i = a..b)
add(f, i = a..b)
mul(f, i = a..b)
```

where f, a, and b are expressions, and i is a name. The expressions a and b must evaluate to numerical constants (except in seq, for which they can be single character strings).

The index name i is successively assigned the values a, a+1, ..., b (or up to the last value not exceeding b). The result returned by seq is the sequence that Maple produces by evaluating f at each value of i.

```
> seq(i, i = 4.123 .. 6.1);
```

$$4.123,\, 5.123$$

```
> seq(i^2, i=1..4);
```

$$1,\, 4,\, 9,\, 16$$

The result returned by add is the sum of the sequence. The result of mul is the product of the sequence.

```
> add(i^2, i=1..4);
```

30

```
> mul(i^2, i=1..4);
```

$$576$$

```
> add(x[i], i=1..4);
```

$$x_1 + x_2 + x_3 + x_4$$

In the case that a is greater than b, the result returned by seq, add, and mul is the NULL sequence, 0, and 1, respectively.

```
> mul(i^2, i = 4..1);
```

$$1$$

You can also use the seq, add, and mul commands with the following syntax.

```
seq(f, i = X)
add(f, i = X)
mul(f, i = X)
```

where f and X are expressions, and i is a name.

Using this form, the index name i is successively assigned the *operands* of the expression X (or the characters of string X). The result returned by seq is the sequence that Maple produces by evaluating f at each value of i.

```
> a := x^3 + 3*x^2 + 3*x + 1;
```

$$a := x^3 + 3\,x^2 + 3\,x + 1$$

```
> seq(degree(i,x), i=a);
```

$$3,\,2,\,1,\,0$$

```
> seq(i, i="square");
```

$$\text{``s'', ``q'', ``u'', ``a'', ``r'', ``e''}$$

The result of `add` is the sum of the sequence. The result of `mul` is the product of the sequence.

```
> add(degree(i,x), i=a);
```

$$6$$

```
> a := [23,-42,11,-3];
```

$$a := [23, -42, 11, -3]$$

```
> add(i^2, i=a);
```

$$2423$$

```
> mul(abs(i), i=a);
```

$$31878$$

This form of the `seq` function can be used to generate a sequence of indexed names.

```
> seq(x[i], i=1..5);
```

$$x_1, x_2, x_3, x_4, x_5$$

Using Specialized Looping Commands

Using the specialized looping commands described in this section can make writing Maple programs simpler and more efficient. However, there are conditions in which it is preferable to use the selection and repetition constructs instead of these specialized commands, and others in which the use of one specialized looping construct is recommended over another. This section illustrates some of these situations.

if versus map   The use of `map` or `zip` to simplify procedure code is not always recommmended. For example, it is common for a procedure to move to the next iteration once a result is determined without performing all the operations. In these cases, use an `if` statement instead of the `map` or `zip` command.

Example Consider the following procedure that uses an **if** statement.

```
> IsStringList := proc( e ) local i;
>     if type( e, 'list' ) then
>             for i from 1 to nops( e ) do
>                     if not type( e[ i ], 'string' ) then
>                             return false
>                     end if
>             end do;
>             true
>     else
>             false
>     end if
> end proc:
```

This procedure can be written in a simpler form by using **map**.

```
> IsStringList := proc( e )
>     type( e, 'list' ) and member( false, map( type, e,
>         'string' ) )
> end proc:
```

However, this "simpler" form allocates storage for a new set that is otherwise unrelated to the problem and tests *every* element of the list. Procedure IsStringList could also be written by using the following code.

```
> IsStringList := proc( e )
>     type( e, 'list' ) and evalb( remove( type, e, 'string' )
>         = [] )
> end proc:
```

Unfortunately, this version also tests *every* element of e to perform the test.

For example, if you call the latter two versions of IsStringList on a 1,000,000 element list whose third member is *not* a string, it performs $1,000,000$ type tests, while the first version of IsStringList (that uses an **if** statement) stops after the third element.

This example illustrates that if a procedure can return early, it is better to implement it by using an **if** statement.

seq, add, and mul versus $, sum, and product The sequence operator, $, and the sum and product commands are very similar to the seq, add, and mul commands. However, they differ in an important way—the index variable i and the end points a and b do not have to be integers.

```
> x[k] $ k=1..n;
```

$$x_k \, \$ \, (k = 1..n)$$

```
> sum(k^2, k=0..n);
```

$$\frac{1}{3}(n+1)^3 - \frac{1}{2}(n+1)^2 + \frac{1}{6}n + \frac{1}{6}$$

These commands are designed for *symbolic* sequences, sums, and products. The index variable k is a global variable to which you must not assign a value. If a previous value was assigned to k, an error message is returned.

```
> k := 10;
```

$$k := 10$$

```
> sum(k^2, k=0..n);
```

```
Error, (in sum) summation variable previously assigned,
second argument evaluates to 10 = 0 .. n
```

Using $, sum, and product   To produce a symbolic sequence, sum, or product, you must use $, sum, or product. For example, if the end points are unknown, use $, sum, or product. If you are producing an explicit finite sequence, sum, or product—that is, when the range points a and b are integers—use seq, add, or mul.[12]

For more information about the $ operator, refer to ?$. For more information about the sum and product commands, refer to ?sum and ?product, respectively.

5.4   Troubleshooting

This section provides you with a list of common mistakes, examples, and hints that will help you understand and avoid common errors. Use this

---

[12]The sum and product commands are *not* built into the kernel. Therefore, in general, they are not as efficient as add and mul. For more information about efficiency, see page 330 or refer to ?efficient.

section to study the errors that you may encounter when entering the examples from this chapter in a Maple session.[13]

Cannot Evaluate Boolean in `if` Statement

The conditional expression in an `if` clause must be a Boolean expression formed by using relational operators, logical operators, and logical names. Maple generates an error if the Boolean expression cannot be evaluated to `true`, `false`, or `FAIL`.[14]

```
> p := proc( x )
>        if x < 0 then
>            -x
>        else
>            x
>        end if
>    end proc;
```

$$p := \mathbf{proc}(x)\, \mathbf{if}\, x < 0\, \mathbf{then} - x\, \mathbf{else}\, x\, \mathbf{end\ if\, end\ proc}$$

```
> p(a);
```

```
Error, (in p) cannot determine if this expression is
true or false: a < 0
```

Instead, you must use a parameter that can be compared to 0 in procedure p.

```
> p(-2);
```

$$2$$

To avoid this error message, use type-checking in the formal parameter list of the procedure definition. For more information, see page 197.

Value in Loop Must Be Numeric or Character

Maple generates an error if the expression in the `from` or `to` part of a `for` statement does not result in a value of type numeric or a character (string of length 1).[15]

---

[13] You can also use the Maple debugger to find errors in programs. For more information, see chapter 8 or refer to `?debugger`.

[14] For more information about Boolean expressions, see page 86 or refer to `?boolean`.

[15] For more information about types, see **2.4 Types and Operands** or refer to `?type`.

```
> for i from a to d do print(i) end do;
```

Error, initial value in for loop must be numeric or
character

```
> for i from 1 to "z" do print(i) end do;
```

Error, final value in for loop must have same type as
initial

Study the following examples to see how to fix these errors.

```
> for i from "a" to "d" do print(i) end do;
```

"a"

"b"

"c"

"d"

```
> for i from 1 to 2 do print(i) end do;
```

1

2

```
> for i from evalf(tan(Pi/8)) to evalf(sqrt(17)) by 1.5
>      do print(i) end do;
```

0.4142135625

1.914213562

3.414213562

Variable Previously Assigned

Maple generates an error if the index variable in a **sum** or **product** command has a previously assigned value. This occurs because the index variable in these commands is the global variable.[16]

---

[16]For more information about the global variables, see **Variables** on page 201.

```
> k := 100;
```

$$k := 100$$

```
> sum(k^2, k=0..4);
```

```
Error, (in sum) summation variable previously assigned,
second argument evaluates to 100 = 0 .. 4
```

It is recommended (and often necessary) that both the expression and index arguments be enclosed in right single quotes to delay evaluation, so that the name (not value) is used.[17]

```
> sum('k^2', 'k'=0..4);
```

$$30$$

Wrong Parameters in Function $

Maple generates an error if the index variable in a statement containing the $ operator has an assigned value. This occurs because the index variable, which is the same as the global variable, is evaluated to its value, and hence cannot be used as a counting variable.[18]

```
> i := 100;
```

$$i := 100$$

```
> a[i] $ i = 1..3;
```

```
Error, wrong number (or type) of parameters in function
$
```

It is recommended that i be enclosed in right single quotes to delay evaluation.[19]

```
> 'a[i]' $ 'i' = 1..3;
```

---

[17]For more information on delaying evaluation, see **Unevaluated Expressions** on page 100.

[18]For more information about the global variables, see **Variables** on page 201.

[19]For more information on delaying evaluation, see **Unevaluated Expressions** on page 100.

$$a_1, a_2, a_3$$

5.5   Exercises

1. Find the product of the square root of all prime numbers less than 100.

   Hint: The function `isprime` determines the primality of an integer.

2. Find the sum of all odd composite numbers less than 150.

3. Find the sum of the first 30 powers of 2.

4. Write a looping structure that finds the four substrings (of a string assigned to the name `MyString`) containing only lower case letters, upper case letters, decimal digits, and special characters.

   Hint: You can use relational operators to compare characters.

5. Write a procedure, `SPLIT`, that, upon input of a product `f` and a variable `x`, returns a list of two values. The first item in the list should be the product of the factors in `f` that are independent of `x`, and the second item should be the product of the factors that contain an `x`.

   Hint: Use the `has`, `select`, `remove`, and `selectremove` commands.

5.6   Conclusion

This chapter discussed flow control in the Maple programming language. Normally, the statements in a procedure body are executed sequentially. However, you can control the order in which operations are executed by using the `if...then...else` selection statement, or the `for...while...do` looping construct. For certain procedures, it is more efficient to use the specialized looping commands: `map`; `select`, `remove`, and `selectremove`; `zip`; `seq`, `add`, and `mul`; and `$`, `sum`, and `product`.

6   Maple Procedures

A Maple procedure definition is a prearranged group of statements entered within a `proc()...end proc` construct. In this construct, you must declare the parameters and variables that the procedure uses, and specify the statements that form the body of the procedure. You can also define simple one-line procedures using functional operators.

In chapter 1, a brief introduction to procedures was presented. This chapter describes the syntax and semantics of a Maple procedure in detail, and discusses how to create mathematical functions using functional operators.

In This Chapter

- Structure of procedures

- Using procedures

- Automatic simplification of procedures

- Procedure return values

- Adding comments, such as copyright statements, and help pages for procedures

- Alternate methods for defining procedures

- The `procedure` object

- Implementing data structures, using procedures, to solve problems

6.1   Defining a Procedure

A Maple procedure definition has the following general syntax.

```
proc( P )
local L;
global G;
options O;
description D;
procedure body
end proc
```

The letter P represents the formal parameter names, which may be NULL (an empty expression). The local variables, global variables, options, description, and procedure body statements are optional.

Example The following is a simple Maple procedure definition. It contains two formal parameters, x and y, and one statement in the body of the procedure, but no local variables, global variables, options, or description.

```
> proc(x,y)
>     x^2 + y^2
> end proc;
```

$$\mathbf{proc}(x,\ y)\ x^2 + y^2\ \mathbf{end\ proc}$$

Naming a Procedure

You can name a procedure by using an assignment statement in the same manner as for other Maple objects. In general, a procedure must be assigned to a name so that you can invoke it with procedure calls. For information about unnamed procedures, see page 232.[1]

```
> f := proc(x,y)
>     x^2 + y^2
> end proc;
```

$$f := \mathbf{proc}(x,\ y)\ x^2 + y^2\ \mathbf{end\ proc}$$

Executing a Procedure

You can execute (or invoke) a procedure assigned to a name by using a procedure call.

---

[1]You can assign a procedure to any number of names. For example, both f and g are assigned the same procedure by using the following commands. `f:=proc(x)` x^2 `end proc; g:=eval(f); map(addressof@eval,[f,g]);`

```
procedureName( A );
```

The **procedureName** is the name to which the procedure definition is assigned, and the letter **A** represents the expression sequence of actual parameters used in the procedure call.

When Maple executes the statements in the body of a procedure, it substitutes the formal parameters P in the procedure definition with the actual parameters **A** in the procedure call. Normally, the result a procedure returns is the value of the *last* executed statement in the body of the procedure.[2]

Note: Maple evaluates the actual parameters before they are substituted for the formal parameters. These parameters are *not* evaluated again during execution of the procedure. Prior to substitution, each actual parameter is also checked against its specified type, if any (see page 197). If the type checking fails, the procedure returns an error. The order in which Maple tests the types of the actual parameters is unspecified. Type checking actual parameters is optional.

In the following procedure call, Maple executes the statements in the body of procedure F and replaces the formal parameters, x and y, with the actual parameters, 2 and 3. The result of the last, and in this case only, statement in the procedure is the returned value of procedure F.

```
> f(2,3);
```

$$13$$

The number of actual parameters need not be the same as the number of specified formal parameters. If too few actual parameters are specified, an error occurs if (and only if) a missing parameter is used during the execution of the procedure body. Maple does not process extra parameters.

```
> f := proc(x,y,z)
>        if x>y then
>            x
>        else
>            z
>        end if
>   end proc:
> f(1,2,3,4);
```

---

[2]For more information about return values, see **6.4 Procedure Return Values**.

3

```
> f(1,2);
```

```
Error, (in f) f uses a 3rd argument, z, which is
missing
```

```
> f(2,1);
```

2

6.2   Procedure Components

The following sections describe the components of a procedure definition in detail. These are the formal parameters, local variables, global variables, options, description, and body statements.

Formal Parameters

```
proc( P )
...
end proc
```

The letter P represents the formal parameter names in a procedure definition. It can be NULL (an empty expression), a sequence of names, or a sequence of names and their type definitions.

Procedures without Formal Parameters   If no input is required to run a procedure, that is, no formal parameters are required, enter empty parentheses in the heading of the procedure definition and in procedure calls.

```
> F := proc()
>          "Hello World"
>   end proc;
```

$$F := \mathbf{proc}()\ \text{"Hello World"}\ \mathbf{end\ proc}$$

```
> F();
```

"Hello World"

Specifying Formal Parameters Procedures that do not require formal parameters usually perform very simple tasks. In general, procedure execution requires input. In these cases, you must enter formal parameters as a sequence of names between the parentheses in the heading of the procedure definition.

```
> F := proc(x, y)
>         gcd(x,y)
>     end proc;
```

$$F := \textbf{proc}(x, y)\, \text{gcd}(x, y)\ \textbf{end proc}$$

You must specify actual parameters between parentheses in the calling sequence.

```
> F(4,6);
```

$$2$$

Type-checking Formal Parameters To restrict the type of parameters, specify the parameter types in the formal parameter list of a procedure definition. To include the type declaration that parameter **p** must be of type **t**, the parameter must be specified by using the following syntax.

```
p::t
```

Although this is optional, it is recommended because it makes the procedure more robust. At invocation, each argument is checked against the type specified for the parameter. If any fail the type check, an error message is generated.[3]

```
> F := proc(x :: integer, y :: integer)
>         gcd(x,y)
>     end proc;
```

$$F := \textbf{proc}(x{::}integer,\ y{::}integer)\, \text{gcd}(x, y)\, \textbf{end proc}$$

---

[3]Maple has many expression types. For more information, refer to **?type**. For more information about parameters and type checking, refer to **?paramtype**.

```
> F(4, 6.3);
```

```
Error, invalid input: F expects its 2nd argument, y, to
be of type integer, but received 6.3
```

```
> F(4, 6);
```

$$2$$

If you do not declare the type of a parameter, it can have any type. For example, `proc(x)` is equivalent to `proc(x::anything)`. In that case it is recommmended that you use the latter form to inform other users that the procedure works for any input.

The closing bracket of the formal parameter list can optionally be followed by `::type_name`; where `type_name` specifies a Maple type. Unlike the case of formal parameters, this is *not* a type declaration, but rather an *assertion*—a statement about the procedure that you assert to be true. This optional assertion facility checks the return value type if you set `kernelopts(assertlevel=2)`. If the type violates the assertion, an exception is raised.[4]

```
> F := proc(x :: numeric ) :: integer;
>        x/2;
>   end proc:
> F(3);
```

$$\frac{3}{2}$$

```
> kernelopts(assertlevel=2):
> F(3);
```

```
Error, (in F) assertion failed: F expects its return
value to be of type integer, but computed 3/2
```

In this case, executing procedure F causes an exception because its definition asserted that the return value must be of type `integer`.

---

[4]For more information about assertions and exceptions, see **8.3 Detecting Errors**.

Evaluation Rules   Parameters play a special role in procedures. Maple replaces them with arguments (actual parameters) when you invoke the procedure.

Examine the following procedure that squares its first argument and assigns the answer to the second argument, which must be a name.

```
> Sqr1 := proc(x::anything, y::name)
>            y := x^2;
> end proc;
```

$$Sqr1 := \mathbf{proc}(x::anything,\ y::name)\ y := x^2\ \mathbf{end\ proc}$$

```
> Sqr1(d, ans);
```

$$d^2$$

```
> ans;
```

$$d^2$$

The procedure squares the value of **d** and assigns the result to the name **ans**.

To demonstrate parameter evaluation, first assign the name **a** the value **b**. Then assign the name **b** the value **c**.

```
> a:=b;
```

$$a := b$$

```
> b:=c;
```

$$b := c$$

Use **a** as the first argument. Reset **ans** to a name so that the procedure type check does not fail.

```
> ans := 'ans';
```

$$ans := ans$$

```
> Sqr1(a, ans);
```

$$c^2$$

```
> ans;
```

$$c^2$$

From the answer, it is clear that the value c is assigned to the parameter x.

Maple evaluates the arguments *before* invoking the procedure.

When you call a procedure, Maple evaluates the arguments as determined by the context of the call. For example, if you call Sqr1 from inside a procedure, Maple evaluates the local variable a to one level. For more information about procedure variable evaluation rules, see page 203. Thus, in the procedure g below, Maple evaluates a to b not c.

```
> g := proc()
>         local a,b,ans;
>         a := b;
>         b := c;
>         Sqr1(a,ans);
> end proc;
```

$$g := \mathbf{proc}()$$
$$\mathbf{local}\ a,\ b,\ ans;$$
$$a := b;\ b := c;\ \mathrm{Sqr1}(a,\ ans)$$
$$\mathbf{end\ proc}$$

```
> g();
```

$$b^2$$

Whether you call a procedure from the interactive level or from inside a procedure, Maple evaluates the arguments to the level specified by the context before invoking the procedure. Once Maple evaluates the arguments, it replaces all occurrences of the corresponding formal parameters with the actual arguments. Then Maple invokes the procedure.

Because Maple only evaluates parameters once, you cannot use them as local variables. This is demonstrated by the following procedure.

```
> Cube := proc(x::anything, y::name)
>             y := x^3;
>             y;
> end proc:
> ans := 'ans';
```

$$ans := ans$$

```
> Cube(2, ans);
```

$$ans$$

```
> ans;
```

$$8$$

Maple replaces each y with **ans**, but does not evaluate these occurrences of **ans** again. Thus, the final line of **Cube** returns the name **ans**, not the value assigned to **ans**.

Use parameters only to pass information into the procedure. Parameters are objects that are evaluated to *zero* levels.

Variables

A *variable* represents a data item, such as a numerical value or a character string, that can change its value during the execution of a program. This section describes local variables, global variables, and their use in Maple procedures.

A *local variable* is a variable that has meaning only within a particular procedure. If the name of a local variable is used outside the procedure, it (usually) refers to a different instantiation of the name. *Global variables* are recognized inside and outside the procedure.

Local and Global Variable Declarations Variables that occur inside a procedure can be global or local to the procedure. Variables that occur outside a procedure are always global. Local variables in different procedure invocations are distinct variables even if they have the same name. Thus, one procedure can change the value of a local variable without affecting variables of the same name in other procedures, or a global variable of the same name. You should always declare variables as local or global by using the following declaration statement in a procedure definition.

```
local L1, L2, ..., Ln;
global G1, G2, ..., Gm;
```

In procedure Max, i and m are local variables.

```
> Max := proc()
>          local i,m;
>          if nargs = 0 then
>             return -infinity
>          end if;
>          m := args[1];
>          for i from 2 to nargs do
>             if args[i] > m then
>                m := args[i]
>             end if;
>          end do;
>          m;
> end proc:
```

Like procedure return values, you can assert the type of each local variable in the local variable declaration statement by using the following syntax.

```
local L1::type1, var2::type2, ...
```

This is *not* a type declaration—it is an *assertion*. If you use this optional assertion facility for checking the local variable types in a procedure and set `kernelopts(assertlevel=2)`, any assignment to a variable with a type assertion is checked before the assignment is performed. If the assignment violates the assertion, an exception is raised.

To illustrate how this facility works, consider the revised procedure `Max` that includes an incorrect type assertion for local variable `m`.

```
> kernelopts(assertlevel=2):
> Max := proc()
>          local i, m :: string;
>          if nargs = 0 then
>             return -infinity
>          end if;
>          m := args[1];
>          for i from 2 to nargs do
>             if args[i] > m then
>                m := args[i]
>             end if;
>          end do;
>          m;
> end proc:
> Max(1,2,3);
```

```
Error, (in Max) assertion failed in assignment,
expected string, got 1
```

In the case of *nested* procedures, where one procedure is defined within the body of another, variables can also acquire local or global declaration from procedures which enclose them. For more information about nested procedures, refer to chapter 1 in the *Maple Advanced Programming Guide* or ?examples,lexical.

Evaluation Rules for Procedure Variables   Maple fully evaluates global variables, even inside a procedure. However, local variables are evaluated in a special way. During the execution of a procedure body, a local variable is *evaluated only one level*. The following examples clarify this concept.

Consider a sequence of Maple statements.

```
> f := x + y;
```

$$f := x + y$$

```
> x := z^2/ y;
```

$$x := \frac{z^2}{y}$$

```
> z := y^3 + 3;
```

$$z := y^3 + 3$$

Since these statements undergo normal full recursive evaluation, the following result is returned.

```
> f;
```

$$\frac{(y^3 + 3)^2}{y} + y$$

The actual level of evaluation is controlled by using the **eval** command. You can use the following commands to evaluate to one, two, or three levels, respectively.

```
> eval(f,1);
```

$$x + y$$

```
> eval(f,2);
```

$$\frac{z^2}{y} + y$$

```
> eval(f,3);
```

$$\frac{(y^3+3)^2}{y} + y$$

Unlike the full evaluation of the sequence of statements in the previous example, in procedures, local variables are only evaluated to one level.

```
> f := proc()
>        local x, y, z;
>        x := y^2; y := z; z := 3;
>        x;
>   end proc:
> f();
```

$$y^2$$

The concept of *one-level evaluation* is important for efficiency. It has very little effect on the behavior of programs because most programs have a sequential structure. In the case that a procedure body requires a full (recursive) evaluation of a local variable, use the `eval` command.[5]

```
> f := proc()
>        local x, y, z;
>        x := y^2; y := z; z := 3;
>        eval(x);
>   end proc:
> f();
```

9

Without the call to `eval`, the value of x is y^2.

In the same manner as global variables, you can use local variables as unknowns. This use is recommended when it is *not* necessary to access the variables. For example, in the RootsOfUnity procedure, the local variable x does not have an assigned value. The procedure uses it as the variable in the polynomial x^n-1.

---

[5]The concept of one-level evaluation does not occur in traditional programming languages. However, in Maple, you can assign to a variable a formula involving other variables (to which you can assign values, and so on).

```
> RootsOfUnity := proc(n)
>                     local x;
>                     [solve( x^n - 1=0, x )];
>  end proc:
> RootsOfUnity(5);
```

$$[1, \frac{1}{4}\sqrt{5} - \frac{1}{4} + \frac{1}{4}I\sqrt{2}\sqrt{5+\sqrt{5}}, -\frac{1}{4}\sqrt{5} - \frac{1}{4} + \frac{1}{4}I\sqrt{2}\sqrt{5-\sqrt{5}},$$
$$-\frac{1}{4}\sqrt{5} - \frac{1}{4} - \frac{1}{4}I\sqrt{2}\sqrt{5-\sqrt{5}}, \frac{1}{4}\sqrt{5} - \frac{1}{4} - \frac{1}{4}I\sqrt{2}\sqrt{5+\sqrt{5}}]$$

Undeclared Variables If a variable is not declared local or global in the one (or more) procedures in which it is enclosed, Maple determines its scope. A variable is automatically made local in the following two cases.

- It appears on the left-hand side of an assignment statement. For example, A in A := y or A[1] := y.

- It appears as the index variable in a **for** loop, or **seq**, **add**, or **mul** command.

If neither of these two rules applies, the variable is a global variable.

To illustrate how Maple reacts to undeclared variables, consider the revised **Max** procedure.

```
> Max := proc()
>         if nargs = 0 then
>             return -infinity
>         end if;
>         m := args[1];
>         for i from 2 to nargs do
>             if args[i] > m then
>                 m := args[i]
>             end if;
>         end do;
>         m;
> end proc:
```

```
Warning, 'm' is implicitly declared local to procedure
'Max'
Warning, 'i' is implicitly declared local to procedure
'Max'
```

Do not rely on this facility to declare local variables. Declare all your local variables explicitly. Use Maple warning messages to identify variables that you have misspelled or neglected to declare.

The `NewName` procedure creates the next unused name in the sequence C1, C2, ... The name that `NewName` creates is a global variable since neither of the two previous rules apply to `cat(C,N)`.

```
> NewName := proc()
>                global N;
>                N := N+1;
>                while assigned(cat(C,N)) do
>                    N := N+1;
>                end do;
>                cat(C,N);
> end proc:
> N := 0;
```

$$N := 0$$

```
> NewName() * sin(x) + NewName() * cos(x);
```

$$C1 \sin(x) + C2 \cos(x)$$

It is recommended that you do *not* assign a value to a global variable in a procedure. A change in the value of a global variable updates all instances of the variable, including those of which you are unaware. Therefore, use this technique judiciously.[6]

Procedure Options

```
proc( ... )
variable declarations
options O;
description
procedure body
end proc
```

The options of a procedure definition must appear immediately after the local and global variable declarations, if any. A procedure can have one or more options. These options are specified by using the **options** clause in a procedure definition.

---

[6]As is the case with any global side effect, assigning to a global variable in a procedure invalidates that procedure for **option remember**. For more information about **option remember**, see page 210.

```
options O1, O2, ...,Om;
```

You can use any symbol to specify an option name. However, the following terms have special meanings.[7]

The arrow Option   The arrow option has meaning only when specified in conjunction with option operator. The arrow option causes the Maple prettyprinter to print the procedure using arrow notation. For more information, see page 209.

```
> f := proc(x, y)
>        option operator;
>        x^2 + y^2
>   end proc;
```

$$f := \mathbf{proc}(x, y) \, \mathbf{option} \; operator; \; x^2 + y^2 \, \mathbf{end} \; \mathbf{proc}$$

```
> f := proc(x, y)
>        option operator, arrow;
>        x^2 + y^2
>   end proc;
```

$$f := (x, y) \rightarrow x^2 + y^2$$

The builtin Option   Maple has two classes of procedures: kernel procedures written in the C programming language, and library procedures written in the Maple programming language. Because the built-in kernel functions are compiled, you cannot view their procedure definitions. The builtin option is used to identify a kernel procedure.

You see this option when you evaluate a built-in procedure. Also, instead of displaying the source code, a number is displayed. This number uniquely identifies each built-in procedure. You cannot create built-in procedures.[8]

For example, the add function is in the kernel.[9]

```
> eval(add);
```

---

[7]For more information about symbols in Maple, see **Names** on page 26 or refer to ?symbol. For more information about procedure options, refer to ?options.

[8]For information on using external compiled code, see the call_external option in this section.

[9]For more information about the Maple system and built-in functions, refer to ?builtin.

$$\mathbf{proc}()\,\mathbf{option}\ \textit{builtin};\ 90\,\mathbf{end}\ \mathbf{proc}$$

You can also use type-checking to determine if a Maple procedure is built-in. An expression is of type `builtin` if it is a procedure with `option builtin`. This type identifies procedures implemented in the Maple kernel, rather than the library.

```
> type(add, 'builtin');
```

$$true$$

```
> type(int, 'builtin');
```

$$false$$

The `call_external` Option To create a link to and call functions that are external to the Maple program, use the `define_external` and `call_external` functions, respectively. The `define_external` function returns a `call_external` procedure. That is, you do not need to construct a procedure with `option call_external`. For more information about defining procedures that call external functions, refer to chapter 6 of the *Maple Advanced Programming Guide* or `?define_external`.

The `Copyright` Option To add a copyright notice to a procedure, use option `Copyright`. Maple considers any option that begins with the word `Copyright` to be a copyright option. The body of a procedure with a copyright option is not printed unless the `interface` variable `verboseproc` is at least 2—this is accomplished with the command `interface(verboseproc=2)`.[10] All Maple library routines have the copyright option.

```
> f := proc(expr::anything, x::name)
>         option 'Copyright (c) 1684 by G. W. Leibnitz';
>         Diff(expr, x);
> end proc;
```

$$f := \mathbf{proc}(\textit{expr::anything},\ \textit{x::name})\ \ldots\ \mathbf{end}\ \mathbf{proc}$$

---

[10]For more information about using the `interface` variable, see page 258 or refer to `?interface`.

```
> interface(verboseproc=2);
> eval(f);
```

> **proc**(*expr::anything, x::name*)
> **option** '*Copyright (c) 1684 by G. W. Leibnitz*';
>   Diff(*expr, x*)
> **end proc**

The `inline` Option To create an inline Maple procedure, include `option inline` in the options field of the procedure definition. An inline Maple procedure avoids the overhead of a procedure call by executing the Maple instructions directly, as if it were written inline, rather than in a separate procedure. By avoiding the overhead of the procedure call, small performance improvements can be achieved. However, not all Maple procedures can be inline. Only procedures whose body consists of a single expression or an expression sequence can be inline—the body cannot consist of a statement or statement sequence. Other restrictions also apply. For more information about procedure inlining, refer to `?inline`.

The `operator` Option Functional operators (or *arrow* operators) provide an alternate method for representing a mathematical function (or mapping) in Maple—they are a special form of a procedure. An arrow operator consists of a sequence of arguments (generally enclosed in parantheses) followed by an arrow (`->`), and then the expression that defines the function.

```
> (x, y) -> x^2 + y^2;
```

$$(x, y) \rightarrow x^2 + y^2$$

If `option operator` is specified in a procedure definition, it identifies the procedure as a functional operator. If `option arrow` is used in conjunction with `option operator` in the procedure definition, the Maple `prettyprinter` prints the procedure using arrow notation. See also page 207.[11]

```
> f := proc(x, y)
>         option operator;
>           x^2 + y^2
> end proc;
```

---

[11]For more information about functional operators, see page 231 or refer to `?operators,functional`.

$$f := \mathbf{proc}(x,\, y)\, \mathbf{option}\; operator;\; x^2 + y^2\; \mathbf{end\; proc}$$

```
> f := proc(x, y)
>          option operator, arrow;
>          x^2 + y^2
> end proc;
```

$$f := (x,\, y) \to x^2 + y^2$$

The remember Option   To associate a *remember table* with a procedure, include `option remember` in the list of procedure options. If a remember table is not explicitly associated with a procedure, the remember table for the procedure is the `NULL` expression. A remember table that is associated with a procedure can be manipulated as other Maple tables.[12]

If you specify the `remember` option in the options field of a Maple procedure, after each invocation of the procedure, an entry that records the result for the specified arguments is made in the procedure's remember table. For subsequent invocations of the procedure, Maple checks whether you have called the procedure with the same parameters. If so, Maple retrieves the previously calculated result from the remember table, instead of executing the procedure.

The use of `option remember` and remember tables can drastically improve the efficiency of recursively-defined procedures. For example, consider the following procedure that calculates the Fibonacci numbers.[13]

```
> Fib := proc( n :: nonnegint )
>              option remember;
>              if n<2 then
>                   n
>              else
>                   Fib(n-1) + Fib(n-2)
>              end if;
> end proc;
```

---

[12]You can also explicitly associate a remember table with a procedure by direct assignment to the table. For example, if `f` is the name of the procedure definition, the commands `f(0):=0; f(2):=1;` creates the remember table `table([0=0, 2=1)]` for procedure `f`. For more information about tables and remember tables in Maple, refer to `?table` or `?remember`.

[13]For a comparison of run-time efficiency with `option remember`, see **Profiling a Procedure** on page 332.

$Fib := \mathbf{proc}(n::nonnegint)$
$\mathbf{option}\ remember;$
$\quad \mathbf{if}\, n < 2\, \mathbf{then}\, n\ \ \mathbf{else}\, \mathrm{Fib}(n-1) + \mathrm{Fib}(n-2)\, \mathbf{end\ if}$
$\mathbf{end\ proc}$

```
> Fib(4);
```

$$3$$

If you enter `interface(verboseproc=3)`, and then view the procedure definition by using the `eval` command, the contents of its remember table are printed below its procedure definition.[14]

```
> interface(verboseproc=3);
> eval(Fib);
```

$\mathbf{proc}(n::nonnegint)$
$\mathbf{option}\ remember;$
$\quad \mathbf{if}\, n < 2\, \mathbf{then}\, n\ \ \mathbf{else}\, \mathrm{Fib}(n-1) + \mathrm{Fib}(n-2)\, \mathbf{end\ if}$
$\mathbf{end\ proc}$
$\#\,(0) = 0$
$\#\,(1) = 1$
$\#\,(2) = 1$
$\#\,(3) = 2$
$\#\,(4) = 3$

Since `Fib` has the `remember` option, if you invoke the procedure again with an argument greater than 4:

- The results for all calls to `Fib` with arguments less than or equal to 4 are read from the `Fib` remember table, and

- All calls to `Fib` with arguments greater than 4 are computed and appended to the `Fib` remember table.

```
> Fib(7);
```

---

[14]An alternate way to view the remember table of a procedure that has option `remember` is to use `op(4, eval(f))`, where `f` is the name of the procedure definition. For more information, see **Procedure Operands** on page 237, or refer to `?procedure` or `?op`.

13

```
> eval(Fib);
```

$$\mathbf{proc}(n{::}nonnegint)$$
$$\mathbf{option}\ remember;$$
$$\quad \mathbf{if}\ n < 2\ \mathbf{then}\ n\ \ \mathbf{else}\ \mathrm{Fib}(n-1)+\mathrm{Fib}(n-2)\ \mathbf{end\ if}$$
$$\mathbf{end\ proc}$$
$$\#\,(0) = 0$$
$$\#\,(1) = 1$$
$$\#\,(2) = 1$$
$$\#\,(3) = 2$$
$$\#\,(4) = 3$$
$$\#\,(5) = 5$$
$$\#\,(6) = 8$$
$$\#\,(7) = 13$$

The system Option   If option system is specified in conjunction with option remember in the options field of a Maple procedure, entries in the procedure's remember table are removed during garbage collection, freeing the space occupied by the remember table and its entries.[15]

```
> Fib := proc( n :: nonnegint )
>              option remember, system;
>              if n<2 then
>                  n
>              else
>                  Fib(n-1) + Fib(n-2)
>              end if;
> end proc;
```

$$Fib := \mathbf{proc}(n{::}nonnegint)$$
$$\mathbf{option}\ remember,\ system;$$
$$\quad \mathbf{if}\ n < 2\ \mathbf{then}\ n\ \ \mathbf{else}\ \mathrm{Fib}(n-1)+\mathrm{Fib}(n-2)\ \mathbf{end\ if}$$
$$\mathbf{end\ proc}$$

The trace Option   If the trace option is included in a procedure definition, Maple shows the entry and exit calls, and all the internal statements

---

[15]For more information about garbage collection in Maple, see page 335 or refer to ?gc.

when the procedure is executed. This effect is independent of the value of the printlevel variable.[16]

```
> Fib := proc( n :: nonnegint )
>              option remember, system, trace;
>              if n<2 then
>                  n
>              else
>                  Fib(n-1) + Fib(n-2)
>              end if;
> end proc:
> Fib(3);
```

```
{--> enter Fib, args = 3
{--> enter Fib, args = 2
{--> enter Fib, args = 1
```

$$1$$

```
<-- exit Fib (now in Fib) = 1}
{--> enter Fib, args = 0
```

$$0$$

```
<-- exit Fib (now in Fib) = 0}
```

$$1$$

```
<-- exit Fib (now in Fib) = 1}
value remembered (in Fib): Fib(1) -> 1
```

$$2$$

```
<-- exit Fib (now at top level) = 2}
```

$$2$$

Procedure Description

---

[16]For more information about tracing a procedure and printlevel, see chapter 8 or refer to ?trace and ?printlevel.

```
proc( ... )
variable and option declarations
description D;
procedure body
end proc
```

The last part of the procedure header is the description field. It is used to specify lines of text that describe a procedure. Its use is optional. However, if used, it must be entered after local variables, global variables, and options, and before the body of the procedure. Descriptions are specified by using the following format, where D is any symbol or string.

```
description string ;
```

The description field has no effect on the execution of a procedure. It is used only for documentation purposes.

```
> f := proc(x :: integer, y :: integer)
>         local a;
>         description "compute the average of two integers";
>         a := (x + y)/2;
> end proc:
> eval(f);
```

$$\mathbf{proc}(x{::}integer,\ y{::}integer)$$
$$\mathbf{local}\ a;$$
$$\mathbf{description}\ \text{"compute the average of two integers"};$$
$$a := 1/2 * x + 1/2 * y$$
$$\mathbf{end\ proc}$$

Maple prints the description field even if it does not print the body of a procedure because there is a **copyright** option.

```
> f := proc(x)
>         option `Copyrighted ?`;
>         description "computes the square of x";
>         x^2; # compute x^2
>   end proc:
> eval(f);
```

$$\mathbf{proc}(x)$$
$$\mathbf{description}\ \text{"computes the square of x"}$$
$$\dots$$
$$\mathbf{end\ proc}$$

You can include more than one line of text in the description field by splitting the description string into smaller strings.

```
> f := proc(x)
>       description "This example shows "
>                   "how to include "
>                   "a multi-line description.";
>       x^2;
> end proc:
> eval(f);
```

$\mathbf{proc}(x)$

description"This example shows how to include a \
multi-line description.";

x^2

end proc

Procedure Body Statements

The procedure body can contain any number of valid Maple statements. The only condition on the procedure body is that it must terminate with end proc.[17]

6.3   Procedure Interpretation

When a procedure definition is entered, Maple does *not* execute the procedure. However, Maple automatically simplifies the body of the procedure, if possible. This simplification is identical to that which Maple performs in interactive mode.

Consider the following procedure.

```
> f := proc(x)
>       local t;
>       t := x*x*x + 0*2;
>       if true then
>          sqrt(t)
>       else
>          t^2
>       end if;
> end proc;
```

---

[17]For more information about statements to perform numeric, symbolic, and graphical computations, refer to the *Maple Advanced Programming Guide*.

$$f := \mathbf{proc}(x)\,\mathbf{local}\,t;\ t := x * x * x;\ \mathrm{sqrt}(t)\,\mathbf{end\ proc}$$

The expression x*x*x simplifies to x^3, the multiplication by zero is omitted, and the if statement simplifies to sqrt(t).

Since Maple does try to simplify the body of a procedure, you should use caution if you try to hard-code a floating-point constant in a procedure body. (This also applies when specifying floating-point constants in interactive mode.) Consider procedures F and G.

```
> F := proc(x) x*(1/100000000000000000001) end proc;
```

$$F := \mathbf{proc}(x)\,1/100000000000000000001 * x\ \mathbf{end\ proc}$$

```
> G := proc(x) x*(1/100000000000000000001.0) end proc;
```

$$G := \mathbf{proc}(x)$$
$$x * 1/0.1000000000000000000010 * 10^{21}1$$
$$\mathbf{end\ proc}$$

If these procedures are executed with Pi as the parameter and then evaluated to a floating-point result, procedure F works correctly, but procedure G does not because the reciprocal has already been computed at 10 Digits of precision. Notice the different results.[18]

```
> evalf[200]( F(Pi) );
```

$$0.3141592653589793238431227456743604951812\backslash$$
$$8571248076697714568160210597397085716 4083\backslash$$
$$8417437428256400659597973712230718300 0511\backslash$$
$$1410748724339923121421833325604712513 8141\backslash$$
$$9193693780498541782254292551744318402 10^{-19}$$

```
> evalf[200]( G(Pi) );
```

---

[18] For more information about floating-point numbers and Digits, see page 65 and refer to ?Digits.

$$0.31415926535897932384312274567436049518128571248076697714568160210597397085716408384174374282564006595979737122307183000511141074872433992312142183332560471251381419193693780498541782254292551744318402 \cdot 10^{-19}$$

6.4   Procedure Return Values

When a procedure is invoked, the value that Maple returns is normally the value of the *last* statement in the statement sequence in the body of the procedure. There are three other types of returns.

- explicit return

- error return

- return through a parameter[19]

In addition to these types of returns, it is also possible for a procedure to return *unevaluated*.

Explicit Returns

An *explicit return* occurs when a **return** statement is executed inside a procedure. The **return** statement causes an immediate return to the point where the current procedure was invoked. It has the following syntax, where **sequence** is a sequence, set, or list of zero, one, or more expressions.

```
return sequence
```

If the procedure executes the **return** statement, the return value is **sequence**.

Example   The following procedure computes the first position i of a value x in a list of values L. If x is not in the list L, the procedure returns 0.

---

[19]It is possible to return a value through a parameter in a Maple procedure, but it is *not* recommended. Parameters in Maple procedures should be treated as *input* parameters—used for input, but not changed in the procedure. For more information, see page 219.

```
> Position := proc(x::anything, L::list) local i;
>               for i to nops(L) do
>                   if x=L[i] then
>                       return i
>                   end if;
>               end do;
>               0;
> end proc:
```

The following GCD procedure computes the greatest common divisor g of two integers, a and b. It returns the sequence g, a/g, b/g. Procedure GCD treats the case a = b = 0 separately because, in that case, g is zero.

```
> GCD := proc(a::integer, b::integer) local g;
>         if a=0 and b=0 then
>             return 0,0,0
>         end if;
>         g := igcd(a,b);
>         g, iquo(a,g), iquo(b,g);
> end proc:
> GCD(0,0);
```

$$0, 0, 0$$

```
> GCD(12,8);
```

$$4, 3, 2$$

You can use the Boolean constants **true**, **false**, and FAIL in a **return** statement. In particular, FAIL is often used in a **return** statement to indicate that the computation failed or was abandoned.[20]

```
> Division := proc(x, y)
>             if y=0 then
>                 return FAIL
>             else
>                 x/y
>             end if;
> end proc:
> Division(2,0);
```

$$FAIL$$

---

[20]For more information about **return** statements, refer to ?return and ?FAIL.

Error Returns

An *error return* occurs when an **error** statement is executed inside a procedure. The **error** statement indicates that an *exception* has occurred, and the execution of the current statement sequence in the procedure is interrupted. Then, control is passed to the next applicable catch clause in the enclosing **try...catch** statement (if one exists) to test whether the error can be handled. If control is not passed to a catch clause at this level, or if the exception cannot be handled by a **catch** clause at this level, the exception is re-raised at the next higher execution handler level (in other words, at the next enclosing **try...catch** statement). This process continues until either the exception is handled or execution returns to the top level (in which case the exception becomes an error). The **error** statement has the following syntax, where **msgString** is the string Maple displays when the error occurs and **msgParams** are the parameters substituted into **msgString**.[21]

```
error msgString
error msgString, msgParams
```

If an exception becomes an error (because the exception was not caught), **msgString** from the **error** statement associated with the exception is returned.[22]

```
> MyDivision := proc(x, y)
>             if y=0 then
>                 error "trying to divide by zero"
>             else
>                 x/y
>             end if;
> end proc:
> MyDivision(2,0);
```

```
Error, (in MyDivision) trying to divide by zero
```

Returning Values through Parameters

You can write a Maple procedure that returns a value through a parameter. *Though creating side effects such as this is possible in Maple, it is not recommended.*

---

[21]For more information, refer to **?error**.

[22]For more information about error returns and handling exceptions, see page 323 or refer to **?error**.

Consider the following Boolean procedure, Member, which determines whether a list L contains an expression x. Moreover, if you call Member with a third argument, p, the position of x in L is assigned to p.

```
> Member := proc(x::anything, L::list, p::evaln) local i;
>          for i to nops(L) do
>              if x=L[i] then
>                  if nargs>2 then
>                      p := i
>                  end if;
>                  return true
>              end if;
>          end do;
>          false
> end proc:
```

If Member is called with two arguments, that is, nargs is 2, the part of the body of Member that is executed does not refer to the formal parameter, p. Therefore, Maple does not return an error.

```
> Member( x, [a,b,c,d] );
```

$$false$$

If Member is called with three arguments, the type declaration, p::evaln, ensures that Maple evaluates the third actual parameter to a name rather than by using full evaluation.[23]

```
> q := 78;
```

$$q := 78$$

```
> Member( c, [a,b,c,d], q );
```

$$true$$

```
> q;
```

$$3$$

---

[23]If the third parameter has not been declared as evaln, enclose the name q in single right quotes ('q') to ensure that the name, and not the value, of q is passed to the procedure.

Maple evaluates the actual parameters only once—*prior* to substituting them for the formal parameters in a procedure call. This means that you cannot use formal parameters in the same manner as local variables in a procedure body. Once you have assigned a value to a formal parameter, you should not refer to that parameter again.[24]

The Count procedure is an example of this behavior. Procedure Count determines whether a product of factors, p, contains an expression, x. If p contains x, Count returns the number of factors that contain x in the third parameter, n.

```
> Count := proc(p::'*', x::name, n::evaln) local f;
>          n := 0;
>          for f in p do
>              if has(f,x) then
>                  n := n+1
>              end if;
>          end do;
>          evalb( n>0 );
> end proc:
```

This version of the Count procedure does not work as intended.

```
> Count(2*x^2*exp(x)*y, x, m);
```

$$-m < 0$$

The value of the formal parameter, n, inside the procedure is always m, the actual parameter that Maple determines when you invoke the procedure. Thus, when execution reaches the evalb statement, the value of n is the name m, and not the *value* of m. Even worse, if you evaluate m one level, you can see that the n:=n+1 statement assigns to m the name m+1.

```
> eval(m, 1);
```

$$m + 1$$

The m in the previous result also has the value m+1.

```
> eval(m, 2);
```

$$m + 2$$

---

[24]For a simple example, see page 200.

Therefore, if m is fully evaluated, Maple enters an infinite loop and returns an error message.

```
> eval(m);
```

```
Error, too many levels of recursion
```

This example shows that, in general, it is *not* recommended that you use parameters to return values in Maple procedures.

Returning Unevaluated

If a procedure cannot perform a computation, the unevaluated function invocation may be returned. For example, procedure Max calculates the maximum of two numbers, x and y.

```
> Max := proc(x,y)
>           if x>y then
>               x
>           else
>               y
>           end if
> end proc:
```

This version of Max requires that its arguments are numerical values.

```
> Max(3.2, 2);
```

$$3.2$$

```
> Max(x, 2*y);
```

```
Error, (in Max) cannot determine if this expression is
true or false: 2*y-x < 0
```

Furthermore, the absence of symbolic capabilities in Max causes problems if you try to plot expressions involving Max.

```
> plot( Max(x, 1/x), x=1/2..2 );
```

```
Error, (in Max) cannot determine if this expression is
true or false: 1/x-x < 0
```

The error occurs because Maple evaluates Max(x, 1/x) before the plot command is invoked. The solution is to make Max return unevaluated when its parameters, x and y, are not numeric. That is, in such cases Max should return 'Max'(x,y).

```
> Max := proc(x, y)
>          if type(x, numeric) and type(y, numeric) then
>            if x>y then
>                x
>            else
>                y
>            end if;
>          else
>             'Max'(x,y);
>          end if;
> end proc:
```

The new version of `Max` handles both numeric and non-numeric input.

```
> Max(3.2, 2);
```

$$3.2$$

```
> Max(x, 2*y);
```

$$\mathrm{Max}(x,\, 2\,y)$$

```
> plot( Max(x, 1/x), x=1/2..2 );
```

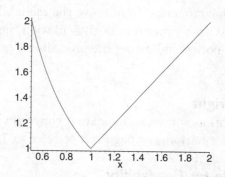

You can improve `Max` so that it can find the maximum of any number of arguments. Inside the revised procedure, **args** is the sequence of actual parameters, **nargs** is the number of actual parameters, and **procname** is the name of the procedure.

```
> Max := proc() local m, i;
>          m := -infinity;
>          for i in (args) do
>            if not type(i, numeric) then
>              return 'procname'(args);
>            end if;
>            if i>m then
>              m := i
```

```
>            end if;
>          end do;
>          m;
> end proc:
> Max(3,1,4);
```

$$4$$

```
> Max(3,x,1,4);
```

$$\mathrm{Max}(3,\ x,\ 1,\ 4)$$

The `sin` function and `int` command (integration) follow the same model as the `Max` procedure. If Maple can compute the result, it is returned. Otherwise, `sin` and `int` return unevaluated.

6.5   Documenting Your Procedures

To minimize the time required to fix code, it is recommended that you annotate code with comments. To improve the readability of the code, include indentation. Other procedure documentation methods include providing a copyright notice, indicating the procedure's purpose, and writing an online help page.

Indicating Copyright
The `Copyright` option is used to indicate a copyright notice for a procedure. For more information, see page 208 or refer to `?options`.

Formatting Code for Readability
In chapter 1, it was shown how you can enter a procedure in a Maple session by entering its definition on one line.

```
> f := proc( x :: integer, y :: integer ) local a;
  description "compute the average of two integers"; a:=
  ( x + y ) / 2; end proc:
```

However, for readability, it is recommended that you enter the procedure on multiple lines.

Entering Multi-line Procedure Definitions To enter a procedure definition on more than one line, hold the SHIFT key and press ENTER at the end of each line.[25] You can indent any of the lines in the procedure by using the spacebar. After you enter the last line, which contains **end proc**, press the ENTER key.

```
> f := proc( x :: integer, y :: integer ) local a;
>        description "compute the average of two integers";
>        a:= ( x + y ) / 2;
> end proc:
```

Using Line Continuation Occasionally, it is not possible to fit a statement on one line. In these cases, use the Maple line continuation character, the backslash (\). For more information, see page 47.

Including Indentation Formatting code increases readability. However, there are no standard rules for when and how to indent procedure statements. The following are some general guidelines.

- Enter every statement on a distinct line.

- Use indentation to indicate that the following line or block of code is a subblock of an **if** or loop statement. Use two spaces for each level of indentation. For more information about **if** statements and loops, see chapter 5 or refer to **?if** and **?do**.

```
> f := proc(x)
>        local a;
>        description "odd or even integer";
>        a := x/2;
>        if type(a, integer) then
>            "even"
>        else
>            "odd"
>        end if;
> end proc:
```

- Enter long comments on a separate line.

- Use continuation lines to ensure that no line exceeds 80 characters in length, or to break a long sequence of digits into groups of smaller sequences to enhance readability.

---

[25] As described in chapter 1, you can enter Maple commands over multiple lines in interactive mode.

Adding Comments

The pound sign (#) marks the characters following it on a line as a *comment*. In other words, Maple does not process anything on the line after the #. If you use the eval command to view the contents of a procedure definition, any comments in the definition are not displayed.

```
> f := proc(x)
>          x^2; # compute x^2
> end proc:
> eval(f);
```

$$\mathbf{proc}(x)\ x^2\ \mathbf{end\ proc}$$

Including a Procedure Description

The desciption field is used to indicate the purpose of a procedure. Unlike a comment, which Maple omits when displaying the code of a procedure, the description field provides a way to attach a one-line comment to a procedure when its code is viewed. For more information, see page 213 or refer to ?procedure.

```
> f := proc(x)
>          description "computes the square of x";
>          x^2; # compute x^2
> end proc:
> eval(f);
```

$$\mathbf{proc}(x)$$
$$\mathbf{description}\ \text{“computes the square of x”;}$$
$$x^2$$
$$\mathbf{end\ proc}$$

Creating Help Pages

The routines in the Maple library all have an associated online help page. To access a help page, enter ?*topic* where *topic* is the name of the function.

If you create a procedure, you can create a corresponding help page. You can convert any text file or Maple worksheet to a Maple help file, and then add it to a help database. For more information on creating help pages, refer to ?helppages.

6.6   Saving and Retrieving Procedures

As you develop a new procedure, you can save your work by saving the worksheet. When you have finished, save (only) the procedure in a file by using the **save** command.[26]

```
> CMax := proc(x::complex(numeric), y::complex(numeric))
>           if abs(x) > abs(y) then
>              x;
>           else
>              y;
>           end if;
> end proc:
```

```
> save CMax, "myfile";
```

The **read** command reads files that contain Maple statements back into a Maple session. The statements in the file are read and executed as if they were being entered directly into a Maple session.[27]

```
> read "myfile";
```

$$\mathbf{proc}(x\text{::complex}(numeric),\ y\text{::complex}(numeric))$$
$$\mathbf{if}\,\mathrm{abs}(y) < \mathrm{abs}(x)\,\mathbf{then}\,x\,\mathbf{else}\,y\,\mathbf{end\ if}$$
$$\mathbf{end\ proc}$$

You can also use the **read** command to read Maple procedures written in your favorite text editor.

6.7   Viewing Maple Library Source Code

An important feature of Maple is its open architecture. You can access the source code of most Maple library routines (only the code for the built-in kernel routines cannot be viewed). This accessibility is helpful for learning the Maple programming language, and it is essential for enhancing existing routines to meet your specific needs. Prior to learning the

---

[26]For more detailed information about Maple I/O features, see chapter 7, or refer to ?read and ?save.

[27]When using the **read** command, the statements are not echoed to the display unless interface(echo) is set to 2 or higher. For more information, refer to ?interface.

commands to display the source code, it is recommended that you learn the evaluation rules for procedures.[28]

Special Evaluation Rules for Procedures

For most named objects in Maple, you can obtain the actual value of the name simply by referring to it.

```
> a := 3;
```

$$a := 3$$

```
> a;
```

$$3$$

In a chain of assignments, each name is fully evaluated to the last assigned expression.

```
> c := b:
> b := a:
> a := 1:
> c;
```

$$1$$

This is called *full evaluation*.

For a procedure (like a table), Maple displays only the name, not its value (the procedure definition). For example, in the previous section, f was defined as a procedure. If you try to view the body of procedure f by referring to it by name, the procedure definition is *not* displayed.

```
> f := proc( x ) x^2 end proc:
> f;
```

$$f$$

This model of evaluation that hides the procedure details is called *last name evaluation*. This approach is used because procedures can contain

---

[28] For more information about the built-in kernel routines, see page 207 or refer to ?builtin.

many subobjects. To obtain the true value of the name f, use the `eval` command, which forces full evaluation.[29]

> `eval(f);`

$$\mathbf{proc}(x)\, x^2 \,\mathbf{end\ proc}$$

Displaying Maple Library Source Code

The `interface` routine is the mechanism by which the Maple computational engine communicates with the user interface. In particular, `interface` is used to set and query all options that affect the format of the output, but do not affect the computation. To view the source code for Maple library procedures, set the `interface` option `verboseproc` to 2.

> `interface(verboseproc=2);`

Then, to view the code for any Maple library routine that is not built-in or local to a module, use the name of the procedure as the argument to the `print` command. For example, use the following command to view the source code for the `blackscholes` routine in the `finance` package.[30]

> `print(finance[blackscholes]);`

---

[29]Last name evaluation applies to procedures, tables, and modules in Maple. For more information, refer to ?last_name_eval.

[30]Viewing the source code in this manner does not display any procedure documentation.

proc(*Amount, Exercise, Rate, Nperiods, Sdev, Hedge*)
local *d1*, *d2*, *Nd1*, *Nd2*;
option'*Copyright (c) 1995 by Waterloo Maple Inc.*\
All rights reserved.';
    $d1 := ($
       $\ln(Amount/Exercise) + (Rate + 1/2 * Sdev^2) * Nperiods)/($
       $Sdev * Nperiods^{(1/2)});$
    $d2 := d1 - Sdev * Nperiods^{(1/2)};$
    $Nd1 := 1/2 * \text{erf}(1/2 * d1 * 2^{(1/2)}) + 1/2;$
    $Nd2 := 1/2 * \text{erf}(1/2 * d2 * 2^{(1/2)}) + 1/2;$
    if nargs $= 6$ **then** *Hedge* $:= Nd1$ **end if**;
    $Amount * Nd1 - Exercise * \exp(-Rate * Nperiods) * Nd2$
end proc

Once you have viewed the code for a procedure, reset the interface variable to the default output level.[31]

```
> interface(verboseproc=1):
```

To view the local routines of a module, set
`kernelopts(opaquemodules=false)`. For more information, refer to
`?kernelopts`.

6.8   Alternate Methods for Defining a Procedure

Encapsulating statements in a `proc...end proc` construct is not the only way to create a procedure in Maple. Alternatively, you can use functional operators or the `unapply` command.

---

[31]You must set the `interface` option `verboseproc` because Maple library routines use the `copyright` option, which suppresses the display of the procedure body. User-defined procedures generally do not use this option. Hence, setting the `interface` option is not necessary to view user-defined procedures. To view the code of a user-defined procedure, use the `eval` command.

Functional Operators: Mapping Notation

Using a functional operator (arrow operator) is another method by which you can create a special form of a procedure in Maple, which represents a mathematical function (or mapping).

```
( P ) -> B
```

The sequence, P, of formal parameters can be empty and the body, B, of the procedure must be a *single* expression or if statement.

```
> F := (x,y) -> x^2 + y^2;
```

$$F := (x, y) \rightarrow x^2 + y^2$$

If the procedure requires only one parameter, you can omit the parentheses around the formal parameter.

```
> G := n -> if n<0 then 0 else 1 end if;
```

$$G := \mathbf{proc}(n)$$
$$\mathbf{option} \ operator, \ arrow;$$
$$\mathbf{if} \, n < 0 \, \mathbf{then} \, 0 \ \ \mathbf{else} \, 1 \, \mathbf{end} \, \mathbf{if}$$
$$\mathbf{end} \, \mathbf{proc}$$

Invoking a function definition is similar to invoking a procedure.

```
> F(1, 2);
```

$$5$$

```
> G(-1);
```

$$0$$

You can also use declared parameters with the functional operator.

```
> H := (n::even) -> n! * (n/2)!;
```

$$H := n{::}even \rightarrow n! \, (\frac{1}{2} n)!$$

```
> H(6);
```

4320

```
> H(5);
```

```
Error, invalid input: H expects its 1st argument, n, to
be of type even, but received 5
```

The arrow notation is designed for simple one-line function definitions. It does not provide a mechanism for specifying local or global variables, or options. If these are required, use the `proc...end proc` construct.[32]

The unapply Command

Another way to create a function in Maple is by using the **unapply** command.

```
unapply(B, P);
```

The sequence, P, represents the formal parameters, and B represents the body of the function.[33]

```
> B := x^2 + y^2:
> F := unapply(B, x, y);
```

$$F := (x, y) \rightarrow x^2 + y^2$$

```
> F(1, 2);
```

5

Unnamed Procedures and the map Command

Procedures are valid Maple expressions. Therefore, you can create, manipulate, and invoke any procedure definition without assigning it to a name.[34]

Consider the following mapping.

```
> x -> x^2;
```

---

[32] For more information about functional operators, see page 209 or refer to `?functional`.

[33] For more information about the **unapply** command, refer to `?unapply`.

[34] For information about named procedures, see page 194.

$$x \to x^2$$

You can invoke this unnamed procedure in the following manner.

```
> (x -> x^2)(t);
```

$$t^2$$

You can use the same method to invoke an unnamed procedure created by using the `proc...end proc` construct.

```
> proc(x,y) x^2 + y^2 end proc(u,v);
```

$$u^2 + v^2$$

When using the `map` command[35], you can use unnamed procedures.

```
> map( x -> x^2, [1,2,3,4] );
```

$$[1, 4, 9, 16]$$

You can add procedures, or, if appropriate, process them by using commands such as the differential operator, D.[36]

```
> D( x -> x^2 );
```

$$x \to 2\,x$$

```
> F := D(exp + 2*ln);
```

$$F := \exp + 2\left(x \to \frac{1}{x}\right)$$

You can apply the result, F, directly to arguments.

```
> F(x);
```

$$e^x + \frac{2}{x}$$

---

[35] For more information on the `map` command, see page 180.
[36] For more information about the differential operator, refer to ?D.

Building a List of Arguments

When you enter a procedure definition, it is not always necessary to supply names for the formal parameters (see page 196). You can access the sequence of arguments (actual parameters) in the procedure by using the special name args.

For example, the following procedure builds a list of its arguments.

```
> f := proc()
>        [args]
> end proc;
```

$$f := \textbf{proc}() \,[\text{args}]\, \textbf{end proc}$$

```
> f(a,b,c);
```

$$[a,\ b,\ c]$$

```
> f(c);
```

$$[c]$$

```
> f();
```

$$[\,]$$

The ith argument is args[i]. Therefore, the following two procedures are equivalent, provided they are called with at least two actual parameters of type numeric.

```
> Max := proc(x::numeric,y::numeric)
>            if x > y then
>               x
>            else
>               y
>            end if;
> end proc;
```

$$Max := \textbf{proc}(x{::}numeric,\ y{::}numeric)$$
$$\textbf{if}\, y < x \,\textbf{then}\, x \ \textbf{else}\, y \,\textbf{end if}$$
$$\textbf{end proc}$$

```
> Max := proc()
>           if args[1] > args[2] then
>               args[1]
>           else
>               args[2]
>           end if;
> end proc;
```

$$Max := \mathbf{proc}()$$
$$\quad \mathbf{if} \, args_2 < args_1 \, \mathbf{then} \, args_1 \, \mathbf{else} \, args_2 \, \mathbf{end \ if}$$
$$\mathbf{end \ proc}$$

The special name **nargs** is assigned the total number of actual parameters passed to a procedure. Using **nargs**, it is possible to write a procedure, Max, that finds the maximum of any number of arguments, but does not have any formal parameters declared in the procedure header.

```
> Max := proc()
>           local i,m;
>           if nargs = 0 then
>             return -infinity
>           end if;
>           m := args[1];
>           for i from 2 to nargs do
>             if args[i] > m then
>                 m := args[i]
>             end if;
>           end do;
>           m;
> end proc:
```

Find the maximum of the three values 2/3, 1/2, and 4/7.

```
> Max(2/3, 1/2, 4/7);
```

$$\frac{2}{3}$$

Find the maximum of the four values 1.3, 4/3, 7/5, and 9/7.

```
> Max(1.3, 4/3, 7/5, 9/7);
```

$$\frac{7}{5}$$

The use of **nargs** is a convenient way of creating a procedure without specifying the number of formal parameters in the procedure definition.

6.9   The Procedure Object

The first part of this chapter described the syntax and semantics of a
Maple procedure. This section describes the procedure object, its type
and operands.

The procedure Type

Maple recognizes all procedures (including those created by using the
mapping notation and any names to which you assign procedures) as
being of type procedure. To verify whether a name or a statement is a
procedure, use the type command.

```
> F := proc(x) x^2 end proc:
> type(F,name);
```

$$true$$

```
> type(F,procedure);
```

$$true$$

```
> type(F,name(procedure));
```

$$true$$

```
> type(eval(F),procedure);
```

$$true$$

As a consequence, you can use the following test to ensure that F is
the name of a procedure.[37]

```
if type(F, name(procedure)) then ... end if
```

The procedure type is *structured*. Therefore, you can also perform
the following types of tests.[38]

```
> G := proc( n::integer, s::string ) print(s); 2*n end proc:
> type( G, 'procedure( integer, string )' );
```

---

[37] For more information about if statements, see page 167 or refer to ?if.

[38] For more information about structured types in Maple, see page 106 or refer to
?structured.

Table 6.1 Procedure Operands

Operand	*op* Command
sequence of formal parameters	op(1, eval(procName))
sequence of local variables	op(2, eval(procName))
sequence of options	op(3, eval(procName))
remember table	op(4, eval(procName))
description string	op(5, eval(procName))
sequence of global variables	op(6, eval(procName))
lexical table	op(7, eval(procName))
return type	op(8, eval(procName))

true

Procedure Operands

Every Maple procedure has seven operands (the value for any of the operands can be NULL). Table 6.1 lists these operands and the corresponding op command that you can use to access them. In the op commands, procName is the name of the procedure.

Example   Consider the following procedure.

```
> f := proc(x::name, n::posint)
>         local i;
>         global y;
>         option Copyright;
>         description "a summation";
>         sum( x[i] + y[i], i=1..n );
>   end proc:
```

The following statements indicate how to access the various parts of a procedure definition.[39,40]

```
> f;    #name of the procedure
```

$$f$$

```
> eval(f);   #procedure
```

---

[39]For more information about remember tables in procedures, see page 210.

[40]The lexical table of a procedure stores information about lexically-scoped variables. For more information, refer to ?examples,lexical.

$$\textbf{proc}(x\text{::}name,\ n\text{::}posint)$$
$$\textbf{description } \text{``a summation''}$$
$$\cdots$$
$$\textbf{end proc}$$

```
> op(1, eval(f));   #formal parameters
```

$$x\text{::}name,\ n\text{::}posint$$

```
> op(2, eval(f));   #local variables
```

$$i$$

```
> op(3, eval(f));   #options
```

$$Copyright$$

```
> f(t,3) := 12;   #place an entry in the remember table
```

$$f(t,\ 3) := 12$$

```
> op(4, eval(f));   #remember table
```

$$\text{table}([(t,\ 3) = 12])$$

```
> op(5, eval(f));   #description
```

$$\text{``a summation''}$$

```
> op(6, eval(f));   #global variables
```

$$y$$

```
> op(7, eval(f));   #lexical table is NULL
```

Alternatively, you can list all of the operands of a procedure with one command.

```
> op(eval(f));
```

$x::name,\ n::posint,\ i,\ Copyright,\ \mathrm{table}([(t,\ 3) = 12]),$
"a summation", y

Note: The body of a procedure is not one of its operands, so you cannot use the **op** command to access it.

6.10 Using Data Structures to Solve Problems

When writing procedures you must decide how to represent the data. Sometimes the choice is straightforward, but often it requires considerable thought and planning. The appropriate choice of data structure can make your procedures more efficient, and easier to write and debug.[41] In chapter 4, you were introduced to the basic data structures, such as sequences, lists, and sets, and shown how to use them in various Maple commands. This section illustrates, by means of examples, how such data structures are useful in writing procedures and solving problems.

Computing an Average

A common problem is to write a procedure that computes the average of $n > 0$ data values $x_1, x_2, \ldots, x_n$ according to the following equation.

$$\mu = \frac{1}{n} \sum_{i=1}^{n} x_i.$$

Before the procedure is written, think about which data structure and Maple commands to use. You can represent the data for this problem as a list. The **nops** command returns the total number of entries in a list X, while the ith entry of the list is found by using X[i].

```
> X := [1.3, 5.3, 11.2, 2.1, 2.1];
```

$$X := [1.3,\ 5.3,\ 11.2,\ 2.1,\ 2.1]$$

```
> nops(X);
```

$$5$$

---

[41]For a list of built-in Maple types, refer to ?type.

```
> X[2];
```

5.3

You can add the numbers in a list by using the **add** command.

```
> add( i, i=X );
```

22.0

Using these ideas, write the procedure **Average** which computes the average of the entries in a list. It handles empty lists as a special case.

```
> Average := proc(X::list) local n, i, total;
>              n := nops(X);
>              if n=0 then
>                  error "empty list"
>              end if;
>              total := add(i, i=X);
>              total / n;
> end proc:
```

Using this procedure you can find the average of list **X** defined above.

```
> Average(X);
```

4.400000000

The procedure also works if the list contains symbolic entries.

```
> Average( [ a , b , c ] );
```

$$\frac{1}{3}a + \frac{1}{3}b + \frac{1}{3}c$$

Testing for Membership

You can write a procedure that determines whether a certain object is an element of a list or a set. Procedure **Member** accomplishes this task by using the **return** statement discussed on page 217.[42]

---

[42] Instead of using procedure **Member**, you can use the built-in **member** command.

```
> Member := proc( a::anything, L::{list, set} ) local i;
>           for i from 1 to nops(L) do
>               if a=L[i] then
>                  return true
>               end if;
>           end do;
>           false;
> end proc:
```

Test procedure Member on a list.

```
> MyList := [1,2,3,4,5,6];
```

$$MyList := [1, 2, 3, 4, 5, 6]$$

Use Member to show that 3 is a member of MyList.

```
> Member( 3, MyList );
```

$$true$$

The type of loop that Member uses occurs so frequently that Maple has a special version of the for loop for it. Compare the previous version of Member to the one below.[43]

```
> Member := proc( a::anything, L::{list, set} ) local i;
>           for i in L do
>               if a=i then
>                  return true
>               end if;
>           end do;
>           false;
> end proc:
```

Test the new for loop version of the procedure Member on a set.

```
> myset := {1,2,3,4};
```

$$myset := \{1, 2, 3, 4\}$$

```
> Member( x, myset );
```

$$false$$

---

[43] For more information about loops, see **5.2 Repetition** or refer to ?for.

Performing a Binary Search

One of the most basic and well-studied computing problems is that of searching. A typical problem involves searching a list of words (a dictionary, for example) for a specific word w. There are many possible methods. One approach is to search the list by comparing each word in the dictionary with w until Maple either finds w or it reaches the end of the list.

Study the code for procedure Search (the first attempt at solving this problem).

```
> Search := proc(Dictionary::list(string), w::string) local x;
>          for x in Dictionary do
>             if x=w then
>                return true
>             end if
>          end do;
>          false
> end proc:
```

Unfortunately, if Dictionary is large (say 50,000 entries), this approach can take a long time.

You can reduce the execution time required by sorting the dictionary before you search it. If you sort the dictionary into ascending order, then you can stop searching as soon as you encounter a word greater than w. On average, it is necessary to search half the dictionary.

Binary searching provides an even better approach. Check the word in the middle of the sorted dictionary. Since the dictionary is already sorted, you can determine whether w is in the first or the second half. Repeat the process with the appropriate half of the dictionary until w is found, or it is determined not to be in the dictionary.

The procedure BinarySearch searches the dictionary D for the word w from position s to position f in D. It also uses the built-in lexorder command to determine the lexicographical ordering of two strings.

```
> BinarySearch := proc(D::list(string), w::string, s::integer,
>                   f::integer) local m;
>                   if s>f then
>                      return false
>                   end if; # entry was not found
>                   m := iquo(s+f+1, 2); # midpoint of D
>                   if w=D[m] then
>                      true;
>                   elif lexorder(w, D[m]) then
>                      BinarySearch(D, w, s, m-1);
>                   else
>                      BinarySearch(D, w, m+1, f);
>                   end if;
> end proc:
```

Test `BinarySearch` on a short dictionary.

```
> Dictionary := [ "induna", "ion", "logarithm", "meld" ];
```

$$Dictionary := [\text{``induna''}, \text{``ion''}, \text{``logarithm''}, \text{``meld''}]$$

Try searching the dictionary.

```
> BinarySearch( Dictionary, "hedgehogs", 1, nops(Dictionary) );
```

$$false$$

```
> BinarySearch( Dictionary, "logarithm", 1, nops(Dictionary) );
```

$$true$$

```
> BinarySearch( Dictionary, "melody", 1, nops(Dictionary) );
```

$$false$$

Plotting the Roots of a Polynomial

You can construct lists of any type of object, including other lists. A list that contains two numbers often represents a point in the plane. The Maple `plot` command uses this structure to generate plots of points and lines.[44]

```
> plot( [ [ 0, 0], [ 1, 2], [-1, 2] ],
> style=point, symbol=point, color=black );
```

---

[44] For more information about plotting in Maple, refer to the *Maple Learning Guide* or `?plot`. For information about graphics programming, refer to chapter 5 of the *Maple Advanced Programming Guide*.

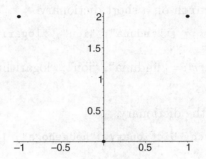

You can use this approach to write a procedure that plots the complex roots of a polynomial.

Example   Consider the polynomial $x^3 - 1$.

```
> y := x^3-1;
```

$$y := x^3 - 1$$

First, find the roots of this polynomial. You can find the numeric solutions to this polynomial by using `fsolve`.

```
> R := [ fsolve(y=0, x, complex) ];
```

$$R := [-0.5000000000 - 0.8660254038\,I,$$
$$-0.5000000000 + 0.8660254038\,I,\ 1.]$$

Next, change this list of complex numbers into a list of points in the plane. The `Re` and `Im` commands return the real and imaginary parts of a complex number, respectively.

```
> points := map( z -> [Re(z), Im(z)], R );
```

$$points := [[-0.5000000000,\ -0.8660254038],$$
$$[-0.5000000000,\ 0.8660254038],\ [1.,\ 0.]]$$

Plot the points.

```
> plot( points, style=point, symbol=point, color=black);
```

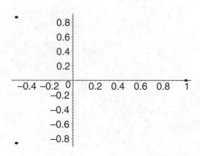

Using the sequence of steps in the previous example, you can write a procedure to automate the process. The input must be a polynomial in x with constant coefficients.

```
> RootPlot := proc( p::polynom(constant, x) ) local R, points;
>             R := [ fsolve(p, x, complex) ];
>             points := map( z -> [Re(z), Im(z)], R );
>             plot( points, style=point, symbol=point,
>             color=black );
> end proc:
```

Test procedure RootPlot by plotting the roots of the polynomial $x^6 + 3x^5 + 5x + 10$.

```
> RootPlot( x^6+3*x^5+5*x+10 );
```

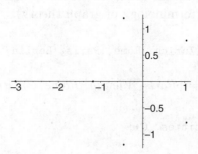

Generate a random polynomial by using the randpoly command, and then test procedure RootPlot again.

```
> y := randpoly(x, degree=100);
```

$$y := 79\,x^{71} + 56\,x^{63} + 49\,x^{44} + 63\,x^{30} + 57\,x^{24} - 59\,x^{18}$$

```
> RootPlot( y );
```

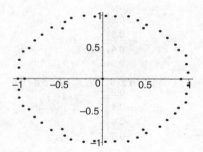

Connected Graphs

Suppose that there is a number of cities, some with roads between them. You want to determine whether travel by road between any two of the cities is possible.

You can express this problem in terms of graph theory by using the Maple **networks** package. You do not need to understand graph theory or the **networks** package to benefit from the examples in this section. The **networks** package is used primarily as a shortcut for drawing graphs.

Example First, load the **networks** package.

```
> with(networks):
```

Create a new graph G using the **new** command and add a few cities (or vertices, in the terminology of graph theory).

```
> new(G):
> cities := {Zurich, Rome, Paris, Berlin, Vienna};
```

$$cities := \{Paris, \; Vienna, \; Rome, \; Zurich, \; Berlin\}$$

```
> addvertex(cities, G);
```

$$Paris, \; Vienna, \; Rome, \; Zurich, \; Berlin$$

To add roads between Zurich and each of Paris, Berlin, and Vienna, use the **connect** command. The roads are automatically named **e1**, **e2**, and **e3**.

```
> connect( {Zurich}, {Paris, Berlin, Vienna}, G );
```

$$e1, \; e2, \; e3$$

Similarly, add roads between Rome and Zurich, and between Berlin and both Paris and Vienna.

```
> connect( {Rome}, {Zurich}, G);
```

$$e4$$

```
> connect( {Berlin}, {Vienna, Paris}, G);
```

$$e5, \; e6$$

Draw the graph of G.

```
> draw(G);
```

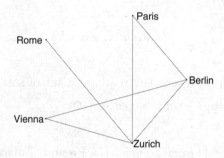

From the drawing, it is obvious that you can travel by road between any two cities. You can also use the **connectivity** command to determine this fact.

```
> evalb( connectivity(G) > 0 );
```

true

The data structures that the **networks** package uses are complicated because the package supports more general structures than this example requires. You must decide what data structure to use to determine how the cities and roads can best be represented in this example.

Representing the Data as a Set   Since cities have distinct names and the order of the cities is irrelevant, represent the cities as a *set* of names.

```
> vertices(G);
```

$$\{Paris,\ Vienna,\ Rome,\ Zurich,\ Berlin\}$$

The `networks` package assigns distinct names to the roads, so it can also represent these roads as a set of names.

```
> edges(G);
```

$$\{e1,\ e2,\ e3,\ e4,\ e5,\ e6\}$$

You can also represent a road as the set consisting of the two cities that the road connects.

```
> ends(e2, G);
```

$$\{Vienna,\ Zurich\}$$

Thus, you can represent the roads as a set of sets.

```
> roads := map( ends, edges(G), G);
```

$$roads := \{\{Paris,\ Zurich\},\ \{Vienna,\ Zurich\},$$
$$\{Zurich,\ Berlin\},\ \{Rome,\ Zurich\},\ \{Paris,\ Berlin\},$$
$$\{Vienna,\ Berlin\}\}$$

However, to determine which cities are directly connected to a city, you must search the whole set of roads. Therefore, representing the data as a set of cities and a set of roads is computationally inefficient for determining whether you can travel between any two cities.

Representing the Data as an Adjacency Matrix   Instead of using a set, try representing the data as an *adjacency matrix*—a square matrix with a row for each city. The (i,j)th entry in the matrix is 1 if the ith and the jth city have a road between them, and 0 otherwise. The following is the adjacency matrix for the graph G.

```
> adjacency(G);
```

$$\begin{bmatrix} 0 & 1 & 0 & 1 & 1 \\ 1 & 0 & 0 & 0 & 1 \\ 0 & 0 & 0 & 0 & 1 \\ 1 & 0 & 0 & 0 & 1 \\ 1 & 1 & 1 & 1 & 0 \end{bmatrix}$$

The adjacency matrix is an inefficient representation if few roads exist relative to the number of cities. In that case, the matrix contains many zeros, representing an overall lack of roads. Also, though each row in the matrix corresponds to a city, you cannot tell which row corresponds to which city.

Representing the Data as a Table   Another way to represent the cities and roads is to consider neighboring cities: Paris has roads between it and both Zurich and Berlin. Thus, Berlin and Zurich are the neighbors of Paris.

```
> neighbors(Paris, G);
```

$$\{Zurich,\ Berlin\}$$

You can represent the data as a table of neighbors; there is one entry in the table for each city.

```
> T := table( map( v -> (v)=neighbors(v,G), cities ) );
```

$T := \text{table}([\mathit{Vienna} = \{Zurich,\ Berlin\},$
$\mathit{Berlin} = \{Paris,\ Vienna,\ Zurich\},\ \mathit{Paris} = \{Zurich,\ Berlin\}$
$,\ \mathit{Zurich} = \{Paris,\ Vienna,\ Rome,\ Berlin\},$
$\mathit{Rome} = \{Zurich\}$
$])$

The representation of a system of cities and roads as a table of neighbors is ideally suited to answering the question of whether it is possible to travel between any two cities. Start at one city and then use the table to efficiently find the cities to which you can travel. Similarly, you can find the neighbors of the neighbors. Thus, you can quickly determine how far you can travel.

You can write a procedure that determines whether you can travel between any two cities. The procedure can use the **indices** command to extract the set of cities from the table.

```
> indices(T);
```

$$[\textit{Vienna}], [\textit{Berlin}], [\textit{Paris}], [\textit{Zurich}], [\textit{Rome}]$$

Since the **indices** command returns a sequence of lists, you must use the **op** and **map** command to generate a set.

```
> map( op, {%} );
```

$$\{\textit{Paris, Vienna, Rome, Zurich, Berlin}\}$$

Write a procedure **Connected** that determines whether you can travel between any two cities and uses the **indices** command.

The **Connected** procedure initially visits the first city, v. It adds v to the set of cities that it has visited and the neighbors of v to the set of cities to which it can travel. It visits the neighbors of v and repeats the process. When **Connected** has no more new cities to which it can travel, it determines whether it has visited all the cities.

```
> Connected := proc( T::table ) local canvisit, seen, v, V;
>              V := map( op, {indices(T)} );
>              seen := {};
>              canvisit := { V[1] };
>              while canvisit <> {} do
>                  v := canvisit[1];
>                  seen := seen union {v};
>                  canvisit := ( canvisit union T[v] ) minus seen;
>              end do;
>              evalb( seen = V );
> end proc:

> Connected(T);
```

$$\textit{true}$$

You can add the cities Montreal, Toronto, and Waterloo, and the highways between them.

```
> T[Waterloo] := {Toronto};
```

$$T_{\textit{Waterloo}} := \{\textit{Toronto}\}$$

```
> T[Toronto] := {Waterloo, Montreal};
```

$$T_{Toronto} := \{\mathit{Waterloo},\ \mathit{Montreal}\}$$

```
> T[Montreal] := {Toronto};
```

$$T_{Montreal} := \{\mathit{Toronto}\}$$

You can no longer travel by road between any two cities. For example, you cannot travel from Paris to Waterloo.

```
> Connected(T);
```

$$\mathit{false}$$

Choosing the Best Data Structure   The importance of this example is not to teach you about `networks`, but to emphasize how the choice of data structures suited to the problem enables you to create an efficient and concise version of the procedure `Connected`. In this case, sets and tables were the best choices. The best choice for the next problem you solve may be very different. Before writing code to perform your task, consider which structures best suit your needs. The first step in good program design is to choose appropriate structures and methods for the data and task.

6.11   Troubleshooting

This section provides you with a list of common mistakes, examples, and hints that will help you understand and avoid common errors. Use this section to study the errors that you may encounter when entering the examples from this chapter in a Maple session.[45]

Missing Argument

Maple generates an error if an argument in a procedure call is missing, but only when it is first required.[46]

---

[45]You can also use the Maple debugger for finding errors in programs. For more information, see chapter 8 or refer to `?debugger`.

[46]For more information about the if statement, see **5.1 Selection and Conditional Execution** or refer to `?if`.

```
> G := proc(x, y)
>        if x > 2 then
>            x
>        else
>            y
>        end if
> end proc:
> G(3);
```

$$3$$

```
> G(1);
```

Error, (in G) G uses a 2nd argument, y, which is
missing

```
> G(1,12);
```

$$12$$

Incorrect Argument Type

When a procedure is invoked, Maple tests the types of the actual parameters, before executing the body of the procedure. Any of these tests can generate an error message. If no type error occurs, the procedure executes.

```
> Max := proc(x::numeric, y::numeric)
>            if x>y then
>                x
>            else
>                y
>            end if
> end proc:
> Max(Pi, 3);
```

Error, invalid input: Max expects its 1st argument, x,
to be of type numeric, but received Pi

Implicitly Declared Local Variable

If a variable is used in a procedure definition, but not declared local or global, Maple determines the type of variable and issues a warning. To avoid these warnings, always declare variables as either local or global in the procedure definition.

```
> F := proc(x)
>       y := x + 1;
> end proc;
```

Warning, 'y' is implicitly declared local to procedure 'F'

$$F := \mathbf{proc}(x)\,\mathbf{local}\,y;\; y := x + 1\;\mathbf{end\ proc}$$

Understanding Names, Functions, and Remember Tables

A common mistake is to confuse names, functions, and remember tables. If no value has been assigned to a name, its value is itself.

```
> phi;
```

$$\phi$$

However, you can assign any expression to a name. Study the following examples to see the difference between assigning a value, function, and remember table to a name.

Assign the value t^2 to the name phi.

```
> phi := t^2;
```

$$\phi := t^2$$

```
> phi;
```

$$t^2$$

```
> print(phi);
```

$$t^2$$

Assign a function of t to the name phi.[47]

```
> phi := t -> t^2;
```

---

[47]Functions can be defined by using the arrow notation ->. For more information, see **Functional Operators: Mapping Notation** on page 231.

$$\phi := t \to t^2$$

```
> phi;
```

$$\phi$$

```
> phi(3);
```

$$9$$

```
> print(phi);
```

$$t \to t^2$$

Create an entry in the remember table for procedure phi.

```
> phi(t) := t^2;
```

$$\phi(t) := t^2$$

```
> phi;
```

$$\phi$$

```
> print(phi);
```

$$\mathbf{proc}()\,\mathbf{option}\,\mathit{remember};\,\text{'procname(args)'}\,\mathbf{end\ proc}$$

```
> op(4, eval(phi));
```

$$\text{table}([t = t^2])$$

```
> phi(t);
```

$$t^2$$

6.12   Exercises

1. Improve the general Max procedure on page 223 so that Max(3,x,1,4) returns Max(x,4). That is, the procedure returns the maximum numerical value along with all nonnumerical values.

2. Implement the function $f(x) = \sqrt{1 - x^{2^3}} - 1$, first as a procedure, and then by using the mapping notation. Compute $f(1/2)$ and $f(0.5)$, and comment on the different results.

3. You can use ab/g to compute the least common multiple of two integers, a and b, where g is the greatest common divisor of a and b. For example, the least common multiple of 4 and 6 is 12. Write a Maple procedure, LCM, which takes as input $n > 0$ integers $a_1, a_2, \ldots, a_n$ and computes their least common multiple. By convention, the least common multiple of zero and any other number is zero.

4. Write a Maple procedure called Sigma which, given $n > 1$ data values, $x_1, x_2, \ldots, x_n$, computes their standard deviation. The following equation gives the standard deviation of $n > 1$ numbers, where μ is the average of the data values.

$$\sigma = \sqrt{\frac{1}{n} \sum_{i=1}^{n} (x_i - \mu)^2}$$

5. Write a Maple procedure which, given a list of lists of numerical data, computes the mean of each column of the data.

6. Write a Maple procedure called Position which returns the position i of an element x in a list L. That is, Position(x,L) should return an integer $i > 0$ such that L[i]=x. If x is not in list L, 0 is returned.

7. Demonstrate that the BinarySearch procedure always terminates.

   Hint: Suppose the dictionary has n entries. How many words in the dictionary D does BinarySearch look at in the worst case?

8. Rewrite BinarySearch to use a while loop instead of a recursive call.

9. The system of cities and roads in **Connected Graphs** on page 246 splits naturally into two components: the Canadian cities and roads between them, and the European cities and roads between them. In each component you can travel between any two cities, but you cannot

travel between the two components. Write a procedure that, given a table of neighbors, splits the system into such components.

Hint: Think about the form in which the procedure returns its result.

10. Procedure `Connected` cannot handle an empty table of neighbors.

```
> Connected( table() );
```

```
Error, (in Connected) invalid subscript selector
```

Correct this shortcoming.

6.13   Conclusion

This chapter discussed the various parts of a Maple procedure when it is created by using the `proc...end proc` construct. Alternate methods to create a procedure, such as using functional operators, the `unapply` command, and the `map` command were also discussed.

Once a procedure is defined, it is beneficial to format and document the code for readability. This saves time in the future when error-correcting or adding enhancements.

When a procedure is invoked, Maple uses particular evaluation rules. Local variables are, generally, evaluated to one level, and global variables are evaluated fully. The arguments to a procedure are evaluated at the time it is invoked. The manner in which they are evaluated depends upon the environment in which the call occurs, and in some cases, the types specified in the procedure definition. Once evaluated, Maple substitutes the values into the procedure, and then executes it. Maple does no further evaluation on the values which it substituted, unless you specifically use an evaluation command, for example, `eval`. This rule makes it impractical to use parameters to store temporary results, as you would use local variables.

7   Input and Output

Input and output (I/O) in Maple can be divided into two categories: screen and keyboard I/O (for communication within Maple, and between Maple and the user), and standard disk I/O (for communication between Maple and other software). This chapter discusses both types of I/O in relation to writing procedures.[1]

In This Chapter

- Displaying output to the screen

- Collecting input interactively from users

- Reading data from files

- Writing data to files

7.1   Screen and Keyboard I/O

This section describes how to present output in various forms on the screen, and how to request input directly from the user during procedure execution. These features make it possible to write interactive procedures.

Printing Output to the Screen

As each complete statement is entered in a Maple session, it is evaluated and the result is printed on the output device, usually the computer terminal. The printing of expressions is normally presented in a two-dimensional, multi-line format (in command-line versions of Maple),

---

[1]The Sockets package contains routines that perform data exchanges between processes on remote hosts on a network. This allows I/O operations over Intranets and the Internet. For more information, refer to ?Sockets.

or as close to typeset mathematical notation as possible (in graphical user interface versions with Maple worksheets). There are several methods for altering the display of expressions: change the `interface` variable `prettyprint`, set the global variable `printlevel`, or use one of the numerous Maple commands that controls the appearance of output, for example, `print`, `lprint`, and `printf`.

The `interface` Command The `interface` command is a mechanism for communication between the computational component and user interface. It is used to set and query all variables that affect the format of the output. However, it does not affect the computation. In particular, the `interface` variable `prettyprint` controls the method that Maple uses to render Maple expressions in the user interface. If the `interface` variable `prettyprint` is set to 0 (zero) by using the command `interface(prettyprint=0)`, expressions are printed in one-dimensional line-printing mode.[2]

```
> interface(prettyprint=0);
> Int(x^2, x=1..10);

Int(x^2,x = 1 .. 10)
```

If the `interface` variable `prettyprint` is set to 1 (one) by using the command `interface(prettyprint=1)`, expressions are printed in two-dimensional character-based format.

```
> interface(prettyprint=1);
> Int(x^2, x=1..10);
```

```
        10
       /
      |     2
      |    x   dx
      |
     /
      1
```

---

[2]For greater control over the format of output, you can set other `interface` variables such as `verboseproc` and `screenwidth`. For more information about the `interface` command and these variables, refer to `?interface`.

If you are using Maple in a graphical user interface (GUI), you can set the value of `prettyprint` to higher values, or you can use the **Options Dialog** in the Maple worksheet to set the `Output Display`.[3]

```
> interface(prettyprint=2);
> Int(x^2, x=1..10);
```

```
> interface(prettyprint=3);
> Int(x^2, x=1..10);
```

The difference between `prettyprint=2` (*Typeset Notation*) and `prettyprint=3` (*Standard Math Notation*) is that with `prettyprint=3` you can select and edit subexpressions of the output.

You can always determine the current value of the `prettyprint` variable by entering the command `interface(prettyprint)`. The default value of the `prettyprint` variable is 1 (for command-line versions) or 3 (for GUI environments). The `prettyprint` variable is reset to its default value if the `restart` command is entered or the Maple session is exited.

The `printlevel` Global Variable The global variable `printlevel` determines how much output is displayed. The default value of `printlevel` is 1. Setting this variable to `-1` prevents the printing of any results. If

---

[3]For more information about the **Options Dialog**, refer to `?worksheet,managing,preferences`.

`printlevel` is set to a value larger than 1, more information, for example, the routines used when execution errors are encountered, is displayed.[4]

The `print` Command The `print` command displays the values of the expressions that appear as its arguments, separated by a comma and a blank space.

```
print( expr1, expr2, ... );
```

It is important to note that the value returned by a call to `print` is NULL. For this reason, the output of the `print` command is not recalled by using a `ditto` operator.

```
> print(apple, banana, orange);
```

$$\text{apple, banana, orange}$$

```
> %;
```

Maple checks the `interface` variable `prettyprint` to determine the print format for expressions. Because the default value for `prettyprint` is 1 for Maple command-line versions, the `print` command normally returns output in a character-based format. Similarly, for Maple GUI versions, the default value of `prettyprint` is 3 so the `print` command normally returns output to a worksheet in an editable typeset format. For more information about these formats and the `prettyprint` variable, see page 258 or refer to `?interface`.

The `print` command is most useful for displaying special objects such as tables, arrays, modules, and procedures. These objects have last name evaluation rules. If they are referenced by name, only their name is printed. The `print` command enables you to see the contents of these objects.

```
> T := table([w,x,y,z]);
```

$$T := \text{table}([1 = w, \ 2 = x, \ 3 = y, \ 4 = z])$$

---

[4]For more information about `printlevel`, see **Tracing a Procedure** on page 315 or refer to `?printlevel`.

```
> T;
```

$$T$$

```
> P := proc(x) x^2 end proc;
```

$$P := proc(x) \ x^2 \ end \ proc$$

```
> P;
```

$$P$$

```
> print(T);
```

$$table([1 = w, 2 = x, 3 = y, 4 = z])$$

```
> print(P);
```

$$proc(x) \ x^2 \ end \ proc$$

The lprint Command   The lprint command displays the values of the
expressions expr1, expr2, ... as valid Maple syntax in a one-dimensional
format.

```
lprint( expr1, expr2, ... );
```

Like the print command, the value returned by a call to lprint is
NULL. For this reason, the output of the lprint command is not recalled
by using a ditto operator.

```
> lprint(apple, banana, orange);
apple, banana, orange
```

```
> %;
```

By setting `interface(prettyprint)=0`, Maple uses `lprint` to print all expressions in the interface. For more information, see page 258 or refer to `?interface`.

The `lprint` command is intended for device-independent printing. To achieve formatted output, use the `printf` command.

The `printf` Command   The `printf` command is used to display output in accordance with indicated formatting specifications. The values of the expressions that appear in the calling sequence are formatted according to the format string in the first argument.[5]

```
printf( formatString, expr1, expr2, expr3, ... );
```

The `formatString` is a Maple symbol or string consisting of a sequence of formatting specifications, possibly separated by other characters. Each formatting specification has the following structure:

$$\%[\text{flags}][\text{width}][.\text{precision}][\text{modifiers}]\text{code}$$

where the options in brackets are optional.

The `%` symbol begins the format specification. One or more of the specifications can optionally follow the `%` symbol. Also, it is important to note that a new line is *not* automatically started at the end of the output. If a new line is required, the `formatString` must contain a new line character (`"\n"`).

The `flags` specify how to format the output. For example, `+` causes the output to appear with a leading positive or negative sign; `-` causes left-justified output.

The `width` indicates the minimum number of characters to display. If the formatted value has fewer characters than `width`, the output is padded with blank spaces.

The `precision` specifies the number of digits that appear after the decimal point for floating-point formats, or the maximum field width for string formats.

The `modifiers` specify the type of the value. For example, `Z` indicates the formatting of a complex number.

---

[5]The `printf` function is based on a C standard library function of the same name.

The code specifies the format of the output object for integer, floating-point number, string, or algebraic formats. For example, d indicates a signed decimal integer, e indicates a floating-point number in scientific notation, s indicates a Maple symbol or string, and c indicates a Maple symbol or string with exactly one character.

For a comprehensive list of permissible formatting specifications, refer to ?printf.

Study the following examples to gain a better understanding of how to use formatting strings in printf.

```
> printf("%d\n", 12345);

12345


> printf("%10d\n", 12345);

     12345


> printf("%+10d\n", 12345);

    +12345


> printf("%-10d %d\n", 12345, 6789);

12345      6789


> printf("%+10d %+5s %-c \n", 12345, hi, z );

    +12345    hi z


> printf("The %-s of the %-s\nis %-a dollars.", price, hat, 10);

The price of the hat
is 10 dollars.
> printf("%-5s is approximately %5.2f.\n", Pi, 3.14159);

Pi    is approximately  3.14.
```

```
> printf("The least common multiple of %a and %a is %a.", 4, 6,
>     lcm(4,6));
```

```
The least common multiple of 4 and 6 is 12.
```

Interactive Input

Input is normally passed to Maple procedures by using parameters. However, you can write a procedure that requests input from the user while the procedure is executing. For example, you can write a procedure that quizes a student (for example, generates random problems, accepts input, and then verifies the student's answers). The input can be the value of a certain parameter or whether a number is positive. Maple has two commands for reading input from the terminal: the **readline** and **readstat** commands.

Reading Text from the Terminal The **readline** command reads *one line of text* from a file or the keyboard. It has the following syntax.

```
readline( filename )
```

If *filename* is the special name **terminal**, **readline** reads a line of text from the keyboard. The text is returned as a string. For example, enter the following statement.

```
> s := readline( terminal );
```

At the next Maple prompt, enter a line of text.

```
> This is my line of text
```

```
                s := "This is my line of text"
```

A simple application of the **readline** command[6] is the following example that prompts the user for an answer to a question.[7]

---

[6]You can also use the **readline** command to read a single line of text from a file. For more information, see page 274 or refer to **?readline**.

[7]The **printf** command is used to print expressions. For more information about **printf**, see page 262 or refer to **?printf**.

```
> DetermineSign := proc(a::algebraic) local s;
>        printf("Is the sign of %a positive? "
>               "Answer yes or no:\n",a);
>        s := readline(terminal);
>        evalb( s="yes" or s = "y" );
> end proc:


> DetermineSign(u-1);
```

Is the sign of u-1 positive? Answer yes or no:

```
> y
```

true

Reading Expressions from the Terminal   You can also write procedures that require the user to input an *expression* rather than a string. The **readstat** command reads *one Maple statement* from the keyboard.

readstat(*promptString*)

If the optional string **promptString** is included, it is displayed as the prompt when the **readstat** command is executed. If you omit this argument, Maple uses a blank prompt.[8]

For example, when the following statement is entered, the **promptString** is immediately displayed, and Maple waits for the user to enter a statement that terminates in a semicolon (or colon). In this case, **n-1;** was entered.

```
> readstat("Enter degree: ");
```

Enter degree: n-1;

n-1

If an incomplete statement is entered (for example, one that does not end in a semicolon or colon), **readstat** redisplays the **promptString** to indicate that further input is required. This continues until a complete statement is entered. If a syntax error is discovered, an error message is returned and **promptString** is redisplayed.

---

[8]For information about other options available to **readstat**, refer to **?readstat**.

Unlike the `readline` command, which reads only one line, the `readstat` command accepts a large expression broken across multiple input lines.

Another advantage of using the `readstat` command is that if the user makes a mistake in the input, the `readstat` command automatically prompts the user for new input, providing an opportunity to correct the error.

```
> readstat("Enter a number: ");
```

```
Enter a number: 5^^8;
syntax error, '^' unexpected:
5^^8;
   ^
```

```
Enter a number: 5^8;
```

$$390625$$

The following procedure shows how to use `readstat` to prompt a user about the derivative of a function.

```
> InteractiveDiff :=
>    proc() local a, b;
>       a := readstat("Please enter an expression: ");
>       b := readstat("Differentiate with respect to: ");
>       printf("The derivative of %a with respect to %a is %a\n",
>              a, b, diff(a,b))
>    end proc:
```

```
> InteractiveDiff();
```

```
Please enter an expression: x^2 + 1/x;
Differentiate with respect to: x;
The derivative of x^2 + 1/x with respect to x is 2*x-1/x^2
```

The final example in this section is an application of the `readstat` command that implements an interface to the `limit` command. The procedure does the following: Given the function `f(x)`, assume `x` is the variable if only one variable is present. Otherwise, ask the user to enter the variable. Ask the user for the limit point.[9]

---

[9]The `indets` command finds the indeterminates of an expression. For more information, refer to `?indets`.

```
> GetLimitInput :=
>   proc(f::algebraic) local x, a, K;
>   # choose all variables in f
>   K := select(type, indets(f), name);
>   if nops(K) = 1 then
>     x := K[1];
>   else
>     x := readstat("Input limit variable: ");
>     while not type(x, name) do
>       printf("A variable is required: received %a\n", x);
>       x := readstat("Please reinput limit variable: ");
>     end do;
>   end if;
>   a := readstat("Input limit point: ");
>   x = a;
>   end proc:
```

The expression $\sin(x)=x$ depends only on one variable, so GetLimitInput does not ask for a limit variable.

```
> GetLimitInput( sin(x)/x );
```

Input limit point: 0;

$$x = 0$$

In the next call to GetLimitInput, the number 1 is entered as the limit variable. Since 1 is not a name, GetLimitInput asks for another limit variable.

```
> GetLimitInput( exp(u*x) );
```

Input limit variable: 1;
A variable is required: received 1

Please re-input limit variable: x;

Input limit point: infinity;

$$x = \text{infinity}$$

The readstat command can also be used to read one statement from a *file*. For more information, refer to ?readstat.

Controlling the Evaluation of Procedure Input   Occasionally, more control is required over how and when Maple evaluates user input to a procedure than the `readstat` command permits (see page 265). In such cases, use the `readline` command to read the input as a string, and then the `parse` command to convert the string to an expression. For information on the `readline` command, see page 264. The `parse` command has the following syntax.

```
parse( string, options )
```

The string must represent a complete Maple expression. When the string is parsed, it becomes an expression.

In the following example, the string "$a * x^2 + 1$" is parsed as an expression.

```
> s := "a*x^2 + 1";
```

$$s := \text{"a*x^2 + 1"}$$

```
> y := parse( s );
```

$$y := a\,x^2 + 1$$

In this case, the expression is a sum.

```
> type(s, string), type(y, '+');
```

$$\text{true, true}$$

The `parse` command does not evaluate the expression it returns. You must use the `eval` command to evaluate the expression explicitly. For example, Maple does not evaluate the variable a to its value 2 until you explicitly use the `eval` command.

```
> a := 2;
```

$$a := 2$$

```
> z := parse( s );
```

$$z := a\,x^2 + 1$$

```
> eval(z);
```

$$2\,x^2 + 1$$

For more information about the `parse` command, refer to chapter 3 of the *Maple Advanced Programming Guide* or `?parse`.

7.2 Standard Disk I/O

Previously, the procedures discussed use keyboard input. However, if a large amount of data must be processed, a different method is recommended. To improve efficiency, use data files to store input and output. This section discusses some basic tools for accessing and storing data in files.

Readable File Formats in Maple

Maple accepts a variety of different file formats. The remainder of this chapter discusses how to use the Maple I/O utilities with the following file types.[10]

- Maple worksheet files

- Maple language files

- general data files created by a text editor

---

[10]For more information about other file formats in Maple, refer to `?filetypes` and `?files`.

Worksheet Files If you are running Maple in a GUI environment, you can save your session as a worksheet file. Worksheet files are identified by filenames that end with the ".mw" extension. You can save and retrieve worksheet files in Maple by using the menus in the GUI environment.[11]

The `Worksheet` package contains tools for generating and manipulating worksheets. For more information, refer to `?Worksheet`.

Note: Maple worksheets use an `.mw` file extension. Previous releases of Maple create worksheets as `.mws` files. The two formats are different, but Maple can open and run both file types. Older worksheets might not behave exactly as they would in the version they were created because improvements to the system sometimes result in different forms of responses.

Language Files A Maple language file is one that contains statements conforming to the syntax of the Maple language. These statements are the same as those that are entered interactively during a Maple session. Reading a language file is identical to entering the same sequence of statements into a Maple session—each statement is executed and its result is displayed.

Maple language files can be created by using a text editor, or by using the `save` statement in Maple. Any filename consisting of letters, decimal numbers, periods, and the underscore (_) can be used to save a Maple language file. The extension *cannot* be ".m", which indicates a Maple internal file (refer to `?filenames`). In addition, like most software programs, special characters are *not* permitted in filenames. This excludes the dollar sign (\$), question mark (?), and exclamation point (!), which can be used.

General Data Files Maple can import and export files that contain formatted numerical data, and files that contain both formatted textual and numerical data. You can create these general data files by using a text editor, and then read them into Maple to perform computations.

Using Filenames in Maple Statements

If a Maple statement expects a filename as a parameter, enter it as a *string*. However, if you are entering the filename and it does not contain a slash (\ or / to indicate the directory location) or a period (to indicate a file extension), you can enter the filename as a *symbol*. In other words, if there

---

[11]For more information about file management with worksheet files in a GUI environment, refer to the *Maple Getting Started Guide* or `?managing`.

are no special characters in the filename, neither single nor double quotes are necessary. For example, MyFile, 'MyFile', and "MyFile" represent the same valid filename.

If a filename contains slashes or periods, then the name must be enclosed in double quotes ("). Backslashes that appear in a filename (the directory separator character on some operating systems) must be escaped by "doubling up" (the first backslash acts as an escape character to the second backslash). For example, the filename C:\Maple\Data\MyFile must be written as "C:\\Maple\\Data\\MyFile". Alternatively, you can use the canonical form "C://Maple/Data/MyFile".[12]

Reading and Saving Data in Maple

You can use Maple without understanding how to access data files for input. However, accessing files from a Maple session, instead of re-entering commands and data, is an important feature (especially for command-line versions). You can save time by reading files that contain Maple statements saved from a previous session, or by accessing general data files that contain formatted data to use in Maple and other applications.

You can interact with the file system either explicitly by using the `read` and `save` statements, or implicitly by executing a command that automatically accesses information from a general data file.

Saving Assignment Statements in a Maple Session You can save the values of a sequence of variables by using the `save` statement. It has the following syntax where `nameseq` is a sequence of names of assigned variables, and `filename` is a valid filename.

```
save nameseq, filename;
```

Maple saves each variable (and its value) in `nameseq` in the file `filename`. Maple evaluates each argument in `nameseq` to a name. The last argument (`filename`) is fully evaluated. It must evaluate to a string (or name) that specifies a valid filename.

For example, clear the Maple internal memory by using the `restart` command and assign new values.

```
> r0 := x^3:
> r1 := diff(r0,x):
> r2 := diff(r1,x):
> r3 := proc(y) local a;
```

---

[12]For more information about backslashes and filenames, refer to `?backslash` and `?filename`.

```
>        a := irem(y, 2);
>        if a=0 then
>            "Even"
>        else
>            "Odd"
>        end if
> end proc:
```

The following statement saves r0, r1, r2, and r3 in the ASCII file named my_file in the current working directory.[13]

```
> save r0, r1, r2, r3, "my_file";
```

Once this statement is executed, the following lines form the contents of file my_file.[14]

```
r0 := x^3;

r1 := 3*x^2;

r2 := 6*x;

r3 := proc (y) local a; a := irem(y,2);
        if a = 0 then "Even" else "Odd" end if end proc;
```

Reading Files Containing Maple Assignments into a Maple Session

You can read files that contain Maple statements into a Maple session by using the read statement. The read statement has the following syntax, where filename is any Maple language file (a sequence of valid Maple statements, separated by semicolons or colons, entered during a Maple session and saved by using the save statement, or created in a text editor and saved as a text file).[15]

```
read filename;
```

The filename must evaluate to the name of a valid file. Reading the file is identical to entering the same sequence of statements interactively into a Maple session, except that the input statements are not echoed to

---

[13]To determine the current working directory, use the currentdir function.

[14]You can also append commands entered in a Maple session to an existing file. For more information, refer to ?appendto.

[15]The read statement is particulary useful for reading long procedure definitions. If you must enter a long procedure that requires much formatting and indentation, it is easier to enter it in a text editor that has a tabulation feature, and then read it into Maple.

the screen. The system only displays the *result* of executing each statement read from the file.

```
> read "my_file";
```

$$r0 := x^3$$

$$r1 := 3\,x^2$$

$$r2 := 6\,x$$

$r3 := \mathbf{proc}(y)$
$\mathbf{local}\, a;$
　$a := \mathrm{irem}(y,\, 2)\,;\, \mathbf{if}\, a = 0\, \mathbf{then}\, \text{"Even"}\, \mathbf{else}\, \text{"Odd"}\, \mathbf{end\ if}$
$\mathbf{end\ proc}$

If you prefer to display both the input assignment statements and their results, you must set the **interface** variable **echo** to 2 or higher. For more information, refer to **?interface**.[16]

```
> interface(echo=2);
> read "my_file";
```

```
> r0 := x^3;
```

$$r0 := x^3$$

```
> r1 := 3*x^3;
```

$$r1 := 3\,x^2$$

```
> r2 := 6*x;
```

$$r2 := 6\,x$$

```
> r3 := proc (y)
>          local a;
```

---

[16]Because the Maple language contains enhancements with each new release, a conversion utility that translates Maple language files from previous releases is shipped with each new version of Maple that requires it. For more information, refer to **?updtsrc**.

```
>         a := irem(y,2);
>         if a = 0 then
>           "Even"
>         else
>           "Odd"
>         end if
> end proc;
```

$$r3 := \mathbf{proc}(y)$$
$$\mathbf{local}\, a;$$
$$a := \mathrm{irem}(y,\, 2)\,;\ \mathbf{if}\, a = 0\, \mathbf{then}\ \text{``Even''}\ \mathbf{else}\ \text{``Odd''}\ \mathbf{end\ if}$$
$$\mathbf{end\ proc}$$

Importing Data from Files

You have already seen how to use `readline` to read text from the keyboard. You can also use `readline` to read *one line of data* from a specified file. Alternatively, you can use the `readdata` command to read *numerical data arranged in columns* from a file.

The `readline` Command The `readline` command has the following syntax.

```
readline( filename );
```

If a `readline` command is entered, Maple attempts to read the next line from the specified file. If successful, a *string* consisting of the line read from the file is returned. However, the new line character at the end of the line is excluded from the string. If there are no more lines in the file to read, `readline` returns 0 to indicate that the end of the file has been reached.[17]

Study the following example to understand how to use `readline` for reading files.

Suppose that the following three lines of data were saved in the file `mydata.txt` in the current working directory.[18]

1   -5.2

---

[17]If the file was not opened for reading when the `readline` command is entered, Maple opens it. Once `readline` returns 0 to indicate that the end of the file has been reached, the file is automatically closed.

[18]To determine the current working directory, use the `currentdir` function.

```
2    6.0

3    7.8
```

You could read this data by entering the following statements.

```
> readline("mydata.txt");
```

$$"1 \ -5.2"$$

The `readline` statement opens file `mydata.txt` for reading, and reads the first line of the file. The `readline` statement returns the data as a *string*. Numerical data is not very useful to Maple in the form of a string. Thus, if you want to use this data for further calculations, use the string formatting command `sscanf` to convert the string to a list of values.

```
> sscanf(%, "%d%f");
```

$$[1, -5.2]$$

The arguments to the `sscanf` command are very similar to the `printf` command. Here, `d` indicates a decimal integer and `f` indicates a floating-point value.[19]

To read the remaining lines in the file, continue to enter `readline` statements.

```
> readline("mydata.txt");
```

$$"2 \ \ 6.0"$$

```
> readline("mydata.txt");
```

$$"3 \ \ 7.8"$$

---

[19]For more information about `sscanf`, refer to chapter 3 of the *Maple Advanced Programming Guide* or `?sscanf`.

```
> readline("mydata.txt");
```

$$0$$

The value 0 is returned because **readline** reached the end of the file. You can automate the process of reading this data by using the following procedure.

```
> readfile := proc(s::string) local line;
>           do
>               line:=readline(s);
>               if line = 0 then
>                   break
>               end if;
>               print(line);
>           end do;
> end proc:

> readfile("mydata.txt");
```

"1 -5.2"

"2 6.0"

"3 7.8"

$$0$$

Since **readline** returns lines read from a file in the form of a string, it is more useful for reading textual data. If a file contains numerical data formatted into columns, it is more appropriate to use the **readdata** command.

The readdata Command The **readdata** command has the following syntax where **filename** is the file that contains numeric data formatted into columns, **format** specifies whether the data is to be read as integer or floating-point values, and **n** is the number of columns of data in **filename**.

```
readdata( filename, format, n );
```

If only one column of data is read, the output is a list of the data. If more than one column is read, the output is a list of lists of data corresponding to the rows of data in **filename**.

```
> readdata("mydata.txt", 2);
```

$$[[1., -5.2], [2., 6.0], [3., 7.8]]$$

The data is automatically returned as floating-point values because no **format** was specified in the calling sequence and Maple detected a floating-point value in the file. You can specify the format of the values in each column by using the following version of the **readdata** command.

```
> readdata("mydata.txt", [integer, float]);
```

$$[[1, -5.2], [2, 6.0], [3, 7.8]]$$

Once you have read the data from a file, use Maple commands to process the data. For example, plot the data points from file **mydata.txt**.

```
> points := %;
```

$$points := [[1, -5.2], [2, 6.0], [3, 7.8]]$$

```
> plot(points, style=point, color=black);
```

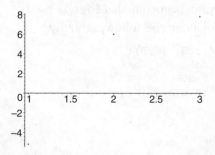

Importing Files Containing Non-uniform Data   Data files frequently contain both numbers and text. These types of data files can be read as formatted input by using the **fscanf** command and the low-level I/O routines. For more information about the low-level routines, refer to chapter 3 of the *Maple Advanced Programming Guide* or the Maple online help system.

Exporting Data to Files

You can use the `writeline` command to write *strings* to a specified file. Alternatively, you can use the `writedata` command to write *numerical data* to a text file.

The `writeline` Command   The `writeline` command writes a sequence of strings as strings separated by new line characters to `filename`. A new line character is also inserted after the last string.

```
writeline( filename, string1, string2,... );
```

A count of the number of characters written to `filename` is returned. If no string sequence is specified in the calling sequence, `writeline` writes a blank line to `filename`. If `filename` exists, the file is overwritten.

The `writedata` Command   The `writedata` command writes `data` to a specified `filename`. The `data` can be in the form of a list or an array. The `format` of the entries in `data` can be `integer`, `float`, or `string`.

```
writedata( filename, data, format );
```

If `filename` exists, the file is overwritten. If `data` is a list of values, each value is printed on a separate line. If `data` is an array or a list of lists of values, the data is printed one row per line, with values separated by a TAB. If no format is specified, `float` is used.[20]

For example, consider the following array.

```
> a := array(1..3, 1..3):
> for i to 3 do
>   for j to 3 do
>     a[i,j] := evalf(i/j,3)
>   end do
> end do;
> print(a);
```

$$\begin{bmatrix} 1. & 0.500 & 0.333 \\ 2. & 1. & 0.667 \\ 3. & 1.50 & 1. \end{bmatrix}$$

To save the entries of `a` to file `arraydata`, enter the following command.

---

[20] For more information about `writedata`, refer to `?writedata`.

```
> writedata("arraydata", a, float):
```

File **arraydata** contains the following data.

```
> writedata(terminal, a, float);
```

1	.500	.333
2	1	.667
3	1.50	1

C, Fortran, Java^TM, MATLAB, and Visual Basic Code Generation
Maple also provides commands to translate Maple expressions to other programming languages: C, Fortran, Java™, MATLAB®, and Visual Basic®. These commands are available in the Maple **codegen** and **CodeGeneration** packages. For more information, refer to chapter 6 of the *Maple Advanced Programming Guide*, **?codegen**, or **?CodeGeneration**.

7.3   Troubleshooting

This section provides you with a list of common mistakes, examples, and hints that will help you understand and avoid common errors. Use this section to study the errors that you may encounter when entering the examples from this chapter in a Maple session.[21]

Syntax Error in readstat

Maple generates an error if the input statement supplied to a **readstat** command contains a syntax error.[22]

```
> readstat("Bad Input: ");
```

Bad Input: a ++ b;

syntax error, '+' unexpected:
a ++ b;
  ^

The **Bad Input** prompt redisplays to request new input. To correct this error, enter a valid statement that ends in a colon or semicolon.

---

[21] For more information about I/O errors in Maple, refer to **?IO_errors**.

[22] For more information about the **readstat** statement, refer to **?readstat**.

Bad Input: a + b;

$$a + b$$

Extra Characters at End of Parsed String

The readstat routine reads as many lines of characters as necessary to parse a complete statement. Maple generates a warning if the last line contains additional characters after the semicolon or colon. Therefore, multiple statements per line are permitted, but those after the first are ignored.

```
> readstat("Extra Input: ");
```

Extra Input: a+b; c+d;

Warning, extra characters at end of parsed string

$$a + b$$

Unable to Read Filename

Maple returns an error message if the filename supplied to the read statement is invalid or if the file does not exist. To correct this error, check that the spelling of the filename is correct and that the file exists in the directory that you have specified.

```
> read MyDataFile;
```

Error, unable to read 'MyDataFile'

7.4   Exercises

1. Write a loop (with a single statement in its body) that prints strings listing the cubes of the integers 1 to 10.

2. Create a file in a text editor that contains the following lines.

```
x := 1;            # valid input line

if := 2;}          # invalid assignment
```

```
y := 3;            # valid input line

two words := 4;  # invalid assignment
```

Save the file. In a Maple session, open the file by using the read statement. Observe how Maple reacts to invalid statements.

3. Create a data file in a text editor that contains the following information.

```
1   2   3

4   5   6
```

Save the file. Read this file into a Maple session, convert the data to a list, and reverse its order. Write the reversed data in the same format to a different file.

7.5   Conclusion

The techniques in this chapter illustrated some of the basic I/O facilities that are available in Maple—how to incorporate interactive input in your procedures, and how to import and export data from Maple. In addition to the commands discussed in this chapter, Maple has many low-level I/O routines, which are useful for reading formatted and non-uniform data from text files.

In Maple, there are packages that generate code in the C, Fortran, Java, MATLAB, and Visual Basic programming languages. For more information, refer to chapter 8 of the *Maple Advanced Programming Guide*. The Sockets and Worksheet packages also contain important I/O routines.

8 Debugging and Efficiency

New programs, whether developed in Maple or any other language, often work incorrectly. Problems that occur in the execution of a program are usually due to syntax errors introduced during implementation, or logic errors in the design of the algorithm. Most errors are subtle and hard to find by visual inspection of the program. Maple provides error detection commands and a debugger to help you find these errors.

Maple provides a variety of commands to help you find errors in procedures. Among these are commands to trace procedure execution, check assertions, raise exceptions and trap errors, and verify procedure semantics and syntax.

Alternatively, the Maple debugger lets you stop execution in a Maple procedure, inspect and modify the values of local and global variables, and continue execution, either to completion, or one statement or block at a time. You can stop execution when Maple reaches a particular statement, when it assigns a value to a specified local or global variable, or when a specified error occurs. This facility lets you investigate the inner workings of a program.

Even when a program is working correctly, you may want to analyze its performance to try to improve its efficiency. Maple commands are available to analyze the time and memory consumption involved in running the program.

In This Chapter
- Using the Maple debugger

- Detailed debugger information

- Additional commands for error detection

- Measuring and improving program efficiency

8.1 A Tutorial Example

The Maple debugger is a tool that you can use to detect errors in your procedures. Using this facility, you can follow the step-by-step execution of your program to determine why it is not returning the results that you expect.

This section illustrates how to use the Maple debugger as a tool for debugging a Maple procedure. The debugger commands are introduced and described as they are applied. Additional information about the commands is provided in **8.2 Maple Debugger Commands**.

As an alternative to the command-line Maple debugger, you can use the interactive Maple debugger available in the graphical user interface (GUI) version of Maple.

The interactive Maple debugger is invoked automatically by Maple when a breakpoint or watchpoint is encountered. An interactive debugger window is displayed, which contains the following:

- a main text box that displays a procedure name and the debugger output

- a text box for entering commands and an associated **Execute** button

- buttons that perform common debugging functions

The interactive Maple debugger functions identically to the command-line Maple debugger. For more information, refer to `?InteractiveDebugger`.

Example Consider the following procedure, `sieve`, which is used as a case study. It implements the *Sieve of Eratosthenes*: Given a parameter n, return a count of the prime numbers less than n (inclusive). To debug the `sieve` procedure, use breakpoints and watchpoints, which cause Maple to stop the execution of the procedure.

```
> sieve := proc(n::integer)
>         local i, k, flags, count,twicei;
>         count := 0;
>         for i from 2 to n do
>             flags[i] := true
>         end do;
>         for i from 2 to n do
>             if flags[i] then
>                 twicei := 2*i;
>                 for k from twicei by i to n do
>                     flags[k] = false;
>                 end do;
>                 count := count+1
>             end if;
```

```
>              end do;
>              count;
>   end proc:
```

Numbering the Procedure Statements I

To use the Maple debugger, you must enter a variety of debugger commands. Many of these debugger commands refer to statements in the procedures that you are debugging. Statement numbers allow such references. The **showstat** command displays a Maple procedure along with numbers preceeding each line that begins a new statement.

```
> showstat(sieve);


sieve := proc(n::integer)
local i, k, flags, count, twicei;
   1    count := 0;
   2    for i from 2 to n do
   3      flags[i] := true
        end do;
   4    for i from 2 to n do
   5      if flags[i] then
   6         twicei := 2*i;
   7         for k from twicei by i to n do
   8            flags[k] = false
            end do;
   9         count := count+1
        end if
     end do;
  10    count
end proc
```

Note: The numbers preceeding each line differ from line numbers that may display in a text editor. For example, keywords that end a statement (such as **end do** and **end if**) are not considered separate commands and are therefore not numbered.

Invoking the Debugger I

To invoke the Maple debugger, start the execution of a procedure, and stop the execution within the procedure. To execute a Maple procedure, call it by using a Maple command at the top-level, or call it from another procedure. The simplest way to cause execution to stop within the procedure, is to set a *breakpoint* in the procedure.

Setting a Breakpoint Use the `stopat` command to set a breakpoint in procedure `sieve`.

```
> stopat(sieve);
```

$$[sieve]$$

This command sets a breakpoint before the first statement in procedure `sieve`. When you subsequently execute `sieve`, Maple stops before executing the first statement. When execution stops, the debugger prompt appears (DBG>).[1]

The following example demonstrates an initial execution of `sieve`.

```
> sieve(10);

sieve:
   1*   count := 0;
```

Preceding the debugger prompt are several pieces of information.

- The previously computed result (This particular execution stopped at the first statement before making any computations, so no result appears.)

- The name of the procedure in which execution has stopped (`sieve`)

- Execution stopped before statement number 1. An asterisk (*) follows this statement number to indicate that a breakpoint was set before the statement.

At the debugger prompt, you can evaluate Maple expressions and invoke debugger commands. Maple evaluates expressions in the context of the stopped procedure. You have access to the same procedure parameters, and local, global, and environment variables, as the stopped procedure. For example, since `sieve` was called with parameter value 10, the formal parameter `n` has the value 10.

---

[1]If a procedure has a remember table, you may have to execute a `restart` command before issuing a second or subsequent `stopat` command. For more information about remember tables, see page 210 or refer to `?remember`.

```
DBG > n

10
sieve:
    1*   count := 0;
```

Notice that for each expression that Maple evaluates, it displays:

- the result of the expression,

- the name of the stopped procedure,

- the statement number where the procedure stopped followed by the statement, and

- a new debugger prompt.

Note: To remove a breakpoint from a procedure, use the unstopat command.

Controlling the Execution of a Procedure During Debugging I

Debugger commands control the execution of the procedure once the debugger is active. Some commonly used debugger commands are next, step, into, list, outfrom, and cont.

The next command executes the next statement at the current nesting level. After the statement is executed, control is returned to the debugger. If the statement is a control structure (an if statement or a loop), the debugger executes any statements within the control structure that it would normally execute. It stops execution before the next statement *after* the control structure. Similarly, if the statement contains calls to procedures, the debugger executes these procedure calls in their entirety before execution stops.

```
DBG > next

0
sieve:
    2    for i from 2 to n do
         ...
         end do;
```

The 0 in the first line of the output represents the result of the executed statement—that is, the result of `count := 0`. A "*" does not appear next to the statement number because there is no breakpoint set immediately before statement 2. The debugger does not show the body of the `for` loop, which itself consists of statements with their own statement numbers, unless execution actually stops within its body. Maple represents the body of compound statements by ellipses (...).

Executing the `next` command again results in the following output.

```
DBG > next

true
sieve:
    4    for i from 2 to n do
           ...
         end do;
```

Execution now stops before statement 4. Statement 3 (the body of the previous `for` loop) is at a deeper nesting level. Therefore, the loop is executed n-1 times. The debugger displays the last result computed in the loop (the assignment of the value `true` to `flags[10]`).

To step into a nested control structure (such as an `if` statement or `for` loop) or a procedure call, use the `step` debugger command.

```
DBG > step

true
sieve:
    5        if flags[i] then
               ...
             end if
```

```
DBG > step

true
sieve:
    6            twicei := 2*i;
```

If you use the **step** debugger command when the next statement to execute is *not* a deeper structured statement or procedure call, it has the same effect as the **next** debugger command.

```
DBG > step

4
sieve:
    7          for k from twicei by i to n do
                  ...
               end do;
```

At any time during the debugging process, you can use the **showstat** debugger command to display the current status of the debugging process.

```
DBG > showstat


sieve := proc(n::integer)
local i, k, flags, count, twicei;
    1*   count := 0;
    2    for i from 2 to n do
    3       flags[i] := true
         end do;
    4    for i from 2 to n do
    5       if flags[i] then
    6          twicei := 2*i;
    7 !        for k from twicei by i to n do
    8             flags[k] = false
               end do;
    9          count := count+1
            end if
         end do;
   10    count
end proc
```

Maple displays a debugger prompt to indicate that you are still working inside the Maple debugger. The asterisk (*) marks the *unconditional* breakpoint. An exclamation point (!) that follows a statement number (see line 7) indicates the statement at which the procedure is stopped.

To continue the debugging process, issue another debugger command. For example, you can use `into` or `step` to enter the innermost loop.

The behavior of the `into` debugger command is between that of the `next` and `step` commands. Execution stops at the next statement in the current procedure independent of whether it is at the current nesting level or in the body of a control structure (an `if` statement or a loop). That is, the `into` command steps into nested statements, but not procedure calls. It executes called procedures completely, then stops. The `into` command is a very useful debugging tool.

```
DBG > into

4
sieve:
   8           flags[k] = false
```

A debugger command that is related to `showstat` is the `list` command. It displays the previous five statements, the current statement, and the next statement, to provide an indication of where the procedure has stopped.

```
DBG > list


sieve := proc(n::integer)
local i, k, flags, count, twicei;
      ...
   3      flags[i] := true
          end do;
   4    for i from 2 to n do
   5      if flags[i] then
   6         twicei := 2*i;
   7         for k from twicei by i to n do
   8 !          flags[k] = false
             end do;
   9         count := count+1
          end if
        end do;
      ...
    end proc
```

You can use the `outfrom` debugger command to finish execution at the current nesting level or deeper. Execution of the procedure is stopped once a statement at a shallower nesting level is reached, that is, after a loop terminates, a branch of an `if` statement executes, or the current procedure call returns.

```
DBG > outfrom

true = false
sieve:
   9        count := count+1
```

```
DBG > outfrom

1
sieve:
   5        if flags[i] then
            ...
            end if
```

The `cont` debugger command continues execution, until either the procedure terminates normally or it encounters another breakpoint.

```
DBG > cont
```

$$9\,l$$

You can now see that the procedure does not give the expected output. Although you may find the reason obvious from the previous debugger command examples, in most cases it is not easy to find procedure errors. Therefore, continue to use the debugger. First, use the `unstopat` command to remove the breakpoint from `sieve`.

```
> unstopat(sieve);
```

[]

Invoking the Debugger II

The procedure `sieve` maintains the changing result in the variable `count`. Therefore, a logical place to look during debugging is wherever Maple modifies `count`. The easiest way to do this is by using a *watchpoint*, which invokes the debugger whenever Maple modifies a watched variable.

Setting a Watchpoint   Use the `stopwhen` command to set watchpoints. In this case, stop execution whenever Maple modifies the variable `count` in the procedure `sieve`.

```
> stopwhen([sieve,count]);
```

$$[[sieve, \ count]]$$

The `stopwhen` command returns a list of all the currently watched variables.

Execute the `sieve` procedure again.

```
> sieve(10);
```

```
count := 0
sieve:
    2    for i from 2 to n do
           ...
         end do;
```

Execution stops because Maple has modified `count`, and the debugger displays the assignment statement `count := 0`. As in the case of breakpoints, the debugger then displays the name of the procedure and the next statement to be executed in the procedure. Note that execution stops *after* Maple has assigned a value to `count`.

This first assignment to `count` is correct. Use the `cont` debugger command to continue execution of the procedure.

```
DBG > cont
```

```
count := 1
sieve:
    5       if flags[i] then
              ...
            end if
```

If you do not look carefully, this also looks correct. Assume that nothing is wrong and continue execution.

```
DBG > cont

count := 2*l
sieve:
    5       if flags[i] then
            ...
            end if
```

This output is suspicious because Maple should have simplified 2*1. Notice that it has printed 2*l (two times the letter l) instead. By studying the source text for the procedure, you can see that the letter "l" was entered instead of the number "1". Since the source of the error has been discovered, there is no reason to continue the execution of the procedure. Use the quit debugger command to exit the debugger, and then use the unstopwhen command to remove the watchpoint from the procedure.

```
DBG > quit
```

```
Warning, computation interrupted
> unstopwhen();
```

[]

After correcting the source text for sieve, issue a restart command, read the corrected version of sieve into Maple, and execute the procedure again.

```
> sieve(10);
```

9

This result is still incorrect. There are four primes less than 10, namely 2, 3, 5, and 7. Therefore, invoke the debugger once more, stepping into the innermost parts of the procedure to investigate. Since you do not want to start at the beginning of the procedure, set the breakpoint at statement 6.

```
> stopat(sieve,6);
```

$$[sieve]$$

```
> sieve(10);

true
sieve:
    6*      twicei := 2*i;
```

```
DBG > step

4
sieve:
    7          for k from twicei by i to n do
                  ...
               end do;
```

```
DBG > step

4
sieve:
    8             flags[k] = false
```

```
DBG > step

true = false
sieve:
    8             flags[k] = false
```

The last step reveals the error. The previously computed result should have been `false` (from the assignment of `flags[k]` to the value `false`), but instead `true = false` was returned. An equation was used instead of an assignment. Therefore, Maple did not set `flags[k]` to `false`.

Once again, exit the debugger and correct the source text.

```
DBG > quit
```

Warning, computation interrupted

The following code represents the corrected procedure.

```
> sieve := proc(n::integer)
>           local i, k, flags, count,twicei;
>           count := 0;
>           for i from 2 to n do
>               flags[i] := true
>           end do;
>           for i from 2 to n do
>               if flags[i] then
>                   twicei := 2*i;
>                   for k from twicei by i to n do
>                       flags[k] := false;
>                   end do;
>                   count := count+1
>               end if;
>           end do;
>           count;
> end proc:
```

Execute procedure `sieve` again to test the corrections.

```
> sieve(10);
```

$$4$$

The `sieve` procedure returns the correct result.

8.2   Maple Debugger Commands

This section provides additional details about the commands used in the tutorial in **8.1 A Tutorial Example** and a description of other debugger commands.

Numbering the Procedure Statements II

The `showstat` command has the following syntax. The `procedureName` parameter is optional.

```
showstat( procedureName );
```

If `showstat` is called with no arguments, all procedures that contain breakpoints are displayed.

You can also use the `showstat` command to display a single statement or a range of statements by using the following syntax.

```
showstat( procedureName, number );
showstat( procedureName, range );
```

In these cases, the statements that are not displayed are represented by ellipses (...). The procedure name, its parameters, and its local and global variables are always displayed.

```
> f := proc(x)
>         if x <= 2 then
>             print(x);
>         end if;
>         print(-x)
>   end proc:


> showstat(f, 2..3);

f := proc(x)
       ...
    2      print(x)
           end if;
    3      print(-x)
end proc
```

Invoking the Debugger III

This section provides additional information about breakpoints and watchpoints.

Setting Breakpoints The `stopat` command has the following syntax where `procedureName` is the name of the procedure in which to set the breakpoint, `statementNumber` is the line number of the statement in the procedure *before* which the breakpoint is set, and `condition` is a Boolean expression which must be *true* for execution to stop. The `statementNumber` and `condition` arguments are optional.

```
stopat( procedureName, statementNumber, condition );
```

This `condition` argument can refer to any global variable, local variable, or parameter of the procedure. These *conditional* breakpoints are marked by a question mark (?) if `showstat` is used to display the procedure.

Since the `stopat` command sets the breakpoint before the specified statement, when Maple encounters a breakpoint, execution stops and Maple engages the debugger *before* the statement. *This means that you* **cannot** *set a breakpoint after the last statement in a statement sequence— that is, at the end of a loop body, an if statement body, or a procedure.*

If two identical procedures exist, depending on how you created them, they may share breakpoints. If you entered the procedures individually, with identical procedure bodies, then they do not share breakpoints. If you created a procedure by assigning it to the body of another procedure, then their breakpoints are shared.

```
> f := proc(x) x^2 end proc:
> g := proc(x) x^2 end proc:
> h := op(g):
> stopat(g);
```

$$[g, h]$$

```
> showstat();
```

```
g := proc(x)
   1*  x^2
end proc
```

```
h := proc(x)
   1*  x^2
end proc
```

Removing Breakpoints The unstopat command has the following syntax where procedureName is the name of the procedure that contains the breakpoint, and statementNumber is the line number of the statement where the breakpoint is set. The statementNumber parameter is optional.

```
unstopat( procedureName, statementNumber );
```

If statementNumber is omitted in the call to unstopat, then *all* breakpoints in procedure procedureName are cleared.

Setting Explicit Breakpoints You can set an explicit breakpoint by inserting a call to the DEBUG command in the source text of a procedure. The DEBUG command has the following syntax. The argument parameter is optional.

```
DEBUG( argument );
```

If no argument is included in the DEBUG command, execution in the procedure stops at the statement *following* the location of the DEBUG command, and then the debugger is invoked.[2]

```
> f := proc(x,y) local a;
>          a:=x^2;
>          DEBUG();
>          a:=y^2;
> end proc:


> showstat(f);


f := proc(x, y)
local a;
   1    a := x^2;
   2    DEBUG();
   3    a := y^2
end proc



> f(2,3);
```

---

[2]The showstat command does not mark explicit breakpoints with a "*" or a "?".

```
  4
f:
    3    a := y^2
```

```
DBG > quit
```

Warning, computation interrupted

If the argument of the DEBUG command is a Boolean expression, execution stops only if the Boolean expression evaluates to **true**. If the Boolean expression evaluates to **false** or FAIL, the DEBUG command is ignored.

```
> f := proc(x,y) local a;
>           a:=x^2;
>           DEBUG(a<1);
>           a:=y^2;
>           DEBUG(a>1);
>           print(a);
> end proc:
```

```
> f(2,3);
```

```
  9
f:
    5    print(a)
```

```
DBG > quit
```

Warning, computation interrupted

If the argument of the DEBUG command is anything but a Boolean expression, the debugger prints the value of the argument (instead of the last result) when execution stops at the following statement.

```
> f := proc(x)
>            x^2;
>            DEBUG("This is my breakpoint. The current value of x\
>   is:", x);
>            x^3
> end proc:


> f(2);

"This is my breakpoint. The current value of x is:"
2
f:
    3    x^3
```

Removing Explicit Breakpoints   The unstopat command cannot remove explicit breakpoints. You must remove breakpoints that were set
by using DEBUG by editing the source text for the procedure.

```
DBG > unstopat

[f, g, h]
f:
    3    x^3




DBG > showstat


f := proc(x)
    1    x^2;
    2    DEBUG("This is my breakpoint. The current value of x is:",x);
    3 !  x^3
end proc



DBG > quit



Warning, computation interrupted
```

Note: If you display the contents of a procedure by using `print` (or `lprint`) and the procedure contains a breakpoint that was set by using `stopat`, the breakpoint appears as a call to `DEBUG`.

```
> f := proc(x) x^2 end proc:
> stopat(f);
```

$$[f, g, h]$$

```
> print(f);
```

$$\mathbf{proc}(x)\,\mathrm{DEBUG}()\,;\,x^2\,\mathbf{end\ proc}$$

Setting Watchpoints The `stopwhen` command has the following syntaxes.

```
stopwhen( globalVariableName );
stopwhen( [procedureName, variableName] );
```

The first form specifies that the debugger should be invoked when the global variable `globalVariableName` is changed. Maple environment variables, such as `Digits`, can also be monitored by using this method.

```
> stopwhen(Digits);
```

$$[Digits]$$

The second form invokes the debugger when the (local or global) variable `variableName` is changed in the procedure `procedureName`.

When any form of `stopwhen` is called, Maple returns a list of the current watchpoints.

Execution stops *after* Maple assigns a value to the watched variable. The debugger displays an assignment statement instead of the last computed result (which would otherwise be the right-hand side of the assignment statement).

Clearing Watchpoints The syntax to call `unstopwhen` is the same as that for `stopwhen`. Similar to `stopwhen`, `unstopwhen` returns a list of all (remaining) watchpoints.

If no arguments are entered in the call to `unstopwhen`, then *all* watchpoints are cleared.

Setting Watchpoints on Specified Errors You can use an error watch-point to invoke the debugger when Maple returns a specified error message. When a watched error occurs, execution of the procedure stops and the debugger displays the statement in which the error occurred.

Error watchpoints are set by using the **stoperror** command. The **stoperror** command has the following syntax

```
stoperror( "errorMessage" );
```

where **errorMessage** is a *string* or a *symbol* that represents the error message returned from a procedure. A list of the current error watchpoints is returned.

If no argument is entered in the call to **stoperror**, the list of current watchpoints is returned.

```
> stoperror();
```

[]

```
> stoperror( "numeric exception: division by zero" );
```

["numeric exception: division by zero"]

```
> stoperror();
```

["numeric exception: division by zero"]

If the special name `all` is used instead of a specific error message as the parameter to the **stoperror** command, execution of a procedure stops when *any* error that would *not* be trapped occurs.

Errors trapped by a traperror construct (**try...catch** statement) do not generate an error message. Hence, **stoperror** cannot be used to catch them. For more information about the **try...catch** structure, see **Trapping Errors** on page 325. If the special name `traperror` is used instead of a specific error message as the parameter to the **stoperror** command, execution of a procedure stops when *any* error that *is* trapped occurs. If the **errorMessage** parameter is entered in the form **traperror["message"]** to **stoperror**, the debugger is invoked only if the error specified by **"message"** *is* trapped.

When execution of a procedure stops due to an error which causes an exception, continued execution is not possible. Any of the execution control commands, such as **next** or **step** (see **Controlling the Execution of a Procedure During Debugging I** on page 287 and **Controlling the Execution of a Procedure During Debugging II** on page 305), process the error as if the debugger had not intervened. For example, consider the following two procedures. The first procedure, f, calculates 1/x. The other procedure, g, calls f but traps the "division by zero" error that occurs when x = 0.

```
> f := proc(x) 1/x end:
> g := proc(x) local r;
>          try
>             f(x);
>          catch:
>             infinity;
>          end try;
> end proc:
```

If procedure g is executed at x=9, the reciprocal is returned.

```
> g(9);
```

$$\frac{1}{9}$$

At x=0, as expected, infinity is returned.

```
> g(0);
```

$$\infty$$

The **stoperror** command stops execution when you call f directly.

```
> stoperror("numeric exception: division by zero");
```

$$["numeric exception: division by zero"]$$

```
> f(0);
```

```
Error, numeric exception: division by zero
f:
   1    1/x
```

```
DBG > cont
```

```
Error, (in f) numeric exception: division by zero
```

The call to f from g is inside a traperror (try...catch statement),
so the "division by zero" error does *not* invoke the debugger.

```
> g(0);
```

$$\infty$$

Instead, try to use **stoperror(traperror)**.

```
> unstoperror( "numeric exception: division by zero" );
```

$$[]$$

```
> stoperror( 'traperror' );
```

$$[traperror]$$

This time Maple does not stop at the error in **f**.

```
> f(0);
```

```
Error, (in f) numeric exception: division by zero
```

However, Maple invokes the debugger when the trapped error occurs.

```
> g(0);
```

```
Error, numeric exception: division by zero
f:
    1    1/x
```

```
DBG > step

Error, numeric exception: division by zero
g:
   3      infinity


DBG > step
```

$$\infty$$

In the case that a particular error message is specified in the form traperror["message"], the debugger is invoked only if the error specified by "message" *is* trapped.

Clearing Watchpoints on Specified Errors   Error watchpoints are cleared by using the top-level unstoperror command. The syntax to call unstoperror is the same as for stoperror. Like stoperror, unstoperror returns a list of all (remaining) error watchpoints.

If no argument is entered in the call to unstoperror, then *all* error watchpoints are cleared.

```
> unstoperror();
```

$$[\;]$$

Controlling the Execution of a Procedure During Debugging II

Once the execution of a procedure is stopped and the debugger is invoked, you can examine the values of variables or perform other experiments (see the following section, **Changing the State of a Procedure During Debugging**). After you have examined the state of the procedure, you can cause execution to continue by using a number of different debugger commands.

The most commonly used debugger commands are into, next, step, cont, outfrom, return, and quit.

The return debugger command causes execution of the currently active procedure call to complete. Execution stops at the first statement after the current procedure.

The other commands are described in the tutorial in **8.1 A Tutorial Example**. For more information about these and other debugger commands, refer to ?debugger.

Changing the State of a Procedure During Debugging

When a breakpoint or watchpoint stops the execution of a procedure, the Maple debugger is invoked. In the debugger mode, you can examine the state of the global variables, local variables, and parameters of the stopped procedure. You can also determine where execution stopped, evaluate expressions, and examine procedures.

While in the debugger mode, you can evaluate any Maple expression and perform assignments to local and global variables. To evaluate an expression, enter the expression at the debugger prompt. To perform assignments to variables, use the standard Maple assignment statement.

```
> f := proc(x) x^2 end proc:
> stopat(f);
```

$$[f]$$

```
> f(10);
```

```
f:
    1*   x^2
```

```
DBG > sin(3.0)
```

```
.1411200081
f:
    1*   x^2
```

```
DBG > cont
```

```
100
```

The debugger evaluates any variable names that you use in the expression in the context of the stopped procedure. Names of parameters or local variables evaluate to their current values in the procedure. Names of global variables evaluate to their current values. Environment variables, such as **Digits**, evaluate to their values in the stopped procedure's environment.

If an expression corresponds to a debugger command (for example, your procedure has a local variable named **step**), you can still evaluate it by enclosing it in parentheses.

```
> f := proc(step) local i;
>           for i to 10 by step do
>               i^2
>           end do;
> end proc:


> stopat(f,2);
```

$$[f]$$

```
> f(3);

f:
    2*     i^2
```

```
DBG > step

1
f:
    2*     i^2
```

```
DBG > (step)

3
f:
    2*     i^2
```

```
DBG > quit
```

```
Warning, computation interrupted
```

While execution is stopped, you can modify local and global variables by using the assignment operator (:=). The following example sets a breakpoint in the loop only when the index variable is equal to 5.

```
> sumn := proc(n) local i, sum;
>              sum := 0;
>              for i to n do
>                  sum := sum + i
>              end do;
> end proc:


> showstat(sumn);


sumn := proc(n)
local i, sum;
   1    sum := 0;
   2    for i to n do
   3        sum := sum+i
        end do
end proc



> stopat(sumn,3,i=5);
```

$$[sumn]$$

```
> sumn(10);

10
sumn:
   3?      sum := sum+i
```

Reset the index to 3 so that the breakpoint is encountered again.

```
DBG > i := 3

sumn:
   3?      sum := sum+i
```

```
DBG > cont

17
sumn:
    3?    sum := sum+i
```

Maple has added the numbers 1, 2, 3, 4, 3, and 4 and returned 17 as the result. Continuing the execution of the procedure, the numbers 5, 6, 7, 8, 9, and 10 are added and 62 is returned as the result.

```
DBG > cont
```

$$62$$

Examining the State of a Procedure During Debugging

There are two debugger commands available that return information about the state of the procedure execution. The `list` debugger command shows you the location within a procedure where execution stopped, and the `where` debugger command shows you the stack of procedure activations.

The `list` debugger command has the following syntax.

```
list procedureName statementNumber[..statNumber]
```

The `list` debugger command is similar to `showstat`, except in the case that you do not specify any arguments. If no arguments are included in the call to `list`, only the five previous statements, the current statement, and the next statement to be executed are displayed. This provides some context in the stopped procedure. In other words, it indicates the *static* position where execution stopped.

The `where` debugger command shows you the stack of procedure activations. Starting from the top-level, it shows you the statement that is executing and the parameters it passed to the called procedure. The `where` debugger command repeats this for each level of procedure call until it reaches the current statement in the current procedure. In other words, it indicates the *dynamic* position where execution stopped. The `where` command has the following syntax.

```
where numLevels
```

To illustrate these commands, consider the following example. The procedure check calls the sumn procedure from the previous example.

```
> check := proc(i) local p, a, b;
>              p := ithprime(i);
>              a := sumn(p);
>              b := p*(p+1)/2;
>              evalb( a=b );
> end proc:
```

There is a (conditional) breakpoint in sumn.

```
> showstat(sumn);
```

```
sumn := proc(n)
local i, sum;
   1    sum := 0;
   2    for i to n do
   3?      sum := sum+i
         end do
end proc
```

When check calls sumn, the breakpoint invokes the debugger.

```
> check(9);
```

```
10
sumn:
   3?      sum := sum+i
```

The where debugger command reveals that:

- check was invoked from the top-level with argument 9,

- check called sumn with argument 23, and

- execution stopped at statement number 3 in sumn.

```
DBG > where
```

```
TopLevel: check(9)
        [9]
check: a := sumn(p)
        [23]
sumn:
    3?     sum := sum+i
```

```
DBG > cont
```

$$true$$

The next example illustrates the use of **where** in a recursive function.

```
> fact := proc(x)
>            if x <= 1 then
>                1
>            else
>                x * fact(x-1)
>            end if;
> end proc:
```

```
> showstat(fact);
```

```
fact := proc(x)
   1    if x <= 1 then
   2        1
        else
   3        x*fact(x-1)
        end if
end proc
```

```
> stopat(fact,2);
```

$$[fact]$$

```
> fact(5);
```

```
fact:
    2*     1
```

```
DBG > where

TopLevel: fact(5)
         [5]
fact: x*fact(x-1)
         [4]
fact: x*fact(x-1)
         [3]
fact: x*fact(x-1)
         [2]
fact: x*fact(x-1)
         [1]
fact:
    2*      1
```

If you are not interested in the entire history of the nested procedure calls, use the numLevels parameter in the call to **where** to print a specified number of levels.

```
DBG > where 3

fact: x*fact(x-1)
         [2]
fact: x*fact(x-1)
         [1]
fact:
    2*      1
```

```
DBG > quit
```

Warning, computation interrupted

The **showstop** command (and the **showstop** debugger command) displays a report of all currently set breakpoints, watchpoints, and error watchpoints. Outside the debugger at the top-level, the **showstop** command has the following syntax.

```
showstop();
```

The next example illustrates the use of **showstop**.

```
>   f := proc(x) local y;
>           if x < 2 then
>               y := x;
>               print(y^2);
>           end if;
>           print(-x);
>           x^3;
>   end proc:
```

Set breakpoints.

```
> stopat(f):
> stopat(f,2):
> stopat(int);
```

$$[f,\ int]$$

Set watchpoints.

```
> stopwhen(f,y):
> stopwhen(Digits);
```

$$[Digits,\ [f,\ y]]$$

Set an error watchpoint.

```
> stoperror( "numeric exception: division by zero" );
```

$$[\text{"numeric exception: division by zero"}]$$

The **showstop** command reports all the breakpoints and watchpoints.

```
> showstop();
```

```
Breakpoints in:
    f
    int

Watched variables:
    Digits
    y in procedure f

Watched errors:
```

```
"numeric exception: division by zero"
```

Using Top-Level Commands at the Debugger Prompt

The `showstat`, `stopat`, `unstopat`, `stopwhen`, `unstopwhen`, `stoperror`, and `showstop` commands can be used at the debugger prompt. The following list describes the syntax rules for top-level commands used at the debugger prompt.

- Do *not* enclose the arguments of the command in parentheses.

- Do *not* separate the arguments of the command with a comma. The arguments must be separated by a space character.

- Do *not* use colons or semicolons to end statements.

- The procedure name is *not* required by any command. Commands that use a procedure name assume the currently stopped procedure if one is not specified.

- For the `stoperror` command, double quotes are *not* required.

Except for these rules, the debugger prompt call for each command is of the same form and takes the same arguments as the corresponding top-level command call.

Restrictions

At the debugger prompt, the only permissible Maple statements are debugger commands, expressions, and assignments. The debugger does not permit statements such as `if`, `while`, `for`, `read`, and `save`. However, you can use `'if'` to simulate an `if` statement, and `seq` to simulate a loop.

The debugger cannot set breakpoints in, or step into, built-in routines, such as `diff` and `has`. These routines are implemented in C and compiled into the Maple kernel. Debugging information about these routines is not accessible to Maple. However, if a built-in command calls a library routine, for example, the `diff` command calling `'diff/sin'`, you can use a breakpoint to stop in the latter.

If a procedure contains two identical statements that are expressions, the debugger cannot determine with certainty the statement at which execution stopped. If this situation occurs, you can still use the debugger and execution can continue. The debugger merely issues a warning that the displayed statement number may be incorrect.[3]

8.3   Detecting Errors

This section describes some simple commands that you can use for detecting errors in procedures that are written in Maple. If you are not successful in finding the error by using these commands, you can use the Maple debugger, which is discussed in **8.1 A Tutorial Example** and **8.2 Maple Debugger Commands**, to display the stepwise execution of a procedure.

Tracing a Procedure

The simplest tools available for error detection in Maple are the `printlevel` global variable, and the `trace` and `tracelast` commands. These facilities enable you to trace the execution of both user-defined and Maple library procedures. However, they differ in the type of information that is returned about a procedure.

The `printlevel` variable is used to control how much information is displayed when a program is executed. By assigning a large integer value to `printlevel`, you can monitor the execution of statements to selected levels of nesting within procedures. The default value of `printlevel` is 1. Larger, positive integer values cause the display of more intermediate steps in a computation. Negative integer values suppress the display of information.

The `printlevel` global variable is set by using the following syntax, where `n` is the level to which Maple commands are evaluated.

```
printlevel := n;
```

To determine what value of `n` to use, remember that statements within a particular procedure are recognized in levels that are determined by the nesting of conditional or repetition statements, and by the nesting of procedures. Each loop or `if` condition increases the evaluation level by 1, and each procedure call increases the evaluation level by 5. Alternatively, you can use a sufficiently large value of `n` to ensure that all levels are traced.

---

[3]This problem occurs because Maple stores all identical expressions as a single occurrence of the expression. The debugger cannot determine at which invocation execution stopped.

For example, `printlevel := 1000` displays information in procedures up to 200 levels deep.

```
> f := proc(x) local y; y := x^2; g(y) / 4; end proc;
```

$$f := \mathbf{proc}(x)\,\mathbf{local}\,y;\ y := x^2\,;\ 1/4 * g(y)\,\mathbf{end\ proc}$$

```
> g := proc(x) local z; z := x^2; z * 2; end proc;
```

$$g := \mathbf{proc}(x)\,\mathbf{local}\,z;\ z := x^2\,;\ 2 * z\,\mathbf{end\ proc}$$

```
> f(3);
```

$$\frac{81}{2}$$

```
> printlevel := 5;
```

$$printlevel := 5$$

```
> f(3);

{--> enter f, args = 3
```

$$y := 9$$

$$\frac{81}{2}$$

```
<-- exit f (now at top level) = 81/2}
> printlevel := 10;
```

$$printlevel := 10$$

```
> f(3);
```

```
{--> enter f, args = 3
```

$$y := 9$$

```
{--> enter g, args = 9
```

$$z := 81$$

$$162$$

```
<-- exit g (now in f) = 162}
```

$$\frac{81}{2}$$

```
<-- exit f (now at top level) = 81/2}
```

$$\frac{81}{2}$$

The amount of information that is displayed depends on whether the call to the procedure was terminated with a colon or a semicolon. If a colon is used, only entry and exit points of the procedure are printed. If a semicolon is used, the results of the statements are also printed.

To reset the value of the **printlevel** variable, reassign its value to 1.

```
> printlevel := 1;
```

$$printlevel := 1$$

By assigning a large value to **printlevel**, the trace of *all* subsequent Maple procedure calls is displayed. To display the trace of *specific* procedures, you can use the **trace** command. The **trace** command has the following syntax, where **arguments** is one or more procedure names.

```
trace(arguments);
```

The `trace` command returns an expression sequence containing the names of the traced procedures. To begin tracing, you must call the procedure.

```
> trace(f,g);
```

$$f, g$$

```
> f(3):
```

```
{--> enter f, args = 3
{--> enter g, args = 9
<-- exit g (now in f) = 162}
<-- exit f (now at top level) = 81/2}
```

```
> f(3);
```

```
{--> enter f, args = 3
```

$$y := 9$$

```
{--> enter g, args = 9
```

$$z := 81$$

$$162$$

```
<-- exit g (now in f) = 162}
```

$$\frac{81}{2}$$

```
<-- exit f (now at top level) = 81/2}
```

$$\frac{81}{2}$$

Like `printlevel`, the amount of information that is displayed during tracing when `trace` is used depends on whether the call to the procedure was terminated with a colon or a semicolon. If a colon is used, only entry and exit points of the procedure are printed. If a semicolon is used, the results of the statements are also printed.

To turn off the tracing of specific procedures, use the `untrace` command.[4]

```
> untrace(f,g);
```

$$f, g$$

```
> f(3);
```

$$\frac{81}{2}$$

If a procedure returns an error message, you can use the `tracelast` command to determine the last statement executed and the values of variables at the time of the error. The `tracelast` command has the following syntax.

```
tracelast;
```

When a procedure returns an error message, the following information is returned from a call to `tracelast`.

- The first line displays which procedure was called and what parameter was used.

- The second line displays the # symbol, the procedure name with the line number of the statement that was executed, and the statement that was executed.

- Finally, if there are any local variables in the procedure, they are displayed with their corresponding values.

---

[4]You can use `debug` and `undebug` as alternate names for `trace` and `untrace`.

```
> f := proc(x) local i,j,k;
>           i := x;
>           j = x^2;
>           seq(k, k=i..j);
> end proc;
```

$$f := \mathbf{proc}(x)$$
$$\mathbf{local}\, i,\, j,\, k;$$
$$i := x;\ j = x^2;\ \mathrm{seq}(k,\, k = i..j)$$
$$\mathbf{end\ proc}$$

```
> f(2,3);
```

Error, (in f) unable to execute seq

```
> tracelast;
```

f called with arguments: 2, 3
#(f2,3): seq(k,k = i .. j)

Error, (in f) unable to execute seq

locals defined as: i = 2, j = j, k = k

You can find the error in this procedure by studying the results of the tracelast command—the assignment to the local variable j incorrectly uses an equal sign (=) instead of an assignment operator (:=).

The information provided by tracelast can become unavailable whenever Maple does a garbage collection. Therefore, it is advisable to use tracelast immediately after an error occurs. [5]

Using Assertions

An *assertion* is a statement about a procedure that you *assert* to be true. You can include assertions in your procedure to guarantee pre- and post-conditions, and loop invariants during execution by using the ASSERT command. You can also use assertions to guarantee the value returned by a procedure or the value of local variables inside a procedure. The ASSERT command has the following syntax.

---

[5]For more information about garbage collection in Maple, see page 335 or refer to ?gc.

```
ASSERT( condition, message );
```

If `condition` evaluates to `false`, an error is generated and `message` is printed. If the first argument evaluates to `true`, `ASSERT` returns `NULL`.

To check assertions, turn on assertion checking prior to executing a procedure that contains an `ASSERT` command. To query the current state of assertion checking, or turn assertion checking on or off, use the `kernelopts` command.[6]

The default state for assertion checking is `false`.

```
> kernelopts(ASSERT);  #query the current state
```

$$false$$

If you enter a `kernelopts` command to turn assertion checking on, `kernelopts` returns its *previous* value.

```
> kernelopts(ASSERT=true);
```

$$false$$

At any time during the Maple session, you can confirm whether assertion checking is on by entering the following command.

```
> kernelopts(ASSERT);
```

$$true$$

If assertion checking is on and a procedure that contains an `ASSERT` statement is executed , the condition represented by the `ASSERT` statement is checked.

```
> f := proc(x,y) local i,j;
>         i:=0;
>         j:=0;
>         while (i <> x) do
>            ASSERT(i > 0,"invalid index");
>            j := j + y;
>            i := i + 1;
>         end do;
>         j;
> end proc;
```

---

[6]For more information about `kernelopts`, refer to `?kernelopts`.

$f := \mathbf{proc}(x, y)$
$\quad \mathbf{local}\, i, j;$
$\quad\quad i := 0\,;$
$\quad\quad j := 0\,;$
$\quad\quad \mathbf{while}\, i \neq x\, \mathbf{do}$
$\quad\quad\quad \text{ASSERT}(0 < i,\ \text{``invalid index''})\,;\ j := j + y\,;\ i := i + 1$
$\quad\quad \mathbf{end\ do};$
$\quad\quad j$
$\quad \mathbf{end\ proc}$

```
> f(2,3);
```

```
Error, (in f) assertion failed, invalid index
```

Use the `kernelopts` command again to turn assertion checking off. (Again, `kernelopts` returns its *previous* value.) When assertion checking is off, the overhead of processing an `ASSERT` statement in a procedure is negligible.

```
> kernelopts(ASSERT=false);
```

$$true$$

Related to assertions are Maple warning messages. The `WARNING` command causes a specified warning, preceded by the string `"Warning,"`, to display. The `WARNING` command has the following syntax.

```
WARNING( msgString, msgParam1, msgParam2, ... );
```

The `msgString` parameter is the text of the warning message and `msgParam`*i* are optional parameters to substitute into `msgString`, if any.

```
> f := proc(x)
>       if x < 0 then
>           WARNING("the result is complex")
>       end if;
>       sqrt(x)
> end proc;
```

$$f := \mathbf{proc}(x)$$
$$\quad \mathbf{if}\, x < 0 \,\mathbf{then}\, \text{WARNING}(\text{"the result is complex"})\,\mathbf{end}\ \mathbf{if};$$
$$\quad \text{sqrt}(x)$$
$$\mathbf{end\ proc}$$

```
> f(-2);
```

```
Warning, the result is complex
```

$$\sqrt{2}\,I$$

You can turn the `WARNING` command off by using `interface(warnlevel=0)`. In this case, the warning is not displayed and the call to `WARNING` has no effect.

```
> interface(warnlevel=0);
> f(-2);
```

$$\sqrt{2}\,I$$

Handling Exceptions

An *exception* is an event that occurs during the execution of a procedure that disrupts the normal flow of instructions. Many kinds of errors can cause exceptions, for example, attempting to read from a file that does not exist. Maple has two mechanisms available when such situations arise:

- the `error` statement to raise an exception, and

- the `try...catch...finally` block to handle exceptions.

Raising Exceptions The `error` statement raises an exception. Execution of the current statement sequence is interrupted, and the block and procedure call stack is popped until either an exception handler is encountered, or execution returns to the top-level (in which case the exception becomes an error). The `error` statement has the following syntax.

```
error msgString, msgParam1, msgParam2, ...
```

The `msgString` parameter is a string that gives the text of the error message. It can contain numbered parameters of the form `%n` or `%-n`, where `n` is an integer. These numbered parameters are used as placeholders for actual values. In the event that the exception is printed as an error message, the actual values are specified by the `msgParams`.

For example, the error message `"f has a 4th argument, x, which is missing"` is specified by the following `error` statement.

```
error "%1 has a %-2 argument, %3, which is missing", f, 4, x
```

A numbered parameter of the form `%n` displays the `n`th `msgParam` in line-printed notation (that is, as `lprint` would display it). A numbered parameter of the form `%-n` displays the `n`th `msgParam`, assumed to be an integer, in ordinal form. For example, the `%-2` in the error statement above is displayed as "4th". The special parameter `%0` displays all the `msgParams`, separated by a comma and a space.

The `error` statement evaluates its arguments, and then creates an exception object which is an expression sequence with the following elements.

- The name of the procedure in which the exception was raised, or the constant 0 if the exception was raised at the top-level.

- The `msgString`.

- The `msgParams`, if any.

The created exception object is assigned to the global variable `lastexception` as an expression sequence.[7,8]

The `error` statement normally causes an immediate exit from the current procedure to the Maple session. Maple prints an error message of the following form.

---

[7]The actual arguments to the `error` statement are also assigned to `lasterror` for compatibility with older versions of Maple. For more information, refer to `?traperror`.

[8]To view the value of the `lastexception` variable inside the debugger, use the `showexception` debugger command.

```
Error, (in procName) msgText
```

In this case, `msgText` is the text of the error message (which is constructed from the `msgString` and optional `msgParams` of the `error` statement), and `procName` is the procedure in which the error occurred. If the procedure does not have a name, `procName` is displayed as `unknown`. If the error occurs at the top-level, outside of any procedure, the `(in procName)` part of the message is omitted.

The `error` statement is commonly used when parameter declarations are not sufficient to check that the actual parameters to a procedure are of the correct type. The following `pairup` procedure takes a list L of the form $[x_1, y_1, x_2, y_2, \ldots, x_n, y_n]$ as input, and creates from it a list of the form $[[x_1, y_1], [x_2, y_2], \ldots, [x_n, y_n]]$. A simple type check cannot determine if list L has an even number of elements, so you need to check this explicitly by using an `error` statement.

```
> pairup := proc(L::list)
>             local i, n;
>             n := nops(L);
>             if irem(n,2) = 1 then
>                 error "list must have an even number of "
>                     "entries, but had %1", n
>             end if;
>             [seq( [L[2*i-1],L[2*i]], i=1..n/2 )]
> end proc:


> pairup([1, 2, 3, 4, 5]);

Error, (in pairup) list must have an even number of
entries, but had 5


> pairup([1, 2, 3, 4, 5, 6]);
```

$$[[1, 2], [3, 4], [5, 6]]$$

Trapping Errors The `try` statement is a mechanism for executing procedure statements in a controlled environment so that if an error occurs, it does not immediately terminate the procedure. The `try` statement has the following syntax (the `finally` clause is optional).

```
try tryStatSeq
    catch catchStrings : catchStatSeq
    finally finalStatSeq
end try
```

If procedure execution enters a `try...catch` block, the `tryStatSeq` is executed. If *no* exceptions occur during the execution of `tryStatSeq`, procedure execution continues with the statement after `end try`.

If procedure execution enters a `try...catch...finally` block, the `tryStatSeq` is executed. If *no* exceptions occur during the execution of `tryStatSeq`, the `finalStatSeq` in the `finally` clause is executed. Execution then continues with the statement after `end try`.

If an exception *occurs* during the execution of `tryStatSeq` (in a `try...catch` or `try...catch...finally` block), execution of `tryStatSeq` terminates immediately. The exception object corresponding to the exception is compared against each `catchString`. Any number of catch clauses can be provided, and each can have any number of `catchStrings` separated by commas. Alternatively, a catch clause need not have a catch string. Any given `catchString` (or a catch clause without one) can appear only once in a `try...end try` construct.

If a matching catch clause is found, or the catch clause contains no `catchStrings`, the `catchStatSeq` of that catch clause is executed, and the exception is considered to have been caught. If no matching catch clause is found, the exception is considered *not caught*, and is re-raised outside the `try` block.

When Maple is looking for a matching catch clause, the following definition of "matching" is used.

- Neither the exception object nor the `catchStrings` are evaluated (the exception object has already been evaluated by the error statement that produced it).

- The `catchStrings` are considered to be prefixes of the exception object's `msgString`. If a `catchString` has n characters, only the first n characters of the `msgString` need match the `catchString`. This permits the definition of classes of exceptions.

- A missing `catchString` matches any exception.

- The "result" of a `try` statement (the value that `%` returns if it is evaluated immediately after execution of the `try` statement) is the result of the last statement executed in the `try` statement.

A `catchStatSeq` can contain an `error` statement with no arguments, which also re-raises the exception. When an exception is re-raised, a new exception object is created that records the current procedure name, and the message and parameters from the original exception.

Under normal circumstances, the `finalStatSeq` of the `finally` clause, if there is one, is always executed before control leaves the `try` statement. This is true in the case that an exception occurs, independent of whether it is caught or whether another exception occurs in the `catch` clause.

This is true even if a `catchStatSeq` re-raises the exception, raises a new one, or executes a `return`, `break`, or `next` statement.

Under certain abnormal circumstances, the `finalStatSeq` is not executed:

- If an exception is raised in a catch clause and this exception is caught by the debugger and the user exits the debugger, the user's command to stop execution overrides everything.

- If one of the following untrappable exceptions occurs, the exception is not caught, and `finalStatSeq` is not executed:

  1. Computation timed out. (This can only be caught by `timelimit`, which raises a "time expired" exception that can be caught. For more information on the `timelimit` command, see page 334.)

  2. Computation interrupted. (In other words, the user pressed CTRL+C, BREAK, or equivalent.)

  3. Internal system error. (This indicates a bug in Maple itself.)

  4. `ASSERT` or local variable type assertion failure. (Assertion failures are not trappable because they indicate a coding error, not an algorithmic failure.)

  5. Stack overflow. (If a stack overflow occurs, there is generally not enough stack space to do anything, such as running cleanup code.)

If an exception occurs during the execution of a `catchStatSeq` or the `finalStatSeq`, it is treated in the same way as if it occurred outside the `try...end try` statement.

Example 1 A useful application of the `try` and `error` statements is to abort an expensive computation as quickly and cleanly as possible. For example, suppose that you are trying to compute an integral by using one of several methods, and in the middle of the first method, you determine that it will not succeed. You would like to abort that method and try another method. The following code implements this example.

```
> try
>    result := MethodA(f,x)
> catch "FAIL":
>    result := MethodB(f,x)
> end try:
```

MethodA can abort its computation at any time by executing the statement error "FAIL". The catch clause will catch that exception, and proceed to try MethodB. If any other error occurs during the execution of MethodA, or if an error occurs during the execution of MethodB, it is not caught.

Another useful application of the **try** statement is to ensure that certain resources are freed when you are done with them, regardless of whether anything went wrong while you were using them.

Example 2   Use the following code to access the Maple I/O facilities to read the lines of a file and process them in some way.

```
> f := fopen("myfile",TEXT,READ):
> try
>    line := readline(f);
>    while line < 0 do
>       ProcessContentsOfLine(line);
>       line := readline(f)
>    end do
> finally
>    fclose(f)
> end try:
```

In this example, if any exception occurs while reading or processing the lines of the file, it is not caught because there is no catch clause. However, fclose(f) is executed before execution leaves the **try** statement, regardless of whether there was an exception.

The next example uses both catch and finally clauses to write to a file instead of reading from one.

```
> f := fopen("myfile",TEXT,WRITE):
> try
>    for i to 100 do
>       fprintf(f,"Result %d is %q\n",i,ComputeSomething(i))
>    end do
> catch:
>    fprintf(f,"Something went wrong: %q\n",lastexception);
>    error
> finally
>    fclose(f)
```

```
> end try:
```

If any exception occurs, it is caught with the catch clause that has no catchString, and the exception object is written into the file. The exception is re-raised by executing the error statement with no msgString. In all cases, the file is closed by executing fclose(f) in the finally clause.

Checking Syntax

The Maple maplemint command generates a list of semantic errors for a specified procedure, if any. The semantic errors for which maplemint checks include parameter name conflicts, local and global variable name conflicts, unused variable declarations, and unreachable code. The maplemint command has the following syntax.

maplemint(*procedureName*);

In the case where the specified procedure is free of semantic errors, maplemint returns NULL.

```
> f := proc() local a,i; global c;
>           for i from 1 to 10 do
>             print(i);
>             for i from 1 to 5 do
>               if (a=5) then
>                 a:=6;
>                 return true;
>                 print('test');
>               end if;
>             end do;
>           end do;
> end proc;
```

```
> maplemint(f);

    This code is unreachable:
      print(test)
    These global variables were declared, but never used:
      c
    These local variables were used before they were assigned
    a value:
      a
    These variables were used as the same loop variable for
    nested loops:
      i
```

Similar to `maplemint`, Maple also has an *external* program utility called `mint`. The `mint` program is called from outside Maple and it is used to check both semantic and syntax errors in an external Maple source file. For more information about `mint`, refer to `?mint`.

8.4 Creating Efficient Programs

After a Maple procedure is debugged, it is often desirable to improve the performance of the code. Maple commands are available to analyze the time and memory consumption involved in executing individual statements. Maple also provides commands to monitor the efficiency of procedures.

During the performance improvement phase, keep in mind that Maple is based on a small kernel written in C, and on large libraries of Maple code which are interpreted. Therefore, whenever possible, it is generally more efficient to perform computations by using the built-in functions in the kernel. The phrase **option** *builtin* is used to identify the built-in functions. For example, the `add` function is a built-in function in Maple. To determine if a function is built-in, use the **eval** command with the function name as its argument.

```
> eval(add);
```

$$\mathbf{proc}()\,\mathbf{option}\;\mathit{builtin};\;90\,\mathbf{end\;proc}$$

The **option** *builtin* phrase identifies this as a built-in function, and the number following *builtin* is a special number that identifies this particular function in the kernel.[9]

Displaying Time and Memory Statistics

A simple way to measure the time and memory requirements of an executed command at the interactive level is to use the `showtime` command. The `showtime` command has the following syntax.

---

[9]For more information about efficiency in Maple programming, refer to `?efficiency`.

```
showtime();
```

Once the `showtime` command is entered, subsequent Maple statements that are executed are evaluated normally with the exception that the input statements are assigned to the global variables 01, 02, 03, ... Immediately after the output, the amount of CPU time taken and the amount of memory used is displayed.[10]

The following statements all return the sum of the same sequence of numbers. However, by using the `showtime` command, it is clear that statement 03, which uses the `add` command, is the most efficient method with respect to time and memory consumption. The `for...do` loop is the least efficient method in this case.

```
> S:=0: #initialize sum
> showtime();
```

```
01 :=  for i from 1 to 100 do S := S + 2^i end do:
```

```
time = 0.10, bytes = 32166
```

```
02 :=  '+'(seq(2^i, i=1..100)):
```

```
time = 0.01, bytes = 13462
```

```
03 :=  add(2^i, i=1..100):
```

```
time = 0.01, bytes = 12450
```

To turn `showtime` off, enter the `off` command. Maple returns to its normal interactive mode using the standard prompt.

```
04 :=  off:
```

An alternate method for measuring the time requirements of an executed command at the interactive level is to use the `time` command. The total CPU time used since the *start of the Maple session* is returned. The units are in seconds and the value returned is a floating-point number. The `time` command has the following syntax.

---

[10]For more information about using the global variables 0i at a later time in a Maple session, refer to `?history`.

```
time();
```

To find the time used to execute particular statements or groups of statements, use the following assignments.

```
st := time():
... statements to be timed ...
time() - st;
```

Therefore, you could use the following set of statements to calculate the amount of time (in seconds) required to add the first 10,000 powers of 2 by using the add command.

```
> st:=time(): add(2^i, i=1..10000): time()-st;
```

$$8.402$$

Profiling a Procedure

Used in conjunction with the profile command, the showprofile command is used to display run-time information about a procedure. The run-time information is displayed in tabular form and it contains the number of calls to the procedure, the nesting level of each call, the CPU time used, and the number of bytes used by each call. To turn on profiling, use the profile command.

```
profile( procedureName );
```

Then, to display the run-time information collected for the specified procedure, use the showprofile command. If no argument is supplied to showprofile, the run-time information for all profiled procedures is displayed.

```
showprofile( procedureName );
```

To illustrate the use of profiling in Maple, consider the following procedures which compute the nth Fibonacci number. Both procedures contain the same code except that fib1 uses option remember.[11]

---

[11] For more information about option remember, see page 210 or refer to ?remember.

```
> fib1:=proc(n) option remember;
>       if n<2 then
>          n
>       else
>          fib1(n-1)+fib1(n-2)
>       end if;
> end proc;
```

$$fib1 := \mathbf{proc}(n)$$
$$\mathbf{option}\ remember;$$
$$\mathbf{if}\,n < 2\,\mathbf{then}\,n\ \ \mathbf{else}\,\text{fib1}(n-1) + \text{fib1}(n-2)\ \ \mathbf{end\ if}$$
$$\mathbf{end\ proc}$$

```
> fib2:=proc(n)
>       if n<2 then
>          n
>       else
>          fib2(n-1)+fib2(n-2)
>       end if;
> end proc;
```

$$fib2 := \mathbf{proc}(n)$$
$$\mathbf{if}\,n < 2\,\mathbf{then}\,n\ \ \mathbf{else}\,\text{fib2}(n-1) + \text{fib2}(n-2)\ \ \mathbf{end\ if}$$
$$\mathbf{end\ proc}$$

Turn on profiling for both procedures.

```
> profile(fib1);
> profile(fib2);
```

Execute the procedures.

```
> fib1(10);
```

$$55$$

```
> fib2(10);
```

$$55$$

Use **showprofile** to display the run-time information about **fib1** and **fib2**.

```
> showprofile();
```

function	depth	calls	time	time%	bytes	bytes%
fib2	10	177	.030	75.00	78232	87.94
fib1	10	19	.010	25.00	10728	12.06
total:	20	196	.040	100.00	88960	100.00

By studying the run-time information, particularly the number of calls to each procedure, you can see that it is more efficient to use `option remember` in a recursive procedure.

To turn off profiling, use the `unprofile` command. If no argument is supplied to `unprofile`, all procedures currently profiled are returned to their original state.

```
unprofile( procedureName );
```

When a procedure is unprofiled, all run-time information for that procedure is lost.

```
> unprofile();
> showprofile();
```

function	depth	calls	time	time%	bytes	bytes%
total:	0	0	0.000	0.00	0	0.00

8.5   Managing Resources

Maple provides a number of commands to use for managing the computer's resources during computation. In particular, `timelimit` controls the maximum amount of time available for a computation, `gc` causes garbage collection, and `kernelopts` provides communication with the Maple kernel.

Setting a Time Limit on Computations
The `timelimit` command is used to limit the amount of CPU time for a computation. The `timelimit` command has the following syntax, where `time` is the time limit (in seconds) to evaluate `expression`.

```
timelimit( time, expression );
```

If the expression is successfully evaluated within the specified time, `timelimit` returns the value of the expression. If the time limit is reached before the expression is evaluated, `timelimit` generates an error message.

```
> f := proc ()
>        local i;
>        for i to 100000 do
>            2^i
>        end do
>    end proc:


> timelimit(0.25, f());

Error, (in f) time expired
```

Garbage Collection

Garbage collection deletes all objects that are no longer in use by the program and are occupying space in memory. In Maple, garbage collection also clears the remember tables of procedures that use an `option system` or `option builtin` by removing entries that have no other references to them.[12]

The Maple garbage collection function is `gc`. The `gc` command has the following syntax.

```
gc();
```

The `gc` command *explicitly* invokes a garbage collection process and returns `NULL`. Otherwise, garbage collections are done *automatically* by Maple every 1,000,000 words used. To change the frequency of automatic garbage collections, use the `kernelopts` command.

The `kernelopts` command can also be used to query other garbage collection information such as the number of bytes returned after the last garbage collection, and the number of times garbage collection has been invoked. The `kernelopts` command is discussed more in the next section.

---

[12]For more information about procedure options, see page 206 or refer to `?options`.

Communicating with the Kernel

The kernelopts command[13] is provided as a mechanism of communication between the user and the kernel. You have already seen how to use kernelopts to include assertions in procedures. Specifically, this command is used to set and query variables that affect computations in Maple.[14] For example:

- kernelopts(gcfreq) sets or queries the frequency of automatic garbage collections.

- kernelopts(gcbytesavailable) queries the number of bytes available after the last garbage collection.

- kernelopts(gctimes) queries the number of times that garbage collection has been invoked.

- kernelopts(memusage) reports the amount of storage used by objects of different types.

- kernelopts(stacklimit) sets the total amount of stack space, in kilobytes, that Maple can consume.

For more information about kernelopts, refer to ?kernelopts.

8.6   Exercises

1. The following procedure tries to compute $1 - x^{|a|}$.

```
> f := proc(a::integer, x::anything)
>      if a<0 then
>          a := -a
>      end if;
>      1-x^a;
> end proc:
```

Determine what is wrong with this procedure.

Hint: Use the Maple debugger described in **8.1 A Tutorial Example** and **8.2 Maple Debugger Commands** to isolate the error.

---

[13]For information about the KernelOpts Maplet application, which provides a graphical user interface to the kernel options, refer to ?Maplets[Examples][KernelOpts].

[14]For more information about kernelopts, refer to ?kernelopts.

2. The following recurrence relation defines the Chebyshev polynomials of the first kind, $T_n(x)$.

$$T_0(x) = 1, \; T_1(x) = x, \; T_n(x) = 2\,x\,T_{n-1}(x) - T_{n-2}(x)$$

The following procedure computes $T_n(x)$ in a loop for any given integer n.

```
> T := proc(n::integer, x) local t1, tn, t;
>        t1 := 1; tn := x;
>        for i from 2 to n do
>            t := expand(2*x*tn - t1);
>            t1 := tn; tn := t;
>        end do;
>        tn;
> end proc:
```

```
Warning, 'i' is implicitly declared local to procedure
'T'
```

This procedure has several errors. Which variables must be declared local? What happens if n is zero or negative? Identify and correct all errors, using the Maple debugger where appropriate. Modify the procedure so that it returns unevaluated if n is a symbolic value.

8.7 Conclusion

This chapter surveyed a variety of Maple commands that are available to help you find errors in procedures, and those available to analyze the time and memory consumption involved in running a program. In particular, the Maple debugger was presented as a tool that you can use to find and correct errors.

9   Introduction to the Maplet User Interface Customization System

A Maplet application is a graphical user interface for Maple, which is launched from a Maple session. It allows a Maple software user to combine packages and procedures with interactive windows and dialogs.

This chapter provides an overview of the `Maplets` package. For detailed information and a tutorial, enter `?Maplets` at the Maple prompt.

In This Chapter

- Uses of Maplet applications

- Structure of the `Maplets` package

- Elements used to construct a Maplet application definition

- Example Maplet applications and authoring tools provided in the package

- Writing and running Maplet applications

9.1   Uses of Maplet Applications

The Maplet user interface customization system can be used to create custom Maple calculators, interfaces to Maple packages and routines, queries, and messages.

Custom Maple Calculators

The Maplet system can be used to create calculators. Students or professionals, who have little or no experience with Maple, can use the calculators.

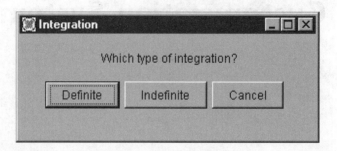

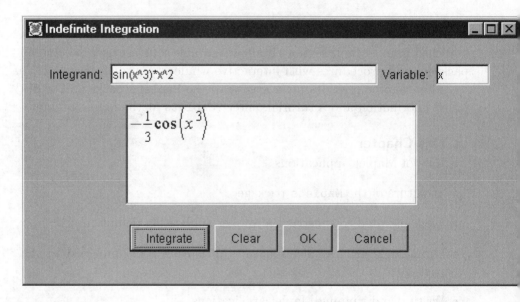

Interfaces to Maple Packages and Routines

A Maplet application can facilitate changing default values and options in Maple packages and routines. For example, a package may have a list of global settings, which users need or want to modify occasionally. A Maplet application to a Maple package can also be created to help users learn about a package. For example, many routines have a myriad of associated options. Giving users an interface to options facilitates the use of a package. The following Maplet application is a graphical interface to a function in the `LinearAlgebra` package.[1,2]

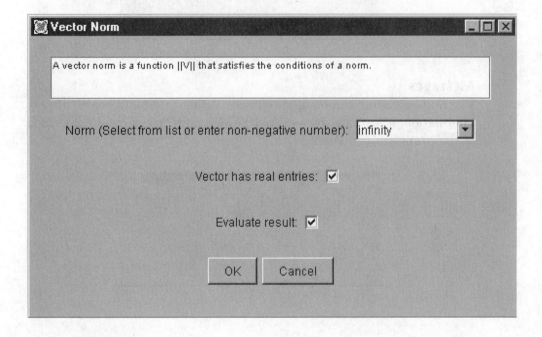

---

[1]For more information on this Maplet application, refer to `?examples/VectorNormMaplet`.

[2]For information on using this Maplet application, refer to `?Maplets[Examples][VectorNorm]`.

Queries

The Maplet system can be used to create queries. Users can be prompted for information, from the basic name and student number query, to *'Is x positive?'* and arguments to a routine.

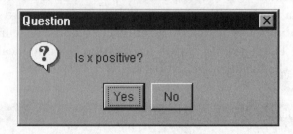

Messages

The Maplet system can be used to create various messages, which display information, a warning, or an error. Additionally, users can be informed of their progress in a session.

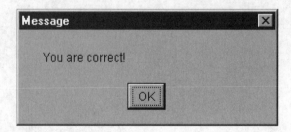

9.2   The Maplets Package

The Maplets package contains three subpackages:

- Elements

- Examples

- Tools

and one top-level function.

- Display

Elements

Elements are the individual components used to create a Maplet application, for example, windows, buttons, and check boxes. A variety of different elements are used in the `Maplets[Examples]` subpackage. Each element has a help page, describing various options.

Examples

Example Maplet applications show how the Maplet system can be used. The more complicated examples have an associated help page and worksheet describing how particular Maplet applications were constructed. The worksheets guide you from simple to complex Maplet applications.

Tools

Tools are aids for Maple software users developing Maplet applications.

Display

The `Display` function is used to display (run) a Maplet application.

9.3   Terminology

Maplet Application   A Maplet application is a collection of elements, such as window, layout, dialog, and command elements. A Maplet application contains windows and dialogs.

Maplet Application Author   A programmer who uses Maple code to write a Maplet application.

Maplet Application User   Someone who interacts with a Maplet application.

Layout   A layout defines how elements within a Maplet application are visually assembled.

Window   A window should not be thought of as the Maplet application, but rather as the top-level element within a Maplet application.

Window Element   An element that creates a window within a Maplet application. A Maplet application can contain more than one window. Each window can contain many elements that control the layout and function of the window. The `Window` element is classified under **Other Elements**.

Window Body Elements   Window body elements is a category of elements that specify viewable elements in a window other than menu bars and toolbars. There are many viewable elements in the window body category, including drop-down boxes, sliders, and tables.

Dialog Element   A dialog element has a predefined layout. For a dialog, a Maplet application author can only specify text. This is different from the `Window` element, which can contain other elements, for example, buttons and layout elements. The dialog elements in the `Maplets` package include the color selection and alert dialogs.

9.4   Elements

Each element belongs to one of seven categories:

- Window Body Elements

- Layout Elements

- Menubar Elements

- Toolbar Elements

- Command Elements

- Dialog Elements

- Other Elements

The most significant element, which can be included in a Maplet application, is the `Window` element. A `Window` element can contain layout, menu, toolbar, and command elements.

The Elements section of this guide provides:

- Descriptions of individual elements.

- A short section on Reference Options.

Window Body Elements
Button   Defines a button that can appear in a Maplet application window. Each button can be associated with an `Action` element, which is run when the button is clicked. The text, font, colors, and other properties of the button can be modified.

CheckBox   Displays a box in a Maplet application window which, when selected, contains a check mark. Like buttons, each check box can be associated with an `Action` element, which is run when the check box is selected or cleared.

ComboBox   Displays a box in which users can enter a value or select from a predefined list of strings. An initial value can be specified, otherwise it defaults to the first element in the list. The predefined list of strings can be entered either by using `Item` elements, or simply as a list of strings. When the combo box is queried for its value, the currently selected string is returned.

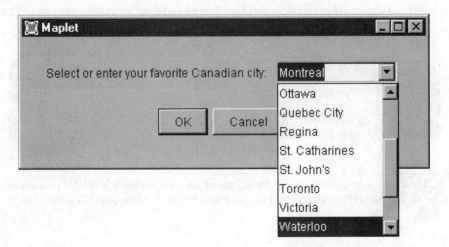

DropDownBox The `DropDownBox` is similar to the `ComboBox`, except that users *cannot* enter a value. This is most useful when users must select from a finite set of objects. To view an example of both elements, compare the `VectorNorm` and `MatrixNorm` advanced example Maplet applications in the `LinearAlgebra` subpackage of the `Maplets[Examples]` package.[3]

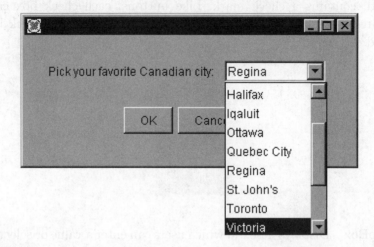

Label Contains either a single line of text or an image. If multiple lines of text are preferred, a `TextBox` element is more appropriate. A `Label` element (text or image) in a running Maplet application *cannot* be highlighted and copied. To create text that can be highlighted and copied within a Maplet application, use the `TextField` or `TextBox` element. For more information, see `TextField` or `TextBox` element later in this section.

This is a label for the TextField

This is also a label *and so is this*

---

[3]For more information on the `MatrixNorm` and `VectorNorm` Maplet applications, refer to `?Maplets[Examples][MatrixNorm]` and `?Maplets[Examples][VectorNorm]`.

ListBox   A list box is similar to a drop-down box, in that the user must select from a list, but more than one selection can be made, and more than one entry appears on the screen. The SHIFT and CONTROL keys are used to make multiple selections. The return value is a comma-delimited (separated) string, which can be converted to a list of strings by using the `ListBoxSplit` function from the `Maplets[Tools]` subpackage.

MathMLEditor   Displays, and allows the user to edit and create mathematical expressions. To enter mathematical constructs, use the input expression templates and keyboard. Subexpressions can be deleted, cut, or copied to the clipboard as MathML. From the clipboard, you can paste them into a Maple session.

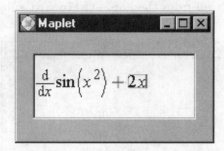

MathMLViewer   Displays MathML expressions. The displayed expression *cannot* be copied and pasted into a Maple session. The expression is displayed by using formatted mathematical notation instead of Maple syntax. For example, the square root symbol is displayed not the Maple function `sqrt`.

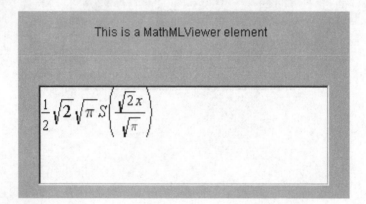

Plotter Displays a 2-D or 3-D static Maple plot in a Maplet application.

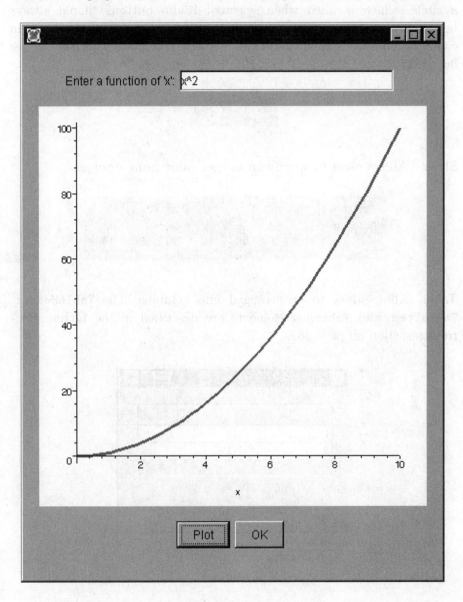

RadioButton A radio button is similar to a check box. It appears as a circle, which is filled when selected. Radio buttons should always be grouped together. This is done by using the `'group'` option, in combination with the `ButtonGroup` element. For more information, see `ButtonGroup` element in **Other Elements** on page 361.

Slider Allows users to specify an integer value from a range.

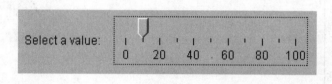

Table Allows data to be arranged into columns. The `TableHeader`, `TableItem`, and `TableRow` elements are described in the **Other Elements** section on page 362.

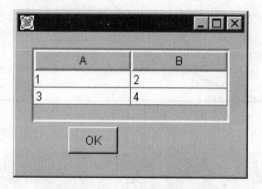

TextBox   A multiple line box for input, output, or labels. The `'editable'`
option can be set to `true` to create input fields and `false` to create output
fields or labels. Text boxes have pop-up menus, which can be accessed by
right-clicking the field. By default, an `editable=true` text box has the
entries **Cut**, **Copy**, **Paste**, **Delete**, and **Select All** in the pop-up menu.
An `editable=false` text box has **Copy** and **Select All** in the pop-up
menu.

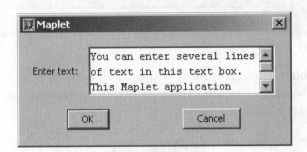

Note: Other entries can be appended to the associated pop-up menu,
by using the `'popupmenu'` option.

TextField A single line input or output field depending on whether the 'editable' option is set to `true` or `false`. Text fields, like text boxes, have pop-up menus, which can be accessed by right-clicking the field. Entries can be appended to the pop-up menu. For more information, see the previous description for `TextBox` or the **Menu Elements** section on page 354.

Enter your name:

ToggleButton A toggle button is similar to a check box, except in appearance. The toggle button can contain text or an image on the face of the button.

Layout Elements

The layout of a window describes how various elements in a Maplet application are positioned. Two different forms of layout are provided by the elements `BoxLayout` and `GridLayout`. Additionally, nested lists can be used to define box layouts. When writing a Maplet application, text strings, user prompts, or text fields are defined as expressions in lists. A Maplet application window definition includes the main list, which contains the lists of text strings, user prompts, and other elements.

The following elements are classified as layout elements:

- BoxCell

- BoxColumn

- BoxLayout

- BoxRow

- GridCell

- GridLayout

- GridRow

For details about each element, see the help pages.

BoxLayout A relative layout scheme in which you can control where items appear horizontally or vertically relative to other elements. For horizontal control in box layout, use the `BoxRow` element. For vertical control in box layout, use the `BoxColumn` element.

GridLayout A square layout where all elements must appear within a square grid. Grid layout is best used for simple layout designs. For complex layout designs, box layout is recommended.

Nested Lists Nested lists (lists of lists) can be used to define box layouts. In Maple, a list is an ordered sequence of comma-delimited expressions that is enclosed in square brackets ([ ]).

For example:

```
> List := [1,5,7];
```

$$List := [1, 5, 7]$$

A nested list is an ordered sequence of expressions that is enclosed in square brackets, in which each expression can be a list.

For example:

```
> NestedList:= [1, [2,3], [4,[5,6]], 7, 8, [9,10]];
```

$$NestedList := [1, [2, 3], [4, [5, 6]], 7, 8, [9, 10]]$$

MenuBar Elements

The following elements are classified as menubar elements:

- MenuBar - Must be defined in a `Window` element.

- Menu - Must be defined in a `Menu`, `MenuBar`, or `PopupMenu` element.

- MenuItem - Must be defined in a `MenuBar` or `PopupMenu` element.

- CheckBoxMenuItem - Must be defined in a `MenuBar` or `PopupMenu` element.

- RadioButtonMenuItem - Must be defined in a `MenuBar` or `PopupMenu` element.

- MenuSeparator - Must be defined in a `MenuBar` or `PopupMenu` element.

- PopupMenu - Must be defined in a `TextField` or `TextBox` element.

A menu bar can contain any number of menus. Each menu can contain items, defined by using the `MenuItem`, `CheckBoxMenuItem`, and `RadioButtonMenuItem` elements, and submenus, defined by nesting `Menu` elements. Separators can be used to group the menu into logically distinct groups separated by horizontal bars.

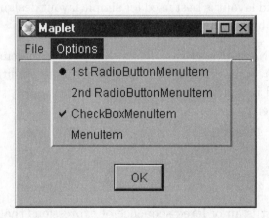

The default pop-up menu contains **Copy** and **Select All**. If the box or field is editable, it also contains the selection items **Paste, Delete,** and **Clear**. Other entries can be appended to the pop-up menu.

ToolBar Elements

A toolbar can contain any number of buttons. The buttons can be grouped into logically distinct groups by using a separator, which produces a large space between adjacent buttons. The following elements are classified as toolbar elements:

- ToolBar - Must be defined in a `Window` element.

- ToolBarButton - Must be defined in a `ToolBar` element.

- ToolBarSeparator - Must be defined in a `ToolBar` element.

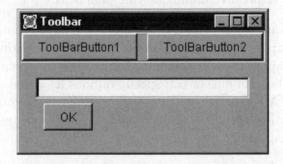

Command Elements

A Maplet application can perform actions in response to user actions such as clicking a button or changing the value in a text field. Each command element is performed before the next one is started. These are non-visual elements. The following elements are classified as command elements:

- CloseWindow

- Evaluate

- RunDialog

- RunWindow

- ShutDown

- SetOption

CloseWindow   Closes a running window by referencing the window.

Evaluate   The `Evaluate` command element runs a Maple procedure with the given set of arguments `args` in the underlying Maple session. An `Evaluate` element can contain `Argument` elements.

RunDialog   Displays a dialog element. The `RunDialog` element takes only one option `'dialog'`, which is a reference to the dialog to be run. If the dialog is already running, nothing happens.

RunWindow   Displays a `Window` element. The `RunWindow` element takes only one option `'window'`, which is a reference to the window to be run. If the window is already running, nothing happens.

Note: There are separate `RunDialog` and `RunWindow` command elements because the `Maplets[Elements][Window]` element is intrinsically different from the `Maplets` dialog elements. A dialog has a predefined structure. A Maplet application author can specify options for a dialog, but *cannot* add elements. A window does not have a predefined structure. A Maplet application author specifies its structure by using elements and options. They also behave differently. For example, a window can be minimized.

SetOption   Allows values of certain options to be changed while the Maplet application is running. For example, if a user clicks a button, the `'onchange'` option of the button can use the `SetOption` element to initiate a change such as clearing a text field. The `SetOption` element is used within a Maplet application and the `Set` routine (see **9.6 Tools**) is used within a procedure.

Shutdown Closes a running Maplet application. Optionally, it can send a return value to the Maple session. It can return specific values stored within the Maplet application, for example, the content of a text field, or a fixed value.

Dialog Elements

Dialogs are small windows that provide information, such as alert or warning messages, and gather input, such as a filename, from users. Users respond to a dialog by clicking a button. The Maplet application author can modify only specific features in the layout, for example, the text in the title bar, in a caption, or on a button. Dialogs are displayed by using the `RunDialog` element.

Important: Dialog element values *cannot* be queried after the dialog closes. As a Maplet application author, it is important to create a Maplet application that returns relevant information to the Maple session.

AlertDialog Draws attention to a potential issue. Allows users to indicate approval to continue (**OK**) or to heed the warning (**Cancel**).

ColorDialog A standard color chooser that provides users with interfaces for choosing a color: Color swatches, RGB palettes, and HSB palettes.

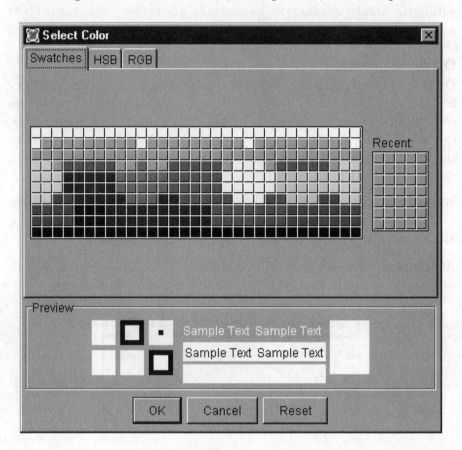

ConfirmDialog Allows users to specify whether an action is performed. A dialog box with a statement like: *"Is x greater than 0 ?"* is displayed with the options **Yes** (and exit), **No** (but exit), and **Cancel** (do not exit).

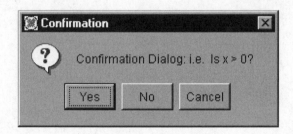

FileDialog A standard file chooser dialog.

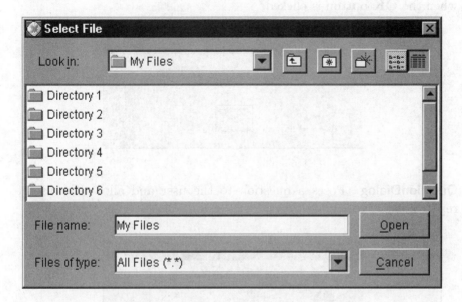

InputDialog The InputDialog element is similar to the AlertDialog element except that it contains a text field in which the user can enter or modify data. An initial value can be included in the text field of the box when it is displayed.

MessageDialog Presents users with information and closes the dialog when the **OK** button is clicked.

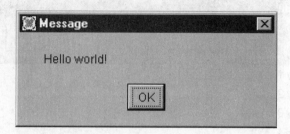

QuestionDialog Poses a question to the user and allows the user to reply, **Yes** or **No**.

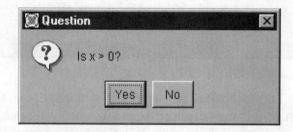

Other Elements

Action Defines an action in a Maplet application. Contains any number of `Action` or command elements to be executed.

Argument Specifies the argument of a Maple function call. It can be used only in an `Evaluate` element.

ButtonGroup A radio button must be associated with a button group so that at any time, only one button in the group can be selected. By using the `'group'` option in combination with the `ButtonGroup` element, radio buttons are grouped, as required.

Font Specifies a font for an element. The fonts available are dependent on your operating system. If you specify a `family` that is not recognized by your system, the **Unrecognized Font** message dialog displays. To view the Maplet application using the default font, click **OK**. To determine which font families are recognized, click **Valid fonts...**.

Image Specifies a *jpeg* or *gif* image in a Maplet application.

Item Specifies an entry in a `ComboBox`, `DropDownBox`, or `ListBox` element. The `Item` element cannot contain other elements.

Maplet Contains the elements defining a Maplet application. The top-level Maplet application element.

Return Encapsulates values to be returned to the Maple session when the Maplet application closes. It can contain any number of `ReturnItem` elements.

ReturnItem Specifies which values are to be returned to the Maple session when the Maplet application closes. It cannot contain other elements.

TableHeader A `Table` element contains up to one `TableHeader` element, which displays the text in the header of the table, and any number of `TableRow` elements.

Note: A table with a header must be specified in a scroll pane, that is, a `BoxCell` or `GridCell` element with the `'vscroll'='as_needed'` option. Otherwise, the header is not displayed. If a table without a header is specified in a scroll pane, default header values are used: **A,...Z, AA,...ZZ...**

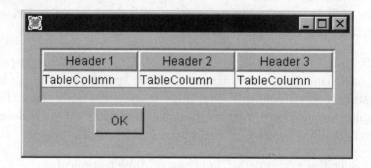

TableItem Specifies an entry in a Maplet application table header or row.

TableRow Specifies a row in a Maplet application table. The individual columns in a row are defined by using the `TableItem` element.

Note: Each `TableRow` must have the same number of `TableItem` elements. The number of `TableItem` elements in the `TableHeader`, if specified, must equal the number of `TableItem` elements in each `TableRow`.

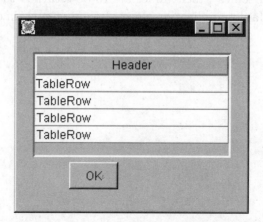

Window   Defines a window in a Maplet application. A Maplet application can contain more than one `Window` element. Each window can contain many elements that control the layout and function of the window. The `MenuBar` and `ToolBar` elements (or a reference to these elements) must be defined within the `Window` element. When creating a window, the Maplet application author can choose from options that control the height, width, and whether the window is resizable, visible, or contains a title. A complete list of options is listed in the `Maplets[Elements][Window]` help page.

Reference Options

Most elements can be given an identifying reference by using the `'reference'` option, or as a short cut, by placing the reference in an index.

Long form: `TextField('reference'= 'TF1', 'value' = "Hello" )`

Short form: `TextField[TF1]( 'value' = "Hello" )`

If references are specified by using both an index and an option, the index reference takes precedence. The reference can be a name or a string. Note that the variable name *TF1* and the string *"TF1"* are interpreted as different references.

9.5   Example Maplet Applications

The `Maplets[Examples]` subpackage provides examples of how Maplet applications can be used to solve problems. These Maplet applications provide information to a user, query a user, or display an interface to a package or routine. The `Examples` package contains the following routines and subpackages:

- Alert

- Confirm

- GetColor

- GetEquation

- GetExpression

- GetFile

- GetInput

- Message

- Question

- Selection

- SignQuery

Advanced Example Maplet Applications:

- Integration

- KernelOpts

- ShowTable

- LinearAlgebra subpackage.

Linear Algebra Subpackage

The LinearAlgebra subpackage contains the following example Maplet applications, which are interfaces for some of the LinearAlgebra routines.

- Constructors - BezoutMatrix and HilbertMatrix

- Queries - ConditionNumber

- Solvers - QRDecomposition

- Eigenvalue Problems - SingularValues

- Standard Routines - MatrixNorm and VectorNorm

Using the Example Maplet Applications

As stated in **9.1 Uses of Maplet Applications**, the Maplet system can be used to create calculators, interfaces to Maple packages and routines, queries, and messages. The following example Maplet applications demonstrate these four major uses.

Creating a Calculator and Interface to a Maple Package The `LinearAlgebra` subpackage shows how Maplet applications can be used to support an existing package.

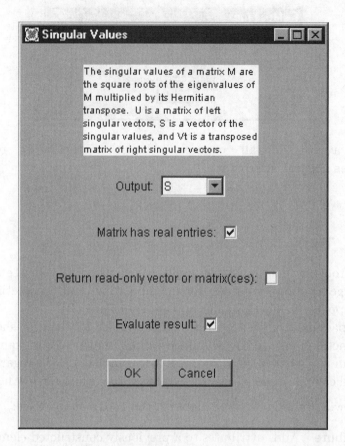

Creating Queries The example `GetEquation` Maplet application prompts the user for an equation. If the user enters an expression, it is set equal to zero when the user clicks **OK**. The equation is returned by the Maplet application.

Creating Messages   The example `Message` Maplet application displays a message to the user.

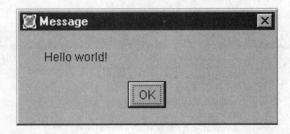

For a list of all example Maplet applications, refer to `?examples,ExampleMaplets`.

9.6   Tools

`Maplets` tools are aids for Maplet application authors. The `Maplets[Tools]` subpackage contains routines for manipulating and interacting with Maplet applications and Maplet application elements.

The package can be accessed by using either the long or short form of the function name in the command calling sequence. For example, the short form is `with(Maplets[Tools])`. For complete details regarding the command calling sequence, see the `Maplets[Tools]`, overview help page.

The following functions are available in the `Tools` subpackage:

AddAttribute   Adds attributes to a previously constructed element. For example, if you have created and run a Maplet application that displays a button, but want to add color to the button, you must add a color attribute (`'color'="#FF00FF"`) to the Maplet application code. Instead of recoding the Maplet application, you can test the look of the Maplet application by using the `AddAttribute` function.

AddContent   Adds content to a previously constructed element.

Get   Retrieves the value of a specified element option from a running Maplet application. Must be used in a procedure. Cannot be used in a Maplet application definition.

ListBoxSplit   Converts a list box value to a list of strings.

Print Prints the XML data structure of a Maplet application. Default values are included. This is useful when investigating why a Maplet application does not display as expected.

Set Cannot be used in a Maplet application definition. Must be used in a procedure. The `Set` function sets the value of a specified element option in a running Maplet application. The `SetOption` (a command element) is used in a Maplet application.

StartEngine Starts the `Maplets` environment.

StopEngine Stops the `Maplets` environment. All running Maplet applications are closed.

Maplet System Global Variables

There are two global variables in the `Maplets[Tools]` subpackage that are useful tools to Maplet application authors:

lastmaplet Each time a user runs a Maplet application by using the `Display` function, the Maplet application is assigned to the global variable, `lastmaplet`. This Maplet application can be used to debug or display the last Maplet application run.

thismaplet Each time a procedure is evaluated by using an `Evaluate` action element, the global variable, `thismaplet` is assigned the handle for the Maplet application that called the procedure. After evaluation, the variable is reset to its previous value.

9.7   Running a Maplet Application

To run a Maplet application, you must use the top-level `Display` function. In the following example, the *"Hello World"* Maplet application is displayed (or run).

```
> Maplets[Display](Maplet["Hello World",
>                  Button( "OK", Shutdown())]);
```

For more information on running a Maplet application, refer to chapter 9 of the *Maple Learning Guide*.

9.8   Writing a Maplet Application

Defining a Maplet Application

Each Maplet application must be defined in a top-level element `Maplet`. For example, a `Button` element is defined in the following `Maplet` element.

```
> Maplet(["Hello World", Button( "OK", Shutdown() )]);
```

Note: To run this Maplet application, use the top-level `Display` function. For more information, see **9.7 Running a Maplet Application**.

Maplet Application Programming Style Guidelines

1. Use only one element definition per line.

2. Indent each subsequent nested element or list.

3. Place closing parentheses, brackets of elements, or nested lists at the same level of indentation as the opening line.

4. The `Font` and `Image` elements can be defined anywhere. The Maplet application code, however, is easier to read if these elements are defined first in the Maplet application. These two elements are listed under the category of **Other Elements** on page 361.

5. Keep attributes separate from the content of an element.

6. Place unevaluation quotes (right single quotes) around any symbols or names used as option names or references. Otherwise, if any of the symbols or names are assigned values in the user's Maple session, your Maplet application definition will generate errors.

7. In a procedure, use the **use** statement rather than the **with** statement. If another user runs your code, the **with** command affects that user's environment, while **use** does not.

The following illustrates correct code structure.

```
> use Maplets[Elements] in
> maplet := Maplet(
>     'onstartup' = RunWindow( 'W1' ),
>     Font['F1']( 'family' = "times" ),
>
>     Window['W1']("Vector Norm",
>         [
>
>             BoxCell( 'left',
>                 TextBox( 'editable' = 'false', 'width' = 50,
>                     'font' = 'F1', "A vector norm is a function
>  ||V|| that satisifies the conditions of a norm."
>                 )
>             ),
>             [
>                 "Norm (Select from list or enter non-negative
>  number):",
>                 ComboBox['CoB1']( ["infinity", "1",
>                     "Euclidean (2)", "Frobenius"] )
>             ],
>             [
>                 "Vector has real entries: ",
>                 CheckBox['ChB1']( 'true' )
>             ],
>             [
>                 "Evaluate result: ",
>                 CheckBox['ChB2']( 'true' )
>             ],
>             [
>                 Button['B1']( "OK", Shutdown(['CoB1','ChB1',
>                     'ChB2']) ),
>                 Button['B2']( "Cancel", Shutdown() )
>             ]
>         ]
>     )
> );
> end use:
> Maplets[Display](maplet);
```

9.9   After Reading This Chapter

When first reviewing the help pages:

1. Read the short *Introduction to Maplets* help page (`?Maplets`).

2. Depending on your experience with the Maple software and `Maplets` package, you can choose from three paths:

- As a Maplet application user, select the *Maplet Application User Hints* link.

- As a beginning Maplet application author, select the *Roadmap to Using the Maplet User Interface Customization System* link. The roadmap guides you through the *Tutorial: Creating a Maplet Application*, *Maplet Application Code Style Guide* worksheet, *Maplet Application Layout Guidelines* worksheet, *Overviews of the Elements* and *Tools* subpackages, and *Example Maplet Applications*.

- If you are an experienced Maplet application author, select the *Maplets Package Index* link. You can navigate to all the `Maplets` help pages and worksheets from this index.

9.10   Conclusion

This book described the basic programming concepts in the Maple language: the construction of expressions and other statements from tokens, data structures, flow control, procedures, I/O, debugging, and efficiency. In this chapter, the Maple `Maplets` package, which provides the tools necessary to create graphical user interfaces to Maple, was introduced.

For more information about programming topics, refer to the Maple online help system and the *Maple Advanced Programming Guide*.

Index